# Figure Mak[ing] Can Be Fun?!!

## By Michael Brose

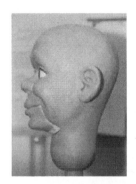

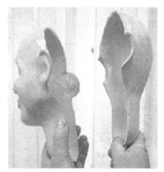

PUPPETS AND PROPS PUBLISHING

**Figure Making Can Be Fun?!?**

**Puppets and Props Publishing**
P. O. Box 250
Benson, AZ 85627

ISBN  978-0974223209

*Printed in the United States of America*

## *Permissions*

Photos of Jimmy Nelson and Paul Winchell used by permission. Photos by Rick Price are used by permission. All other photos and illustrations are by the author unless otherwise indicated in the text.

# *Of Vital Importance! Read This!*

The materials and procedures outlined in this publication are potentially dangerous. The author is not a scientist, engineer or safety consultant and has no certification involving any of the materials, processes, procedures, machinery or the like, outlined in this book. This book is intended to describe the author's mold making, casting and figure making experience for informational purposes only. The publisher and author assumes no liability for any loss, damages, deaths or injuries to persons, entities or property caused directly or indirectly, or alleged to be caused directly or indirectly as a result of using this information.

# *General Safety Information*

It is up to the reader of this publication to obtain and read all Material Safety Data Sheets (*MSDS*) for each material or chemical compound that you purchase and to strictly follow *all* of the safety recommendations and precautions therein as outlined by the manufacturer. Failure to do so can be detrimental to your health. Use of impermeable gloves and aprons, safety goggles/face shield, as well as a respirator with organic or other filters recommended in the *MSDS* literature, are vital. Work in a well-ventilated area and have a properly maintained fire extinguisher on hand. Periodic reminders will be repeated throughout the pages of this publication, however it is up to you, the reader, to become fully aware of all the potential hazards associated with the particular material you are working with and to heed the recommended safety precautions given for said material. Some procedures and processes require basic shop skills. Teaching those basic shop skills is beyond the scope of this publication. If you feel that any of the procedures are beyond your current capabilities, you are strongly urged to seek out appropriate guidance and assistance from those qualified to give it.

# Table of Contents

# Info on the 'World Wide Web'

## FIGURE MAKING CAN BE FUN?!?
### An engaging series of figure making articles

# By Michael Brose

For more Figure Making Info log onto:

**http://www.puppetsandprops.com/FigMakInfo.html**

# Introduction

Hi! My name is Michael Brose, and I enjoy making ventriloquist figures. The first step to getting treatment, I've heard, is admitting that one has a problem (tongue planted firmly in cheek)! Most figure makers (hobbyist and professional figure makers) who have been bitten by the figure making 'bug', have been bitten, and bitten hard! The majority never seem to recover. I am certainly one of those.

My interest in this fascinating art of figure making (as well as the the art of ventriloquism), began when I was 10 years old, in the early 60's. I had already been exposed to ventriloquism quite a bit on TV, and hard figures seemed to be in their heyday. Early on, I saw clips of Edgar Bergen with his faithful side kicks (most notably Charlie McCarthy and Mortimer Snerd). I was intrigued to say the least. I really did not fully appreciate Bergen's talents until later as an adult.

Around the same time, Jimmy Nelson caught my attention, as he was regularly on the tube with his companions, Danny O' Day and Farfel. My first vent figure ever was a Danny O' Day ventriloquist doll. What warm and fuzzy memories I have of that time! Jimmy also had quite an impact on an impressionable young boy. I'm sure he never knew that at the time. Whenever he appeared

**Jimmy Nelson with Danny O'Day and Farfel**

on TV, nothing else existed around me. I was totally mesmerized by what he was doing and the life he was putting into his inanimate friends. Jimmy is a very kind and gracious gentleman and continues to serve the vent community with a willingness to share with other vents. He very generously provided photos for me when I told him about this project I was working on. Thank you Jimmy!

Also on TV in the early 60's, was Paul Winchell. I guess you could say that he had the greatest influence on my life at that time, and it continues until this day. I initially learned how to be a ventriloquist from Paul's

book, 'Ventriloquism for Fun and Profit'. It was such a boost in self-confidence and self-esteem when I learned from his book this most fascinating art. I won first place in a talent contest at age 11! The next year, I had the privilege of meeting Winch in person at a special appearance in southern California. I was able to shake hands with Jerry and Knuck, and, of course, got Paul's autograph. That is one of my most treasured memories.

But what happened after that had the most impact on my life. In Paul Winchell's book, there were instructions on making your own ventriloquist figure. This started a quest for

Paul Winchell with his partners, Jerry Mahoney and Knucklehead Smiff

learning as much as I could about this process, as well as sculpting, mold making and casting. His book gave me the self-confidence that I could do it! This quest has continued until now. It has taken me down some roads I would never have traveled had it not been for this book. Until recently, Paul had no idea what an impact he had on my life. In addition to these early influences, I continue to get immense joy from building vent figures and am still learning new methods at this late date. I also have had the privilege of earning a good portion of my income as a sculptor and mold maker. I strongly feel that none of this would ever have happened without this early influence in my life.

I still feel this influence. Paul has said that he was 'pleased that he had inspired me in my craft'. He further encouraged me by saying that 'my dedication to the art helps keep ventriloquism alive'. This has helped give me the boost needed to finish writing this book, which has been a huge undertaking. I feel I have come around full circle now. It started with Paul Winchell's book, and now I have tried to return something to him, and the vent community, with the publication of this volume. Thank you, Dr. Paul Winchell! I am deeply indebted to you.

This book is aimed at the beginner, intermediate and professional figure maker. I think all will find some useful information packed in the pages of this book. My forte is mold making and casting, and I hope that what I have shared here will help further the fine art of figure making, especially as it pertains to a cast figure. Many who have tried their hand at figure making have found this to be one of the more challenging areas of the craft. At first glance, making a head, hand, or foot casting may not seem that hard

to do. Those who have tried it know otherwise. The attempt here is to take the mystery out of this and replace it with a good working knowledge of mold making and casting principles. Of course, other aspects of the art of figure making will be covered too.

Another aim has been for this to be a progressive book that will hopefully provide the reader with more than one way to make a figure. Most figure makers have their favorite materials and methods which work well for them, and have generously shared their techniques for doing this. Many, however, would like to know, 'What else can I use, or is there another way to do this?!?" Each person likes something different. Also, depending on previous experience, some will want to start with an easier technique, and some will want to try something a little more advanced right away. One of the basic ideas of this book is to provide you with enough choices so you can find what best suits you personally, and to advance at your own pace.

This book has been produced mainly because of my love for the art of figure making. I humbly acknowledge that there are many figure makers out there who know much more than I do, and I do not, by any means, pretend to 'know it all'! I merely wish to present what I do know, that might be helpful for the furtherance of this art.

There has been, in the past, a somewhat secretive nature about this interesting and fascinating art form, which has caused some information to be hidden. This has usually been based on fear. I have seen however, the lines of communication opening up in the past few years, and wish to further encourage an interchange and sharing of such knowledge. Hopefully it will encourage others to consider doing the same. By doing this, I think the quality of figures made will continue to improve. In my opinion, this will benefit *all* in the vent community.

### Acknowledgments

There are many people who have helped to make this volume possible. I'm sure I will forget someone, and if I do, I sincerely apologize in advance. At any rate, here is my attempt to thank them.

I would like to acknowledge the influence and/or direct help from the following people: Paul Winchell, Jimmy Nelson, the memory of Edgar Bergen, Rick Price, Ray Guyll, Conrad Hartz, Alan Semok, Tim Selberg, Joel Leder, Larry LaFontsee, Al Stevens, Gary Koepke, Chris Rund, Dave Boiano, and Steve Weber. Thank you so much!

I have to mention Rick Price's name again. A special thanks to Rick for his help, advice, and patience throughout the duration of this project. He generously let me bounce ideas and thoughts off of him and was a great help in keeping me grounded in many ways. Rick is very knowledgeable about vent figures and figure making in general. Rick has a high commitment to quality and this is very evident in the figures he has made over the years. He originally learned the craft from noted figure maker Chuck Jackson (who has since retired), and became a very well respected figure maker in his own right. I'm sure he does not know fully to what extent he has helped. But I do! Thanks again for all your help Rick.

Noted figure maker Ray Guyll has also been very generous in taking the time to discuss various topics on figure making, and encouraged me in many ways. Ray also has a very strong background in mold making and casting, so it is always a pleasure to talk with him on those subjects as they relate to figure making. He has a wealth of knowledge about the history of various famous vent figures and has worked on almost all of them. If enough of us keep twisting his arm, maybe we can get him to publish something on this subject eventually! I think what I appreciate the most about Ray is his fine artistry when it comes to figure making. Being a sculptor and having been involved with artistic pursuits all my life, I can really admire not only his attention to detail, but the fine artwork in the figures he has made. Thanks for all your help and insights Ray.

There are many other mentors and influences over the years that have brought me here. Many have not been in the vent community. There are too many to mention here. I would be amiss, however, if I did not mention the loving encouragement from my Mom and Dad over the years. They have always encouraged me with my artistic pursuits (no matter how crazy it might have seemed), both while growing up and as an adult. This continues to this day, without which, I'm not certain where I would be. Love you both!

### Figure Making can be Fun?!?

Figure making can be one of the most challenging and rewarding activities in which one can engage. One will find many hurdles along the way. The intent in this volume is to help the reader past as many of these hurdles as is possible. Hopefully, I have succeeded in doing that. The rewards? They are immense! Making your own figure can be *extremely* rewarding. When it is all done, you will look at it and say, "Hey, I did that!! I made him myself!" It's a feeling that is hard to describe.

One word of advice: Start simple and progress to more difficult projects later on. Many would like to start with a figure that has all the bells and whistles (moving mouth, eyes, eyebrows, winkers, flapping ears, etc.). Learn how to do a less complex figure first, and learn to do that well. Then add another animation in the next figure that you build, and so on. You will learn a great deal from each level of mechanics that you try. Strive for quality, both in the molding and casting of your figure, as well as all of the various mechanics that you install.

It is a lot like learning how to juggle. In a class on juggling, how many objects does the instructor start you out with? Three? No, they start you out with one object only (one scarf, bean bag or ball, etc.). They do not have you go on to two until you can do one the correct way. In the same way, you do not go on to three until you can do two flawlessly. Juggling is not complicated when learned step-by-step. Most people try to do too much too soon, and think it is just too hard to learn. The same applies to many aspects of figure making. Start out simple and work up to the more complex figure making skills. You will save yourself a lot of frustration and enjoy your journey much, much, more.

There will be mistakes along the way. That is a natural part of the process. Using the juggling analogy again, a ***drop*** (on the floor) is actually a sign of progress. It means you are experimenting, learning, and trying to find out what *does* work. If you analyze a drop, and you know why it occurred, you can then figure out how to correct it and make good progress. Don't let a *drop* or mistake stop you from continuing. It really is a sign of progress. Rest assured that those who have succeeded at figure making have had their share of *drops*, and they did not learn it all overnight.

You will need patience, persistence, and above all a strong desire to succeed. I'm assuming you already have the strong desire to make a vent figure, or you wouldn't be reading this book. Take your time, do quality work, and most of all, have some fun along the way! Please know that my personal wishes for your success go with you. May your quest be as enjoyable and as rewarding as mine has been over the years. Yes indeed. Figure making can be fun!!! Happy figure making!

*'For my wife Catherine, my son Aric, and my daughter Katrina, whose patience, encouragement and love, made this book possible.'*

# CHAPTER ONE

# *VENT FIGURE PROPORTIONS*

Professional ventriloquist figures come in a variety of shapes and sizes. So the first question that usually comes to mind is, "How big should my figure be?" The size of your completed figure will of course depend on your own personal preferences. So the only aim in this chapter will be to give you a place to start. The measurements outlined here are based on an average size 38"- 40" figure. You can certainly adjust these measurements up or down to make a larger or smaller figure.

You are the artist when making your own figure, so it will be up to you to decide on the size and shape of your character. However, there are some general rules of thumb you might want to consider when designing your figure.

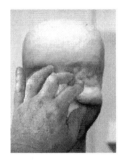

It should be noted that the traditional vent figure is not proportioned the same as a real live human would be. The head is usually life-size, but is often a caricature of sorts. The body is usually somewhat shorter than a life-sized body. The arms are definitely shorter than in real life (see Chapter Eight).

The legs are also somewhat shorter, but closer to the proportions of real legs. The hands are pretty close to being life-sized. The feet, however, are generally foreshortened (from heel to toe), as the ventriloquist doesn't want the feet sticking way out there while they

are performing. Look at the feet on a quality figure sometime and notice that they are quite a bit smaller in length from what a real pair of feet would be.

The following illustrations will show the basic measurements of a fairly well-proportioned figure. Again, these are only very general guidelines to get you started. You can certainly change any of these as you wish. Let's start with the measurements for the head.

Here are some measurements taken from a classic cheeky boy figure which will work for a nice 38" - 40"professional-size vent figure.

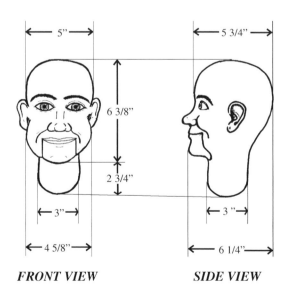

**FRONT VIEW**          **SIDE VIEW**

Next, take a look at the basic measurements for the body of a professional-size vent figure. It should be noted that these illustrations are for the purpose of showing the general size, and not for illustrating what the finished body will necessarily look like. The body illustrated would be fine for a cast fiberglass or resin body; a wood-framed body would look a bit different (see Chapter Eight).

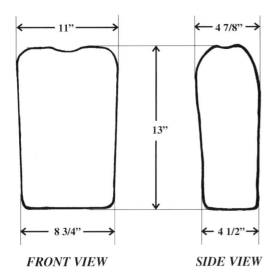

*FRONT VIEW*      *SIDE VIEW*

The hands are next. Notice the indentation a few inches below the wrists. This is where the cloth arms (muslin fabric) will be attached to the hands when making your figure. Details on attaching the hands and feet will be discussed in Chapter Eight. (Note: *the hands and feet are shown in a slightly larger scale than the body for clarity of illustration*)

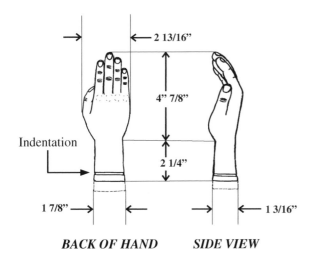

*BACK OF HAND*      *SIDE VIEW*

And, last but not least, here are the measurements for the feet. Again, notice the indentation several inches above the ankle. This is where the cloth leg (muslin fabric) would be attached if you make molded or carved feet for your figure.

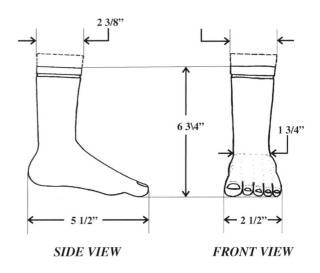

*SIDE VIEW*      *FRONT VIEW*

You will notice at the bottom of the hand illustration and at the top of the feet illustration a little dotted line area that extends beyond the given dimensions. This is the size the models (described in the next chapter) for the hands and feet need to be if you are making a molded figure. After you make the molds and later cast the hands and feet (described in subsequent chapters), these extra areas would be trimmed to the dimensions as given in the illustrations.

In this chapter the focus has been on the dimensions for the parts that will later be cast from molds. Some parts are not cast parts, so no models will be needed. The soft parts of the arms and legs (muslin fabric) will be covered in Chapter Eight. The dimensions given in this chapter for the various parts (head, body, hands and feet) will be used for making the models described next in Chapter Two, the first step in making a cast figure. These same dimensions could be used for making a traditional basswood figure as well.

# CHAPTER TWO

# *MODELS FOR FIGURE MAKING*

The next few chapters (including this one) will be dealing with the steps that are necessary for making a molded or cast figure. Read Chapters 2-6 one time through first, and then decide which methods you like best.

The next step for making a molded figure is to make a model of what you want to mold (i.e., head, hands, feet, etc.). In the previous chapter we talked about proportions, or the size your figure will be when completed. The measurements from Chapter One (or other measurements that you came up with on your own) can normally be used as is, or they may have to be adjusted slightly, depending on the casting materials you will be using.

If you will be casting the different parts of the figure in a material that does not shrink very much (urethane plastic, fiberglass, etc.), you can make the models basically the size you want your finished figure to be. If you are using a material that has high shrinkage, such as liquid neoprene, that is cast in plaster molds using the absorption process, you need to know in advance how much shrinkage there will be. Ask the distributor of these materials for the amount of shrinkage to expect (usually about 10%). You will then need to make the models slightly larger to compensate for this shrinkage that will occur in the molding and casting process (see photo, above right).

### *Clay Models and Armatures*

Clay models are the easiest and fastest to make. Oil base, reusable clays are recom-

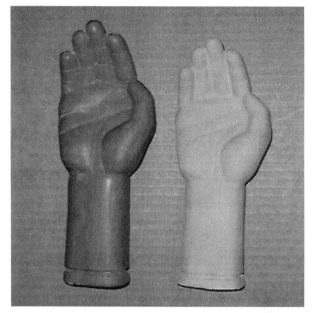

**Original model**        **Neoprene casting**

mended (see the suppliers list at the end of the book). You can work with this type of clay for hours, days, or months and it will not dry out, unlike water based clay. This is what the Hollywood special effects workshops use for model making, with good reason.

There are two basic types of oil base clays generally used: Oil base clay with sulfur, and oil base clay without sulfur. The first type is the easiest to find and can be purchased at most Arts and Crafts stores. The second type is a little more difficult to find, but can be found at places that sell *'mold making and casting'* supplies. One of the brand names is 'KLEAN KLAY'. (See suppliers list at end of book)

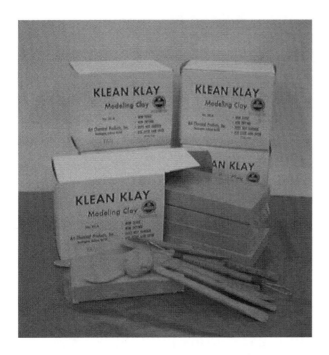

**Klean Klay and clay modeling tools**

The type of oil base clay you use can be important. Many oil base clays contain sulfur, which can react with some of the mold making materials that are used for figure making. Some silicone mold making materials for instance, will not cure where they have come in contact with clay that has sulfur in it. Platinum based silicones (*see Chapter Five*) are generally very sensitive to sulfur. So if you will be making a mold with this type of silicone rubber you will need to use a sulfur-free clay or seal the clay with a good sealer.

Latex molding rubber (*see Chapter Four*) can be sensitive to the oils in both types of clay. It would be a good idea to seal the clay model (after you're done sculpting, of course) if you are going to make a latex mold, whether it is sulfur based clay or not. The latex will still cure if you do not use a sealer, but the oil residue from the clay can attack the latex and possibly cause the latex mold to degrade or age prematurely. More about sealing models in Chapter Three.

### Use of Armatures

Clay all by itself, without an armature, can droop and sag as you try to sculpt. Armatures support the clay underneath so it will stay in place as you sculpt. With a little wood, Styrofoam®, or coat-hanger wire, simple armatures can easily be made. Armature wire can also be purchased from a supplier (see suppliers list). There are really no rules when making an armature. It just has to be strong enough to support the clay adequately. Also, an armature can take up some of the space that would normally have to be filled in with clay. The price for several pounds of a good quality oil base clay can add up!

The trick is to make the armature just slightly smaller than the model you are trying to create. You want the armature big enough so that you do not have to use a lot of clay, and yet not so big that it interferes with your sculpting of the model. A little advanced planning is necessary. As you sculpt you will find yourself making changes here and there. If the armature is too close to the surface of the clay it might not be possible to make those desired changes. So be sure to give yourself enough room to work. As a general rule, you should allow at least 1/4 to 1/2 inch of clay covering the armature. Of course, if you have a lot of clay on hand and you are not worried about it, there is no need to try to make the armature so big. As long as you have the support needed, an armature could be quite thin, with a lot of clay being used.

Hand or foot armatures are not too hard to make. The ones pictured (on the next page) were done on a wood lathe, but that is certainly not necessary. A wood dowel the right size can work just as well. Make a loop in some coat-hanger or armature wire and a screw can be used to attach it to the wood dowel. The wire can then be bent in the general shape of a hand

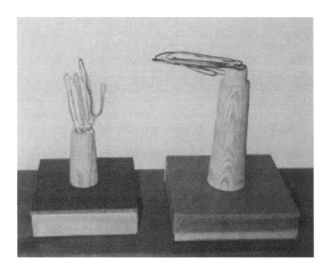

**Hand and foot armatures**

or foot, as the case may be. Notice that they are attached to a wood base or work board, to keep everything upright while you are sculpting.

Next, let's consider some armature methods for the model of the head. The first idea involves the use of Styrofoam® insulation which is easy to find. You can get scrap pieces from a construction site sometimes for free. Here's how to do it: Cut the Styrofoam® insulation into squares or rectangles. Glue these cut Styrofoam® pieces together with Aleene's White Glue for Styrofoam® (craft store item). You now have one big block of Styrofoam®. See illustration below.

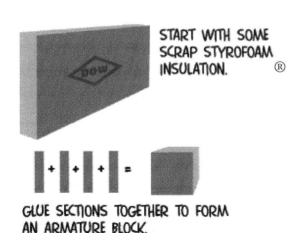

**START WITH SOME SCRAP STYROFOAM INSULATION.** ®

**GLUE SECTIONS TOGETHER TO FORM AN ARMATURE BLOCK.**

Make a hole in the right spot for a control stick and glue the appropriate size dowel in place. Then, cut and shape this composite block of Styrofoam® into the general shape of the head. Styrofoam® insulation is fairly easy to carve. Use drawings or templates to guide you in shaping the rigid foam. Remember to make it slightly undersized to allow for 1/4 to 1/2 inch minimum of clay. (*This idea along with accompanying diagram and photo contributed by Chris Rund*)

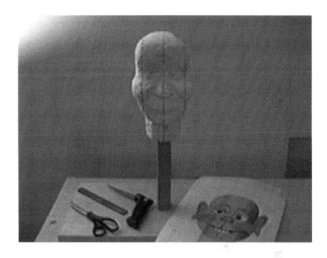

**General shape of head carved in Styrofoam block**

Here is another way a head armature could be made: A series of wood discs could be cut out (use a band saw, scroll saw, saber saw, etc.) with a hole drilled in the middle of each and then glued to a large dowel. (*See illustration, next page*) This makes for a strong armature that will be very stable as you sculpt. The dowel should be the same size as the finished head stick will be, or slightly larger if you will be casting the head in a material that has high shrinkage.

There are certainly many ways an armature could be made. You just need something to support the clay adequately. You could use a Styrofoam® ball (glued to a head stick), a wig stand (also made of Styrofoam®), an old doll

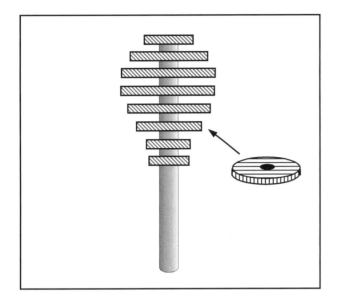

Wood discs used to make head armature

Using a template to shape the clay for the neck as described above works pretty well. But if you want a perfectly rounded neck (as well as a perfectly smooth neck) for a ball and socket type neck joint, take a block of wood and turn a half sphere on a wood lathe. You can make this part of the armature. This could be attached to the Styrofoam® block armature, wood disc style (see illustration at left) or other armature that you come up with on your own. I like to use a metal frame (pictured below) with this arrangement. It's certainly not necessary, and it might be a bit of overkill, but I don't like things moving while I sculpt! Drill a hole the right size in the half sphere and glue it to the head stick dowel.

head, or....???. Use your own imagination in coming up with a way to support the clay model for sculpting. There is no one correct way for making an armature. It just has to be strong enough to work.

For shaping the clay on the bottom of the neck, take a piece of wood or Plexiglas® and make a cut-out the shape of the neck (a quarter round cut-out for a rounded ball shape). You will have to trim the template a little to allow for the thickness of the head stick. Add a little clay to the armature around the neck area, just slightly more than what is needed. Push the template against the head stick and carefully pull it all the way around the neck. As you do this the excess clay will be scraped away leaving the right shape. The final smoothing can be done with your fingers. You have to be careful, though, not to distort the shape you just made.

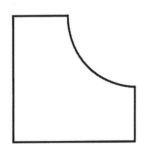

Neck template

**Head armature with lathed wood piece for neck**

When you are adding clay to this special type of armature, you can blend where the clay and lathed wood piece meet. After you have made your first figure, you can use this same armature for your next project. There are distinct advantages to making such a sturdy, durable armature with a lathed wood piece. This will save you a lot of work, as such an armature can be used again and again.

Whatever style of head armature you settle on, a simple jig can be made to hold the armature upright while you sculpt. Take two ordinary 2 X 4's, nail and glue the two pieces together as shown. Drill a hole through the middle of the boards (but not all the way through!) the same diameter as the head stick on the armature.

This jig can then be clamped to your work table using two good size "C" clamps on both ends of the jig. Just insert the head stick portion of the armature into the hole and you are ready to add clay and sculpt. You could also add cross pieces (about 1 foot long) to the ends of the bottom board and eliminate using the clamps altogether. The cross pieces are also made of 2 X 4's. Screw and glue these cross pieces to the bottom board. Now this special jig will sit on your work bench and can be easily moved around. You can put a screw through the front of the top board to keep the head stick from rotating while you are sculpting.

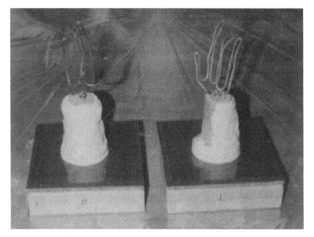

**Adding clay to hand armatures**

basic shape of the model (head, hand, foot, etc.). Add or remove clay as needed. Continually rotate the sculpture to see the model from all angles. Any errors in symmetry or anatomy will then stand out. Reshape as necessary. If you have some drawings of your figure (to scale) of the head, hands or feet, you can compare these to the sculpture in progress. Noted figure maker Ray Guyll takes this a step further and cuts out an outline of the drawing in poster board, which is then used to compare against the clay sculpture in progress.

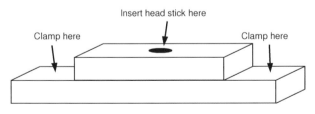

**Simple jig for holding head armature**

### Sculpting in Clay

After you have finished making your armatures, you can start the sculpting process. The first step is to add pieces of clay tightly around the armature and begin to form the

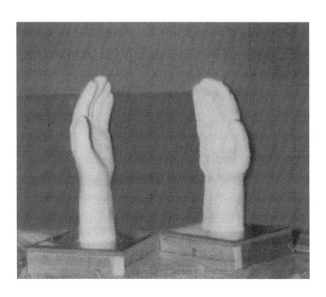

**Left hand getting refined  -  Right hand still rough**

As you get closer to the right size for the model you are working on, start adding some details. Don't try to get too intricate with fine detail work at this point. A mistake that many beginning sculptors make is doing the fine detailing too early in the sculpting process. Make sure first that there are no large changes in the general shape of the sculpture to be made. Then, and only then, should you start on the final details and smoothing.

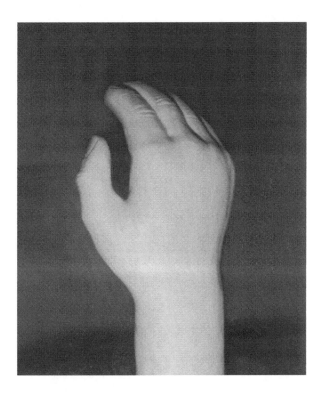

**Detailed hand - final smoothing pretty much done**

Final smoothing is best done with the fingers for the most part. Hard to reach areas can be done with wood modeling tools that are made for sculpting. You can purchase these at most arts & crafts stores or you can make your own. Sometimes objects found around the house or shop can work well, too. The end of a writing pen cap, either end of a eating utensil, things you find in your junk drawer, etc. You just have to try different things.

Some like to use isopropyl alcohol, mineral oil, or a small amount of Vaseline to help with the smoothing process. The key is *very* small amounts. Another trick is to put the sculpture in a refrigerator for awhile (if it will fit in there!). This will make the clay firmer. Most oil base clays will smooth better when they are not quite as soft. You can take small pieces of ordinary sandpaper and draw it against the surface of the clay. This will help the peaks and valleys to show up in the clay, indicating where more smoothing may be required.. Start with course sandpaper and work on down to fine sandpaper. This technique works best with firmer clay as well.

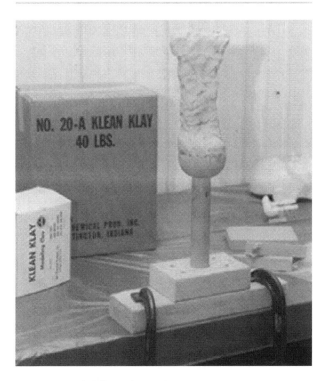

**Adding clay to head armature**

Go to your local library and check out some books on drawing or sculpting. These can have some excellent information on proportions for the face, hands, feet, etc. Some figure makers rely heavily on such references, others sculpt away intuitively and just seem to know where the different features should fall into place. You will find what works best for you as you try it.

Note: To help with the shape of the eye sockets for the head model, insert some eye ball models that are the size the eyes will be, or the size they need to be to allow for a material that shrinks a lot. Later, when you go to fit the eye mechanics inside the head, the eye socket will be the right size and shape. The eyes in the photo below are mounted to a piece of Plexiglas® to keep them the right distance apart while sculpting.

Prior to making a mold, you may also want to scribe some lines in the clay head for the outline of where the mouth will be cut out. That way, each time you do a casting, it is already marked. This saves a lot of time if you are going to make several castings. See Chapter Seven under *'Making a separate*

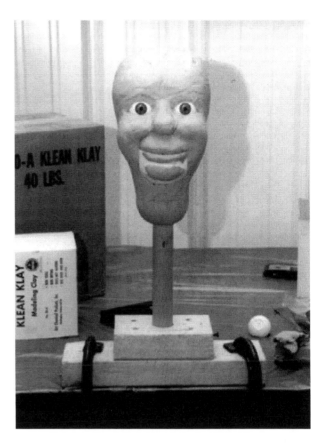

**Not too handsome yet - rough features added.**

**Yikes!! Eyeball models inserted into the clay model**

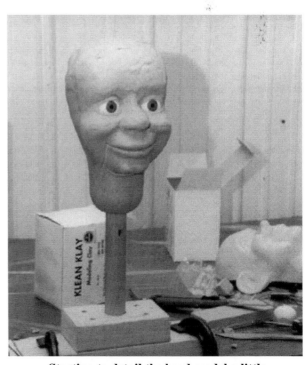

**Starting to detail the head model a little**

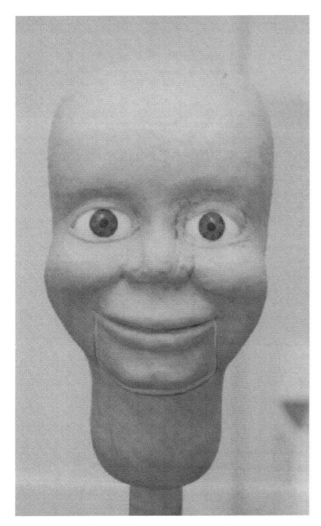

**Right side of face beginning to shape up**

model with few problems. So you might want to carefully check the chapters on mold making and casting techniques (Chapters Three, Four, Five and Six) before deciding whether to mold the ears separately or not. In general, however, you will find it is easier to make a mold of a head model that does not have the ears sculpted in place.

You may feel a little awkward about trying your hand at sculpting. Do not feel that you need to go to art school and take years of classes to learn how to do this. I had the rare privilege of meeting Disney sculptor Blaine Gibson, considered one of the foremost sculptors in the world, and had quite a fascinating conversation with him. He sculpted many, many, items for Disney. He sculpted almost all of the figures for the animatronics at Disneyland, Disney World, etc., including

*mouth piece'* for details on how to do this accurately. Also, see ***Appendix A*** for some further information on making a precision mouth setup from the start of the process.

Some figure makers recommend sculpting and molding the ears separately and then gluing them on later. There are advantages and disadvantages to doing the head this way. The reason for this recommendation usually has to do with the typical two piece-mold that is made for head castings. It is more of a challenge with the ears attached. There are other types of molds, however, that can allow one to sculpt the ears right on the original head

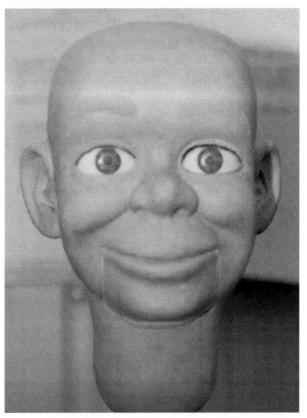

**Looking much better!  He's about ready to talk.**

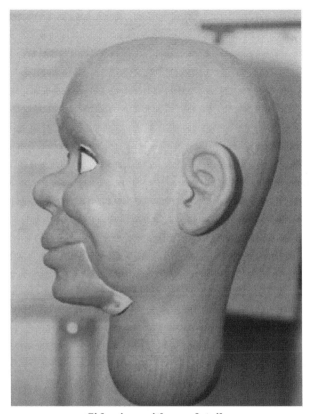

**Side view with ear detail**

Pirates of the Caribbean, Hall of Presidents, and more. The nice bronze statue of Walt Disney standing with Mickey Mouse at the theme parks was done by Blaine. They kept calling him out of retirement for various projects. A very interesting gentleman! At one point I asked him how he learned his craft. I was expecting him to say something about years of training through high school, college, and through special art schools. To my surprise, it turned out he learned his craft by trial and error, sculpting animal models while growing up on a farm! So, give it a try. You may be better at it than you think, with a little practice.

You do not really need to make a model for the body (or torso) unless you plan on making a molded body. Many figure makers find that a wood-framed body is quite satisfactory (See Chapter Eight). One advantage to a molded body, is being able to make the figure's body pre-molded with just the right contours and realism. A molded body, however, takes considerably more time, effort, and skill to produce. You may want to wait until you have a fair amount of mold making and casting experience before attempting to make a molded body. The principles for making a model for a molded body are the same as for making the head or other parts. A carefully constructed armature that eliminates the need for using a lot of clay can help.

### Rigid Model Ideas

Another way to make a model is with a rigid material, as opposed to making a soft clay model. There are a variety of materials that could be used. Here are a few ideas that might be useful.

The first method is that of carving a rigid model out of carving wax. This is a wax that is manufactured just for this purpose. It has no grain to it like wood does, so it can be carved easily in any given direction. You do not need any specialized carving tools. One or two inexpensive carving tools will work just fine. This material makes carving quite enjoyable.

A rigid model offers the advantage of not being as easily damaged as a clay model could be. It is also sometimes easier to make molds from a rigid model rather than a soft clay model, depending on the item being made and the type of mold you're doing. After reading Chapters Four, Five and Six, you will know if a rigid model or a clay model would work best for the type of mold you want to make.

Carving wax is an excellent medium for making quality original hand and foot models. With reasonable care, the wax models will last for years. Carving wax is somewhat impractical, however, for larger parts of the figure (head or body). There are newer materials, such as Balsa Foam®, that carve easily and make nice models (available from Dick Blick Art Materials; See suppliers list).

The first step in making a wax model is to make a wax block of the approximate size of the model. You will need to melt the carving wax on a stove and pour it into a pre-made form. Make a wooden form in the general shape or profile of the item you are trying to make (e.g., a hand or foot). Take some scrap wood the right thickness (or several scrap pieces glued together) and cut an outline out of the material with a band saw, saber saw, etc.

The outline of the hand or foot model should be 1/8" to 1/4" larger than the final size for the model as the wax will shrink as it cools. This is the cavity where you will pour in the wax. Line this cavity along the bottom and sides with aluminum foil. Use one continuous piece of foil, as opposed to two or three sheets of foil. This will help prevent the liquid wax from leaking out of the form.

Melt the carving wax in a large pot or double-boiler (follow the manufacturer's directions). Be careful not to overheat the wax. You do not need to heat the wax any more than what it takes for it to liquefy. ***Carefully pour the wax into the cavity of the form (wear long sleeves, gloves, and safety glasses). Hot wax can scald you easily, so take the right precautions.*** Let the wax completely cool to room temperature before removing it from the form (several hours or overnight). The wood form may have to be cut away. Expect that some of the aluminum foil will stick to the wax. This is not a problem as you will be carving away the outer surface as you begin to carve your model anyway.

Take your time carving. Carve the rough, general shapes and outlines first, and then the details. Take off small amounts of wax with the carving tool, especially as you get closer to the final dimension of the model. I personally like using a small, 1/2 inch wood chisel with a short handle. It is just a simple flat blade, but used carefully, you can get a lot of control in carving the wax. The wax hands and feet pictured were both done with just such a tool. Remember, you can always take more off. You

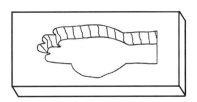

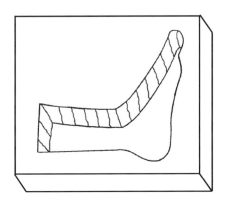

**Forms for hands and feet**

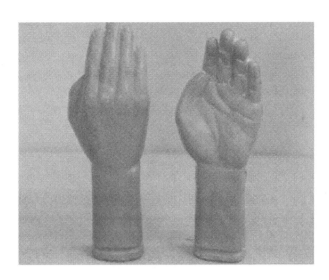

**Carved wax hands**

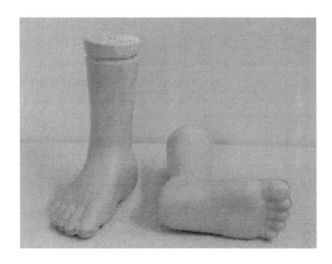

**Carved wax feet**

can not put more wax back on (at least not very easily).

When you have carved as much detail as you think you need, you can finish off the wax model by sanding it to make it smooth. Yes, you *can* sand carving wax!. Regular sandpaper will work, but the wax tends to clog regular sandpaper fairly quickly. Synthetic steel wool (looks like the scrubbers on the backside of some kitchen sponges) seems to work best for this, and is available at most hardware stores.

Some professional model makers will do a quick sculpt in clay first and then make a quick mold. Melted carving wax is poured into the mold. When the wax model has cooled, it is removed from the mold and then refined further and further, until they get a grade 'A' sculpt. Wax can be better smoothed and refined, than clay can.

For a larger part, such as a head model, you make a quick mold of latex (see Chapter Four), and then make a hollow casting of the head (see Chapter Six), out of urethane, Magic Sculp, fiberglass or other suitable material. This model or casting can be sanded, patched, and otherwise refined to your satisfaction. From such a refined model, a very high quality

mold can be made. (See Chapters Four and Five) This is a secret from the toy making industry. If you are going to try to produce a lot of the same figure from one mold, this would be the best way to go. It will save a lot of refining work on each casting.

If all of this sounds a bit daunting, there is yet another way to create a rigid model that some figure makers like to use. It is called **direct modeling**. The idea is to use a soft clay like material that becomes rigid. There are clays that become rigid after sculpting when heated in an oven (Sculpey™, Fimo™, and Cernit™, as well as other brands of polymer clays). There are advantages and disadvantages to these types of clays. Some shrink when heated. Some do not sculpt as nicely as a good oil based clay would. You should experiment with a small amount before buying larger quantities. Be sure that the material has the qualities that you like first.

Another product that has excellent possibilities for *direct modeling* is a material called Magic Sculp (see suppliers list), that was first introduced to me by noted figure maker Rick Price. It molds just like clay, takes great detail and has a good amount of working time. It also does not require an oven to harden! Sculpt a general shape first, then add details later if you'd like. Freshly mixed Magic Sculp will stick to previously hardened material. This way you can add details a little at a time until you get just what you want. If you mix up too much at one time you take a chance that it will begin to set up before you are finished sculpting. Do a test batch with the material first to get used to working with it.

Cured Magic Sculp can be drilled, filed, carved, sanded, etc. It has the advantages of clay (can easily be sculpted) and the advantages of other rigid materials after it cures (it can be sanded, refined, and made very smooth). It is a very versatile material. It stays nice and pliable while you are working with it and does not get dry and crumbly like wood dough. It has no nasty fumes and can be cleaned up with soap and water. It can also be used to make a casting (see Chapter Six). This can be a great way to make a well refined rigid model without having to make a mold first, and make a useable head casting in the process. See Chapter Six, page 94, on 'Mold-less castings' for details.

### *Summary on Models*

There are a variety of ways to make suitable models from which to make molds. Again, use your imagination. A model does not have to be made all out of one material. It could be made from a combination of wood, clay, plastic, etc. This might look kind of peculiar in the model stage, but will not matter when you do the final casting. No one will be able to tell what the original model looked like. And it doesn't matter. A model is typically just a temporary form, from which to make a mold.

A figure maker will use different techniques at different times depending on the desired result. Your approach to model making will change with the task at hand. If you were making a one-time custom figure, a clay model might be best because of its simplicity. If you were thinking of doing production figures, at some point you would want a good quality rigid model that has been well-refined, from which you could make a nice, quality mold. In the end, it saves you a lot of time in the finishing process. A lot of patching, sanding and other refinements can be minimized.

After you have made suitable models of the different parts of your figure that you wish to reproduce (head, hands, feet, or body), the next step is to make molds of these parts. The next few chapters will cover in detail different types of molds that are good for making molded or cast figures. The finished molds will only be as good as the models you make. Go the extra mile and make quality models. It will show in your finished figure!

These finely detailed, quality figures by Rick Price, started with nicely detailed models.

# CHAPTER THREE

# *PLASTER MOLDS*

There are a variety of ways to make a ventriloquial figure. What will be described in this chapter and the ones to follow is how to make a cast or molded figure, which can be made out of a number of materials. This would include, but is certainly not limited to: liquid neoprene, wood dough, epoxy putty (Magic Sculp), fiberglass (with polyester or epoxy resin), and urethane resin. After suitable models have been made, you can make a mold from a given model (head, hand, foot, etc.), from which a replica or casting (the final product) can be molded.

There are different types of molds that can be made, depending on what it is you want to do. There are rubber molds made of latex, silicone, or urethane, which can be used to produce hundreds of castings if you wish. There are also molds that are made of rigid casting materials (fiberglass, urethane, epoxy, etc.), but these take a lot of mold making experience to make and use successfully. For the most part, this book will be dealing with the types of molds that are not too difficult to make, or to use.

In the succeeding chapters there will be several different types of molds described that can be useful for figure making. The advantages and disadvantages of each will be discussed in the chapter for that particular type of mold.

### Plaster 'Waste Molds'

The advantages of a plaster *waste mold* are that it is inexpensive compared to other mold making materials and in many ways fast and easy to make. The disadvantage is that generally you can only get one good casting from the mold. The exception to this is if you are using a waste mold to cast liquid neoprene, using the absorption casting process (Chapter Six). You can get several castings out of a waste mold this way. How many castings can depend on how well you make the mold.

A *waste mold* is usually made of plaster and is generally used only once. This is because it is typically broken into many pieces in order to remove the part (head, hand, foot, etc.) from inside the mold. Thus the reason for the name 'waste mold'. A waste mold is normally used if you are going to make only one part instead of casting several parts from the same mold. It is kind of a 'quick and dirty' way of making a mold from which a casting can be made.

A waste mold is also used for casting your model into a more solid form, which can be an in-between step for making a more intricate mold out of another material, as described later, or for making a more permanent model. For instance, if you have sculpted a hand or foot model out of clay and you would like it to be in a more permanent or a rigid medium (like urethane, fiberglass, wax, etc.) you would first make a waste mold of your clay model. You would then remove the clay from inside the waste mold, use an appropriate mold release if needed, and pour in the casting material of choice, to make a solid or hollow model. (See Chapter Six)

After the material sets up, you break or chip away the plaster to release the casting inside, and then do whatever refinements are necessary, such as sanding and smoothing this new model. Because the new model is made from a rigid material, it will now be easier to work with, as opposed to a clay model which is very easily damaged. There are some mold making techniques that are very difficult to do with a soft model, as you will see in the succeeding chapters.

### How to make a Waste Mold

The first step is to make a clay model, as described in Chapter Two. As outlined in that chapter, the model is probably modeled out of clay over an armature. There should be enough thickness of clay over the armature to be able to insert some plastic shims into the clay. Shims are used to divide the model into two halves when making a waste mold.

In some of the older books on model and mold making, they recommend using metal shims for separating the two halves of a waste mold. These will work just fine, but they can be somewhat sharp, are harder to cut out, and generally more difficult to work with. Plastic shims are much easier to work with and much easier to come by. One idea is to find some old video cassette boxes that are made of plastic (some are black and some are clear). Some of these plastic boxes are thicker than others. You will find that the thinner ones work better for shims. You can also purchase acetate sheet from A-R Products (see suppliers list at end of

book), which is sold specifically for making plastic shims.

Take an ordinary pair of scissors and cut out some rectangles approximately 1" X 1 1/2". Also cut some plastic rectangles that are angled. Some smaller plastic rectangles, 1 1/2" X 1/2", can be useful as well. Basically, you want enough shapes on hand to handle going around all the contours on the model, with a minimal amount of gaps. The less gaps you have between the shims, the better.

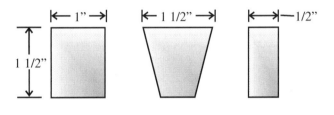

Plastic shims

First, you need to decide where the mold is going to come apart (commonly called the parting line) for a two-piece mold of the head. Normally, for other types of molds, the parting line has to be determined very carefully as well as *undercuts* and *draft* (discussed near the end of this chapter). Otherwise, you will have problems getting the mold apart later. Not so with a waste mold. Because the model is made out of clay, it will typically come apart with few problems. Basically, you just need to divide the model approximately in half for your parting line. See the end of this chapter (***parting lines, draft and undercuts***), if you are making a plaster mold that will be reused.

The parting line can be marked in the clay to help guide you before inserting the shims. On a head model this is generally along the sides of the head (near where the ears are) and going over the top (as opposed to having a parting line going from front to back). See illustration below.

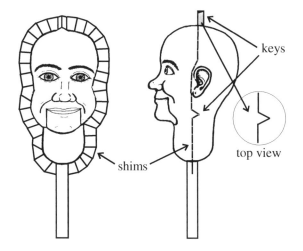

**Shims inserted in parting line of clay model**

Begin inserting shims into the clay head using a combination of straight cut and angle cut shims, getting them as close together as possible without overlapping. It is also a good idea to make some keys. A key is a shape that helps with alignment when putting a two-piece mold back together for casting. One way is by inserting two shims in a "V" shape which will make a key along the parting line. Put some keys in appropriate places along the parting line with the plastic shims. (See illustration above) Usually one at the top of the head and one or two on each side will suffice. You want enough keys to hold things in place but not so many that you clutter the parting line with them.

A-R Products (see suppliers list) sells *bubble stock* acetate sheets which are perfect for keys. These sheets have half-spheres of various sizes vacuum formed into the acetate sheet. You just cut out as many as you need for keys and insert them into the clay the same as the regular shims. See photo at right. One rule of thumb with bubble stock keys or other

styles of keys: the larger the keys, the easier it is to align the mold when putting it back together.

After you have put all the shims along the parting line in the clay model, you will notice some small gaps between the shims. Take pieces of scotch tape just slightly longer than the exposed portion of the shim and carefully tape over the gaps. It will take two pieces of tape per gap, one on each side of the shims, front and back. This will prevent any plaster from leaking through the shims, and also helps keep everything in place while you are making the waste mold. (See photo below)

**Foot model with shims, tape, and bubble stock keys**

If you have sculpted the head out of water-based clay, there is no further preparation of the head model necessary. If you have used an oil-based clay you may want to seal the clay model before proceeding. Some casting materials require that the mold be free of contamination (oils, dirt, wax, etc.). This is true when casting liquid neoprene or other absorption type casting materials (see Chapter Six) into plaster molds. If the plaster gets contaminated, the absorption process will not work properly and you will get poor results.

To seal the oil-based model, purchase some wood sanding sealer or clear acrylic sealer (Krylon brand seems to work well) in a spray can from the hardware store. Spray the model with several light coats. Follow the directions on the can carefully (*especially the safety precautions!*). Let the sealer dry completely before proceeding to make your mold.

The first step in actually making the waste mold is doing what is called a splash coat. A splash coat is a small batch of plaster that is literally spattered onto the model. You have to make sure that this thin coat of plaster covers the model completely with no air holes or bubbles. Often times food coloring is added to the splash coat to color it (blue works quite well). Subsequent coats (as described shortly) are not colored, but left the original white color of the plaster. That way when you start chipping away the completed waste mold after making a casting, you will know when you are getting close to the surface and not accidentally damage the casting inside.

### Mixing Plaster

Purchase some No. 1 pottery plaster (which is slightly harder than plaster of Paris) from your local hobby store, building materials supply company listed in your yellow pages, or see the supplier's list in the back of the book. Purchasing plaster in larger quantities (50 to 100 lbs.) will save you money. You can also use the plaster to make *mother molds* (see Chapter Four). When not using the plaster, keep it stored in a dry place, as plaster is hygroscopic (seeks water). A large, clean, plastic trash can with a lid, or a *box-shaped,* storage container with a lid, works well for storage of dry plaster.

To mix the plaster for the splash coat, first find a small plastic bowl you don't care about (a used food container that's been thoroughly cleaned works well). Fill the plastic container with about one pint of water, or more depending on the size of the model. You will probably have some plaster left over. It is better to have too much than too little when working with plaster. The idea is to have enough plaster to cover the entire part of the model you are working on in one step. You can always throw away the excess, as plaster is relatively inexpensive.

*Note:* Never pour excess plaster down the plumbing or rinse mixing containers in your sink. Put it in the trash! It will *for a certainty* clog your plumbing. Some artists that work with plaster like to have a barrel of water on hand to rinse their plaster mixing utensils in. This can be used many times for rinsing plaster mixing containers. At a later time you can separate the solids from the water by pouring the barrel's contents through a screen. The solids can be discarded in the trash.

*Caution: always wear a dust mask when working with plaster. Breathing in plaster dust can be hazardous to your health. Wearing gloves is also recommended. Read and carefully observe all precautions from the manufacturer.* Next, start adding plaster to the water (this is the traditional way of mixing plaster; another method will be covered in Chapter Four). Sprinkle it slowly into the mixing bowl, letting it sink to the bottom. Keep adding plaster until it no longer sinks and just starts rising above the level of the water. It will look kind of like a dry riverbed on the surface of the water. This is the correct amount of plaster. Using this method you will always have the right amount of water to plaster ratio without any weighing or measuring. (See illustration below)

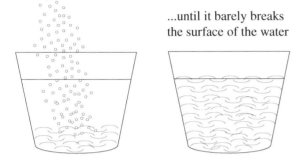

Sprinkle in plaster...

...until it barely breaks the surface of the water

**Measuring plaster the easy way**

Let the plaster sit undisturbed for about 2-3 minutes. This is called *slaking*. The idea is to let all of the particles of plaster become completely soaked with water before any mixing takes place. Otherwise, you can get lumps in the plaster mixture. When the plaster and water mixture has finished slaking, it is ready to be mixed. Add a few drops of food coloring.

Take an old spoon, spatula, stirring stick or other suitable implement and mix the plaster thoroughly for about 5-7 minutes (the longer the plaster is mixed the harder it will be when it sets up). If you are using a mechanical mixer (large hand drill with mixing head attached) mix for only 1-3 minutes. While you are stirring, occasionally scrape the bottom and sides of the mixing container to make sure the plaster and water are completely mixed throughout. Try not to whip an undue amount of air into the plaster.

You are now ready to apply the splash coat. The idea is to take some of the mixed plaster and spatter it all over the model evenly, both front and back. One good way to do this is to first take your hand *(with a rubber glove)* and stick it into the mixing bowl to cover your fingers completely with wet plaster. Then make a fist, remove your hand from the mixing bowl, open your hand quickly, flicking plaster onto the model. Continue until the entire model is completely covered with a thin layer (1/16", approximately) of plaster.

Another way to apply the splash coat is to take a clean paint brush and, using a dabbing motion, carefully apply plaster to the model making sure to work out any air bubbles. Do not pull the brush back and forth. Use only a dabbing motion, as this will ensure filling all the cracks, crevices, and other details of the model. Whatever method you use, make sure to get a coat of plaster on the shims as well. You will have to work somewhat quickly as the plaster might begin to set up soon after being mixed. Let the splash coat set up a little (about an hour should be fine) before continuing.

The next step is to add more plaster over the splash coat. On a big model, like a head, it is easier to do this in several smaller batches, as opposed to one large batch. If you have too large a batch of plaster, you risk having it set up before you get all of it spread onto the model. Mix up another batch of plaster in a clean mixing container. If you use a container with even a small amount of cured plaster remnants in it, the next batch of plaster will set up much faster than normal. Sometimes you can use this to your advantage after you become more adept at working with plaster.

Use at least twice the amount of water than you used for the splash coat. Add plaster to the water the same way as before, until the plaster just begins to rise above the level of the water. Let it slake for 2-3 minutes and mix as previously described. There is no need to put food coloring in this batch or any of the follow-up batches after the splash coat. The coloring is for the first coat only.

Take an old spoon, putty knife, or even your hand *(wear rubber gloves)* and begin covering the model with more plaster. When the plaster is first mixed it will have a fairly thin consistency, like cream from the dairy. As soon as plaster is mixed it begins to go through its cycle of setting up. It starts out thin and starts getting thicker and thicker as the minutes go by. Eventually it will become like the consistency of sour cream and then closer to cream cheese. Past this it gets too difficult to work with. If the mixing water is warm, it will set up faster than if you used room temperature water. When first learning to work with plaster, use room temperature water so that you have enough working time.

It is difficult to build up a thick layer of plaster while it is still thin and runny. Sometimes you have to wait until the material has thickened slightly. The tricky part is that when the plaster is just getting thick enough to work with, it is also about to completely set up. So when it gets to this point you have to work very quickly to get the plaster spread all over the model evenly, before it becomes too stiff to work with. If that happens you'll have to mix up another batch.

The eventual goal here is to build up the plaster to a thickness of 3/4" to 1" thick. Depending on how much plaster you just mixed and applied to the model, you may need 1 or 2 more batches of plaster to build up to this thickness. With these thicker layers of plaster there is no need to let them fully set up before applying the next layer. In fact it is better if you do not. The longer the previous layer has had a chance to set up, the more it will draw moisture out of the next layer, which can give you problems. By the time you get the

next batch mixed up, the previous layer should be quite stiff. Sometimes it helps to have someone assist you who can get help get the next batch of plaster ready.

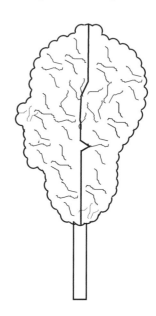

**Plaster built up 3/4" to 1" on model**

As you get closer to the final thickness of plaster, be careful not to cover over the edges of the plastic shims. After applying the final layer of plaster, just before it sets, dip your hand in some water and carefully smooth the outside of the plaster waste mold. This is not absolutely necessary, but it makes the mold nicer to work with. It is best to let the waste mold set for about 24 hours and build a lot of strength before trying to separate the two halves of the mold.

After the mold is strong enough, you can begin to separate the mold halves. First, remove the plastic shims all the way around the mold. Make or obtain some wooden wedges, 1" wide by about 3" long works well. The mold can be separated with only one or two wedges, however, a half dozen wedges make

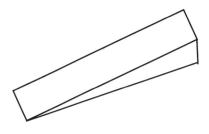

**Wooden wedge**

the job easier. Very carefully begin tapping the wedges in along the parting line where the plastic shims used to be. Go all around the edges of the waste mold, tapping each wedge just a little bit and the mold halves should start to separate. Keep going around and tapping each wedge a little until the mold halves completely separate.

Next, clean out the inside of the mold halves. If some clay is stuck inside the waste mold halves, carefully peel it out, trying not to get get any oil from the clay on the inside of the mold. If you used water-based clay for your model, wash out any remnants of clay with a sponge or damp rag.

Let the waste mold dry out completely before use. If you are going to use a casting material that uses the absorption properties of plaster (liquid neoprene), there is no further preparation of the mold necessary.

If you are going to cast other types of materials it would be best to let the mold dry out for about four days or so, and then seal the insides of the mold halves. Several coats of sanding sealer or *orange shellac* (A-R Products) work well for this. Several light coats are better than one or two heavy coats that run and sag. You do not want to ruin the detail on the inside of the mold. Use an appropriate mold release agent (the dealer where you purchase your casting material can tell you what would work

best), which is brushed or sprayed inside the mold prior to using the mold for casting.

A plaster waste mold can serve many useful purposes. Also, the techniques that you learned in this chapter for making waste molds can be helpful for making plaster *mother molds* or *back-up shells* as they're sometimes called. A mother mold helps hold the shape of a flexible rubber mold such as latex or silicone when doing a casting. (See Chapters Four and Five)

### *Parting lines, Draft and Undercuts*

In making a waste mold, it is not necessary to be too concerned with parting lines, draft and undercuts, as the mold is broken in the process. But, what if you wanted to make a mold of plaster (or other rigid mold material) that you could use more than once? Then these three items become very important. A brief overview of these can be very helpful for this and other parts of the figure making process.

These are principles that most seasoned mold makers understand and use to their advantage daily. Take the time to read and understand this brief overview and you will be way ahead of the game. You will also save yourself a lot of aggravation and grief. Problems such as having models or castings getting locked inside of molds can be avoided by learning about parting lines, draft and undercuts.

A *parting line* is where a mold separates on a two-piece mold. There can be additional parting lines for multiple-piece molds. For example, a three piece mold would have one additional parting line. *Draft* and *undercuts* determine where a two-piece mold will separate the best and whether there is a need for more than two pieces.

Let's cover *draft* first. Draft is the ability for a mold to release easily from a given model or casting because of its shape. We'll use a one-piece mold to show how this works, but the principle works the same for two, three, four or more, piece molds. Although what is shown here is a two-dimensional drawing, the same thing applies in principle to a three-dimensional model and mold. In the illustration below, notice the square-shaped object with a one-piece mold around it. If you tried to separate the mold from the model, there will be a tremendous amount of friction. The arrows in the illustration show which direction the mold would separate from the model.

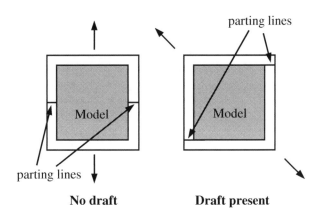

**No draft**　　　　　**Draft present**

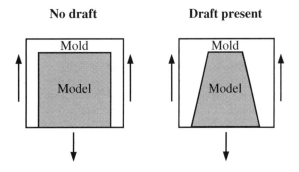

**No draft**　　　　　**Draft present**

To further illustrate the principle of draft, look at the model above on the right with angled sides (exaggerated for the sake of illustration). This model will release quite easily from the mold. The model with no draft will have friction until the mold is pulled all the way off. The model with draft present will have no friction as soon as the mold is pulled away even just 1/16 of an inch. Some models naturally have draft, some do not.

Sometimes draft can be created by how the mold is designed. A given model can be changed from *no draft* to *draft present* according to where the parting line for a two-piece mold is put (parting lines will be discussed in detail later). Let's use the example of a square model again to show how this can be accomplished. In this case we are looking at a *two-piece* mold which can either be easy or diffi-

cult to remove from the model depending on how the mold is made. In the illustration above, the mold on the left has the parting line on the sides of the mold in the middle. If you tried to pull the two halves of the mold away from the model (the direction the arrows are pointing), there will be a tremendous amount of friction, as there is no draft present.

The mold on the right, however, has the parting lines at the corners. When you try to separate the mold, it will come apart easily as there is a good amount of draft present in each half of the mold.

You can be thinking about draft as you are sculpting and sometimes try to create good draft where possible. Too often, however, that is not a realistic option. So careful placement of the parting line as shown above, or in some cases, going to a *three* or *four* piece mold can create the desired amount of draft allowing the mold and model to separate easily. A given model has to be studied carefully to anticipate how the mold and model (or a casting later on) will separate when completed.

*Undercuts* can not only determine if a mold will come apart easily, but in many cases whether it will come apart at all! Undercuts can also determine how many mold pieces a given model might require. We'll use the example of a one-piece mold again to demonstrate the principle of undercuts. In the drawing below, the model on the left has good draft but an obvious undercut. In this case, the model would be locked inside a one-piece mold and would not come apart unless you broke it! The solution is to go to a two-piece mold as shown on the right. The mold halves will now pull away from the model easily.

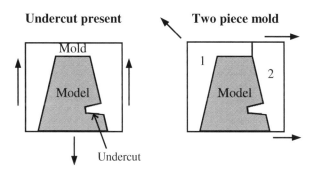

Some undercuts aren't so obvious. Take a sphere or cylinder (which in some ways would be similar to the cross section of a hand, foot or head model), for example. With a sphere (or cylinder), if the parting line is not exactly in the middle, it can create an undercut of sorts as in the illustration below. The fact that an incorrect parting line can create undercuts makes it very important that the parting line be determined carefully.

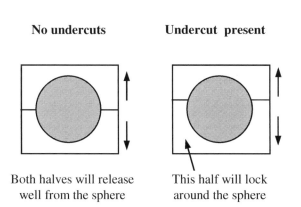

How does one know if you need to go to a three or four-piece mold? The model will tell you. In some cases a model has enough complexity to require more than two pieces. Sometimes the location of undercuts alone make it necessary to go to a three or four-piece mold. But often times it is a combination of undercuts *and* draft that makes it necessary to go to a three or four piece mold to solve the problem. Notice the model in the next illustration below. A four-piece mold was necessary to solve the problems of both **undercuts** and **draft**. Remember to keep a given mold to as few pieces as possible. In this case, four was the least amount of pieces one could go to and still have the mold separate from the model without problems.

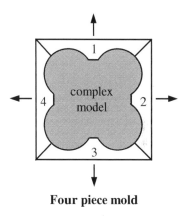

**Four piece mold**

Finally, let's discuss the **parting line**. The parting line, as has been previously mentioned, is where a piece mold comes apart. Obviously, the more pieces there are, the more parting lines there will be. To keep things simple, let's use a two-piece mold to illustrate the principles of how to establish a parting line correctly. The principles, when once learned, can be applied to multiple-piece molds as well.

One easy way to get a good general idea of where the parting line should be is to sight the edge of the model from above. Set your model on the work table and look down at the model directly from above. Sight along one edge of the model. There will be a point where you can just see the edge of the model and a point where you can not see what's below. It is between these two points where the parting line will be as in the illustration below.

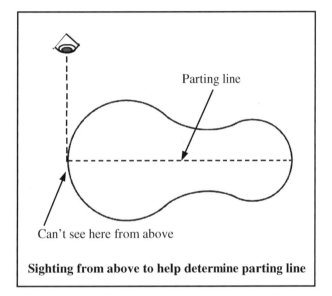

**Sighting from above to help determine parting line**

This same method can also be used to check for undercuts on a given model. Again, set the model on your work table and sight around it from above. If you cannot see an area on the model from above, it is undercut. (See illustration above right) In this illustration, the undercut area is pretty obvious. On some models, it might not be so apparent where the undercuts are. Sometimes they are small or in some cases, there can even be a slight amount of **reverse draft** (the angle of the draft would be going the opposite of what would make for easy mold withdrawal).

A more precise method of establishing the parting line is to lay the model on the work surface and follow around the model with a square. See where the square contacts the

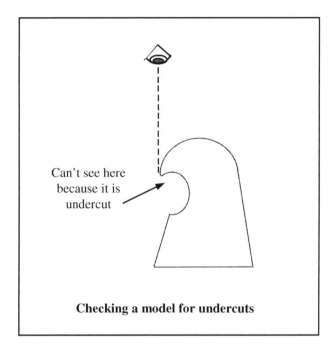

**Checking a model for undercuts**

model and make a mark with a permanent marker. Slide the square on the work table, around the model (as illustrated below) and make a dot or mark with a permanent marker every half inch or so apart. Then connect the dots with the marker to clearly identify the parting line. Some parting lines are straight, some are undulating (go up and down, kind of wavy in appearance).

The parting lines for the feet models shown on the next page, were determined with a square, setting them on the work table two

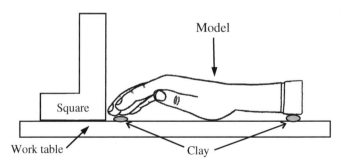

**Determining the parting line with a square**

different ways. These models were used to make plaster molds for casting with liquid neoprene (see Chapter Six) and ended up being three piece molds with two parting lines.

For more complicated shapes, it may be necessary to use a combination of the two methods (sighting from above and using a square) to establish the parting line or lines, as

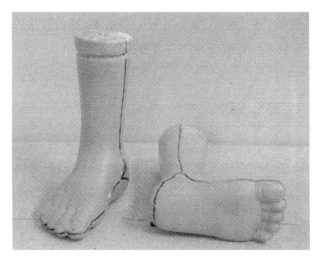

**Parting lines drawn for three part foot molds**

the case may be. Start by sighting the model from all angles to help determine where the parting line(s) should be and how many pieces might be required. Look for the obvious undercuts as well as the *not-so-obvious* undercuts as these will help you to determine where the mold might need to separate. See if the mold can possibly be made in two pieces. If not, make the mold in as few pieces as possible. Do not go to a four-piece mold when a three piece mold will work just fine. The more pieces there are the more complicated it will be to make and use the mold.

This is just a **brief** summary of **parting lines, draft** and **undercuts**. A general understanding of these principles will help not only with making plaster or other rigid molds, but also for making *mother molds* as described in Chapter Four. The molds described in the next few chapters are flexible mold materials, which, in general, are much more forgiving when it comes to parting lines, draft and undercuts. The mold making material, **latex rubber**, will be covered in the next chapter.

**Betty and Jimmy Nelson with Humphrey Higsbye,
Danny O'Day and Farfel**

# CHAPTER FOUR

# *LATEX MOLDS*
## *(and 'mother molds')*

Latex rubber is one of the easiest molding materials to work with and can have some good uses in making vent figures. Latex molding rubber is a liquid or semi-paste rubber that is brushed onto the model (head, hand, foot, etc.) one coat at a time until a thickness of about 1/8" to 3/16" is achieved. Unlike a waste mold which is usually broken after use, a good latex mold can be used to make numerous castings. In this chapter, *'mother molds'* or *'back-up shells'* (as they are sometimes called) will be covered in detail. Most types of rubber molds require a mother mold, so this is a good place to introduce them.

*Advantages of latex molding rubber are:* (1) Ease of use. Because it is fairly easy to use, you are pretty much assured that you will be successful in making a mold from latex molding rubber. (2) Low cost as compared to other mold making materials. A gallon of good quality latex mold rubber will cost you about $35 as of this writing. (3) Low in toxicity and odor compared to other mold making materials. (4) A very strong rubber when cured. If you have tried the hobby store latex before, put that out of your mind. People who do not like latex, have usually tried this type and figured that it was just a poor material for any type of mold making. They have never tried the real thing. Pro quality latex is a whole different deal, and will make

a very durable mold, which can have a much better tear strength than silicone or urethane rubber (see Chapter Five).

*Disadvantages of latex molding rubber are:* (1) Relatively high shrinkage compared to some other mold making materials. Silicone or urethane RTV mold rubber (see Chapter Five) have very low shrinkage compared to latex, and, in some cases, no shrinkage at all. The shrinkage of latex in general, however, is not much of a problem for figure making. Pro-quality latex shrinks much less than the hobby latex. There are some techniques that will help compensate for the shrinkage related problems, which will be covered in this chapter. (2) Length of time it takes to make a mold. It takes several days to make a good latex mold. With latex you can only apply so many coats in a day, and the average mold will need many coats to make a mold that's about 1/8" thick or so. Plan on 4-6 days to make a latex mold.

*Uses in figure making:* (1) One-piece latex hand or foot molds. These molds can be used for slush casting (see Chapter 6) urethane resin. (2) One-piece 'slit' latex head mold. You can slush cast urethane plastic in this type of mold. (3) Two-piece head mold. Standard two-piece mold construction which can be use to hand lay up of fiberglass resin and cloth, brushing or troweling (buttering) thickened resins, slush or roto casting ure-thanes, or pressing wood dough or epoxy putty inside to make a casting. (See Chapter Six for details on these casting techniques) (4) A special 'open' latex head mold. This can be used for all of the same techniques as number 3, but has the advantage of not having to deal with seams where the ears are. This is my personal favorite and can have many advantages over other types of molds.

The techniques for making a latex rubber mold are fairly easy to learn. The only part that might be considered a little difficult is making a *mother mold*. A latex mold all by itself without support can easily distort when making a casting. A rigid shell or mother mold helps to support the latex rubber so it will not distort while it is being used to make castings. In this chapter you will learn how to make latex rubber molds and the mother mold as well, step-by-step.

### Latex 'Open' Head Mold

Take note of this particular mold design. It is probably one of the more useful types of molds to make and use for casting a vent figure head. When casting in this type of mold it is possible to do fiberglassing, slush casting or rotational casting, and buttering of a thickened resin (see Chapter Six), all with this one style of mold. As it is described, you'll see why.

If you have a clay head model you can use plastic shims (see Chapter Three) where you want the opening to be. On the head model, insert shims in the outline of where the trap-door will be. Use a combination of *bubble stock* and regular flat plastic shims that will follow the outline of the trap door area. (See photo above right) Use Scotch Tape to cover any gaps between the shims. When you make the latex mold, you will apply the latex on

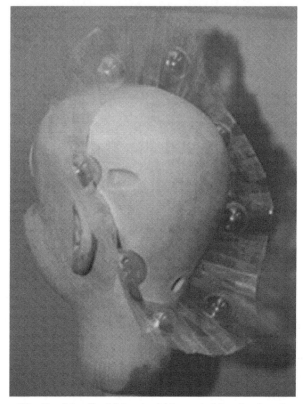

**Plastic shim 'bubble-stock' inserted in clay head**

both sides of the shims. The shims will make a separation for the two parts of the mold. One part of the mold will cover most of the head and another part will be just for the trap-door area. This will make more sense when you see the completed mold.

If you haven't already done so, seal the model with sanding sealer or clear acrylic sealer. Unsealed oil based clay models can leave a residue on the inside surface of the mold, which can potentially attack the latex rubber over time and cause it to deteriorate.

If you are going to go to all the time and trouble of making a latex mold, ***get the right kind of latex!*** This is one of the biggest secrets in working with latex rubber. The hobby store latex has very high shrinkage, and will give you much grief when trying to make something like a head mold. In all honesty, if you are going to try the techniques in this chapter with a cheap latex, it would be better to go to one of the other materials (silicone or urethane, as described in Chapter Six). It's just not worth it. You will end up very frustrated and waste much time.

The #74 Latex Molding Compound available from A R Products is very high in solids, which first of all reduces shrinkage. Second, it adheres well to vertical surfaces without running or sagging because of the high solid content. This allows you to build a mold much faster than the inexpensive, thin hobby latex. It is also of very good quality and nice to use. I have personally tried many different brands and types of latex rubber and have found the #74 Latex to be the best in terms of quality, lowest shrinkage, and ease of use. There are many other mold makers who would agree with me on this. (See suppliers list in the back of the book) Douglas and Sturgess, Inc., has this type of latex also.

For the first coat of latex use a 1/2" flat artist's brush of medium flexibility (not too stiff and not too flexible). Dissolve a little dish washing soap in a cup of water. Dip your brush in this soapy solution and then shake out the brush pretty well. Swirl the dampened brush in the latex container, just at the surface, attempting to get the excess water in the brush well distributed.

Begin by applying latex to the shim area (if you were latexing a hand or foot model, you would apply it to the mounting board near the wrist or ankle of the model). ***This is a general rule of thumb:*** your first few strokes with the brush when starting a new coat, should always be applied to shim area (or the mounting board on other models). That way if there is any dirt or debris in the brush it will end up there and not on the more important model area. You can also see if

there is too much water in the brush. The latex will look watery and there will be obvious bubbles that are a little hard to brush out if there is too much water.

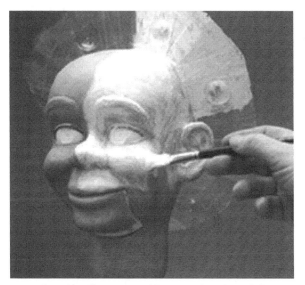

**Starting first coat of latex on head model**

When you are sure that the brush is just a little damp and not too full of water, then start brushing the latex evenly over the whole model, just one coat. This first coat should be spread thinly, taking care to eliminate any bubbles or pockets of air that might form. This is a combination of brushing and dabbing. Watch carefully not to trap air in *undercut* areas, cracks, crevices, and the like. Work these areas somewhat slowly, but keep making progress towards other parts of the model. If you stay working with the brush in any one place too long, the latex can start to set up a little, and you might create a rip or a tear. If this happens you will have to wait for the latex to dry completely, carefully strip the damaged first coat off, and then start over. This is generally only a concern on the first coat.

Let the latex and model sit undisturbed until the first coat of liquid rubber has dried.

The first layer should dry fairly quickly, as it is a thin coat. This will probably take just an hour or two. How quickly it dries depends on ambient room temperature and relative humidity. You can speed this process up a little by aiming a fan on low speed at the model. Do not use heat to speed the drying of the latex. It's too easy to overdo.

You can tell if the latex is partially cured as its appearance will change. The recommended #74 Latex will become slightly darker in color and become somewhat translucent (can see the model through the dried latex). It will also no longer appear to be wet. You can touch it lightly with your finger (make sure your hands are clean when doing this!). If, after touching it, you do not have any wet latex on your finger, it is dry. Check in the cracks and crevices of the model to make sure there are no wet spots, as the latex tends to build up in these areas and takes longer to dry.

**First coat complete and dry**

On subsequent coats, the latex will start looking opaque as the rubber gets built up on the model. Since it will no longer be translucent, the main thing you will be looking for is a change in color from a light cream color to a more beige color. Be careful not to touch the curing latex between coats with dirty fingers. Also, do not kick up any dust or allow sawdust or other such particles to come in contact with the curing latex surface. Any of this can cause the next layer not to adhere properly to the previous layer. Make sure there are no *wet* spots of latex visible anywhere on the model before applying the next coat. If you apply more latex over a wet area it is possible the last layer will seal over the previous layer and the *wet* spot will take forever to fully cure.

### Cleaning the Brush

Be sure to clean the brush out after each coat. Clean the brush in a jar or small pail of warm water being careful to get all of the latex out. Squeeze the brush with your fingers and get the remaining latex out that hides inside the middle of the bristles. Rinse thoroughly. Do not rinse the brush in your sink as latex residue can clog up your plumbing. After rinsing, you can use a wire brush, if necessary, to help get some of the dried latex out of the brush.

As the brush is used again and again it inevitably will collect some hardened latex that is next to impossible to get out. Discard the brush and use a new one. *Tip:* here's how to make your latexing brushes last longer. Each time you dip the brush into your latex container, dip it into the latex all the way up to and slightly past the metal on the brush. This keeps wet latex surrounding all the bristles while you are working and helps keep a hard layer of latex from building up on the brush when you clean it. Also, after cleaning a brush, store it in the cup that has the soapy water solution.

### *Subsequent Coats of Latex*

When you get to the second coat, change over to a 1" wide disposable bristle brush. This next coat can be thicker, but still take care to eliminate any bubbles or pockets of air that might form. The first two to three coats are the most critical as far as air bubbles are concerned. First of all, it preserves the detail of the original model (a good surface without bubbles or air pockets). Secondly, if there are bubbles in the second or third layer of latex these can eventually show through the first or second layer (which are the surface layers on the inside of the mold) after you have made several castings The first or second layer of latex near a bubble will be quite thin and can wear or tear through with use. A latex mold will last longer if you are very careful with the first three coats.

**Second coat of latex being applied with 1" brush**

Apply the second coat in the same way as you did the first. The main difference will be that succeeding coats should be thicker than the first coat. It is like putting on a fairly heavy coat of paint, but not globbed on! Subsequent coats will have to cure longer than the first coat as they are thicker. With the #74 Latex two coats per day is generally recommended. This would equate to one coat in the morning (8:00 am for example) and one in the evening (8:00 pm for example). On a warm day it is possible to do three coats.

As a general rule, when you first start latexing a model, on the ***first day*** you would do your first coat (very thin coat) early in the morning, second coat an hour or two later, and the third coat later in the evening. This would be all in one day, as the first coat usually dries so quickly. Then on day two, apply one coat in the morning and one in the evening as outlined above. The timing does not have to be precisely at 8:00 am and 8:00 pm. You could do a coat at 9 am or 10:00 am, and the second coat at 4:00 pm or 5:00 pm. This will not hurt anything. If you are pushing the two coating times a little closer together this way, it would be best to aim a fan at the piece between coats during the day (keep the mold you are working on out of direct sunlight). You most likely would not need a fan on the piece overnight.

As mentioned, it is possible to speed the curing process slightly by moving the air around the mold using a fan. When using a fan, keep turning the model 90 degrees every half hour or so. This will help the latex to dry evenly. Keep in mind that applying too many coats in one day or using too high a speed on the fan can cause the latex to have higher shrinkage than normal. If you push your latexing schedule to three coats in one day, it would be best to spread out the time between coats. You could do a first coat at 8:00 am, second coat at 2:00 pm, and the third coat at 8:00 pm. You should definitely run a fan on the piece between coats when doing three coats in one day.

---

### *Suggested Latexing Schedule*

#### *First Day*

**8:00 a.m. - *Very Thin Coat to Start***

**9:00 - 10:00 a.m. - *Regular Coat***

**4:00 - 5:00 p.m. - *Regular Coat***

#### *Second Day (normal schedule)*

**8:00 - 9:00 a.m. - *Regular Coat***

**4:00 - 5:00 p.m. - *Regular Coat***

#### *Second Day (accelerated schedule)*

**8:00 a.m. - *Regular Coat (with fan)***

**2:00 p.m. - *Regular Coat (with fan)***

**8:00 p.m. - *Regular Coat (with fan)***

#### *Remaining days of Latexing*

***Use same schedule as second day (normal or accelerated)***

---

You can tell how thick the latex mold is getting by looking at the flange or shim area or the mold. *Remember that you are looking*

*at two thickness' of latex* (one on each side of the shims). About 1/8" is thick enough for most latex molds. On a head mold it is better if it is closer to 3/16" thick (on each side of the shims, for a total of 3/8" thick). This can take anywhere from five to seven days to get the mold to this thickness. (See photo below) It's not that much work, just a fair amount of time between coats. So a little patience is needed.

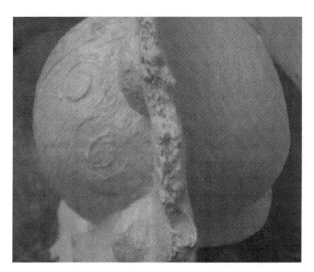

**Check shim area for thickness of latex mold**

At some point during the molding process, you might want to check for undercuts on the latex rubber mold (see Chapter Three). Undercuts can create problems when you go to make the mother mold. In some cases, the mother mold will lock up and not release easily from a latex mold that has a rigid casting in it. Again, you need to plan ahead. If you find some small undercuts, they can be filled in with clay after you are done latexing and just before you make the mother mold.

Larger undercuts you might want to fill in with thickened rubber. This is made by adding ground tire rubber or other such thickening agent to the latex, and filling in the undercuts. A-R Products has a rubber filler available made just for this purpose. Wood flour also works to make a heavy latex paste. Follow the manufacturer's instructions for making the latex paste. It is best if a couple of unfilled layers of latex are applied over the spots where you filled in the undercuts. So plan ahead as you are making the latex mold.

An alternative to this would be filling in *large* undercuts with thickened (thixotropic) urethane rubber or silicone rubber applied with a putty knife. This is done after you have finished applying all of the coats of latex. Mix up the urethane or silicone rubber according to the manufacturer's directions and then add Cab-O-Sil® (fumed silica), which is a thickening agent. (See Chapter Five for details on working with silicone rubber, urethane rubber and Cab-O-Sil®) Mix in the Cab-O-Sil® until the rubber will no longer run off of the mixing spatula (the material is now thixotropic). With urethane rubber, apply some Vaseline® to the area first, so it won't stick to the latex mold. Silicone is self-releasing and will not stick to the latex. The cured rubber undercut 'inserts' can be held in place by the mother mold (described shortly) when doing a casting.

Although the above is a viable method for handling the undercuts, it is best if you do not have to do this. It makes more pieces for reassembling the mold and parts that can be misplaced or lost. It is also sometimes difficult to get these little rubber inserts to be seated in just the right place when putting the mother mold back in place. In the section on making the mother mold for the head, you will notice there are no inserts or thickened latex added behind the ears. The latex is thick enough not to need support in that area for most casting situations. Some clay was temporarily put behind the ears while making the mother mold, and was removed later. (See photo on page 47, in the section on making a fiberglass mother mold)

Let the final coat of latex cure for a day or two. You can test to see if it is cured enough by lightly pressing your fingernail into the curing latex. If it leaves a mark, let it cure for another day and test again. This is best if done to the latex flange where the shims are (or on the mounting board on other types of molds) where it will not hurt anything. After the latex has passed the above test, you can proceed to make the mother mold.

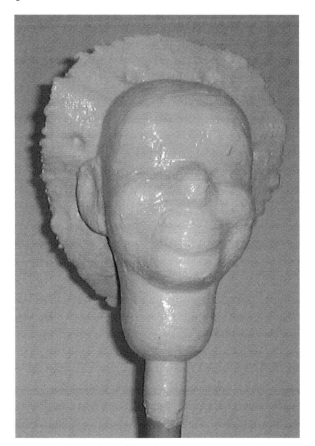

**Latexing of head model complete**

*Note:* If you had a solid or rigid model of a head (made of something other than clay), instead of using plastic shims, you could

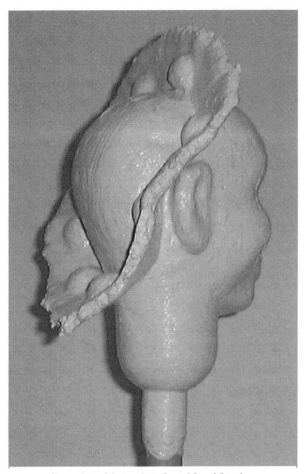

**Completed latex head mold - side view**

make a clay wall of sorts where the trap-door will be. This serves the same purpose as the shims on a clay model. There will be a few extra steps because of this, but it's not a big deal. You will need to make the latex mold of most of the head first, along with the two or three-piece mother mold (the clay wall creates an opening in the latex and mother mold where the trap-door goes, the same as the plastic shims). Keep undercuts and draft in mind as you design where the mother mold will part (see next section). After you have completed all of that, remove the clay wall and make a latex mold of the just the trap door area. Then, finally, make a mother mold for this small trap-door portion of the mold. You can also do this same technique

on a clay model if you did not want to use shims for some reason.

### *Fiberglass Mother Mold*

First of all, it needs to be noted that a *mother mold,* or *back up shell,* serves a very important purpose. Any type of rubber mold, whether it be latex rubber, silicone or urethane rubber, usually needs to be supported to hold its shape when used for casting. A rubber mold all by itself with no support is floppy, and next to useless. If a mother mold is not made well enough or strong enough, the castings produced from that mold can be distorted, and you will only be able to make poor copies of your original model.

A fiberglass mother mold is very lightweight, strong, dimensionally stable and in most cases will outlast mother molds made of other types of materials. Slush casting or rotational casting (as described in Chapter Six) is done more easily with a light weight mold. Not to say that it cannot be done with a heavier mold, but you will be more than just a little worn out, after making just one casting. Some other types of mother molds will be covered later in the chapter, so you will have those options as well.

In a nutshell, a fiberglass mother mold is made like this: A clay wall is formed, mold keys are placed or cut into the clay. A coat of Vaseline® on the latex and clay wall will keep the fiberglass from sticking. The resin and fiberglass cloth are built up 1/16" to 1/8" thick for the first piece of the mother mold. Remove the clay wall and apply a coat of Vaseline® where the clay wall was. If additional clay walls are needed, these are formed next as well. Build up the next section of fiberglass mother mold the same way as the you did the first section. Continue this way until all sections are complete.

A more complete explanation follows: You will be taken step-by-step through the making of a professional style mother mold. We're going to do this for two reasons: **1.)** There are many figure makers and those interested in learning figure making that have never had this adequately explained or demonstrated before. **2.)** There is much to be learned from seeing how a slightly more complicated mother mold is made. After seeing this process and having some understanding of the principles involved, you will then be ready to take on any type of mother mold situation you might be confronted with. These important principles, when once learned, will never be forgotten.

The description here will be for the 'open' latex head mold. It has a few more mother mold sections or pieces than some other types of mother molds, because of the opening in the back of the head. Also, the cheeks are very wide across the front of the face as is typical of many so called 'cheeky boy' style figures. If one were to build a rigid shell (mother mold) over the front of the face in one piece, it would mechanically lock in place, because of undercuts (the cheeks). This would make it impossible to remove the castings from the mold without breaking something. (See Chapter Three on **parting lines, undercuts and draft**) Please bear with me and follow the process through. Some simpler mother molds will be covered later in the chapter. After seeing what is probably the hardest thing you'll come up against in mold making for figures, and seeing that the solutions are not really that difficult, you'll be ready to handle all else with ease. The fundamentals of using fiberglass will also be described as we go through the process here. The use of other materials will be discussed later.

*Clay walls:* To start, clay walls are formed to divide off one half of the front of the head. Keys in the photo (above right) are made from bubble stock. You can also make keys by making half-sphere shapes in the clay. By spinning the head of a spoon in the clay, you can make some nice keys. When the walls are complete, apply a healthy coat of Vaseline® to the exposed latex. Apply a thin layer of Vaseline® to the clay and key area.

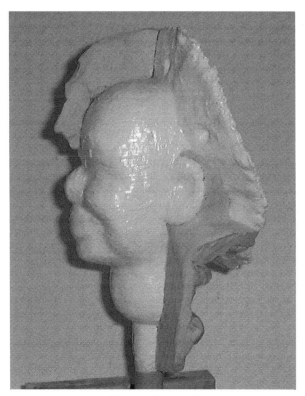

**Clay wall started**

*Note:* You will notice that the space behind the ears (this is an undercut area) is filled in with clay before making the mother mold. There will be a space between the latex (behind the ears) and the mother mold when it is reassembled for casting. That is not a problem. This small area of latex will hold it's shape just fine for casting, especially if the mold is pushing 3/16" thick. This is an

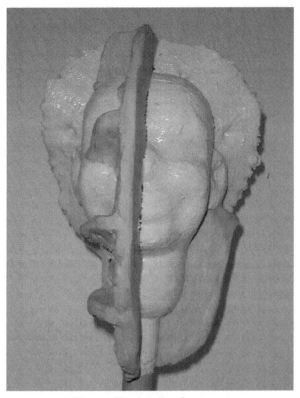

**Clay wall - details of support**

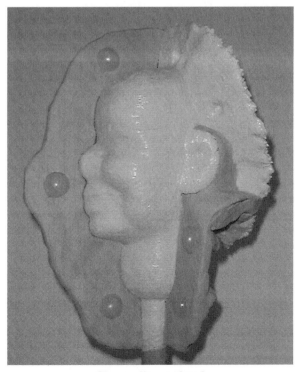

**Clay wall completed**

old mold makers trick. A mother mold does not always have to cover 100% of the rubber mold in all cases. It depends on the mold and the type of castings you will be doing.

The back of the head does not need any clay walls and can be fiberglassed at the same time as the first half of the front of the head. Before getting into doing the actual fiberglassing, there are a few things to know about fiberglass that can help you decide on the best way to go, as there are a few choices. This will help you sort out what can otherwise be a bit of a technical jungle.

***Fiberglass basics:*** A fiberglass mother mold can be made from polyester or epoxy resin. Epoxy resin is more pleasant to work with in terms of fumes, but there are still potential health hazards to be aware of. Also, epoxy is very sensitive to temperature. If you try to use epoxy resin at cooler temperatures (below 75 to 80 degrees F.), it will not cure properly or at all. This can be a consideration, depending on where you have to do the fiberglassing work.

The easiest, cheapest, and generally the most fool-proof resin material for fiberglassing is polyester resin (available at many hardware stores and automotive supply stores). You can adjust the amount of catalyst for the polyester resin so it will cure even at cooler temperatures. However, it has a very strong chemical odor and the potential health hazards to match.

***Fiberglass cloth & mat:*** Epoxy or polyester resin without reinforcement is very brittle and has no real strength. Resin combined with glass fiber is very strong. There are two basic choices. Standard fiberglass cloth (woven cloth) or fiberglass mat (fiberglass strands that are chemically bonded together in a random pattern). Cloth takes more layers than mat to get the thickness you want (usually between 1/16" and 1/8" thick), thus taking more time to make. When you look at cloth and mat side by side (without any resin applied), it would appear that the cloth would be easier to work with, as it bends easily and is somewhat pliable. Mat, in comparison, is very stiff and appears unworkable in its dry state. Once saturated with resin, however, mat will go around the contours of the mold easier and stay in place better than cloth will. Cloth is easier to find in the stores, but mat will make life easier for you. Either can make a nice, strong mother mold.

*Cloth:* Fiberglass cloth comes in a variety of weaving patterns, but for most mold making and casting work, a plain weave will do just fine. Cloth also comes in various weights (which refers to the thickness of the cloth) per square yard and is rated in ounces. Start with cloth in the six to ten *ounce* range if you are purchasing it from a boat making or mold making supplier. It goes without saying that the thicker the cloth, the less layers you will need to achieve the desired thickness. Keep in mind, however, that the heavier (thicker) the cloth, the harder it is to get it to conform around the curves on the mold when fiberglassing. You can buy the cloth that is sold at some hardware stores and sometimes automotive stores. Many times it is sold in a kit with the polyester resin. The cloth in these kits is usually of average weight and should work all right for a mother mold.

*Mat:* Fiberglass mat is glass fiber in a random pattern (as opposed to cloth which is woven in a specific pattern) and is sold in weights per square foot rather than per square yard. The 1.5 ounce mat works very well for making mother molds. Two layers will make an extremely durable fiberglass shell. As a comparison, to produce a fiberglass mother mold that is about 3/32" to 1/8" thick, it would take two layers of 1 1/2 ounce mat or about *four to six layers* of 10 ounce fiberglass cloth. It is definitely less labor to work with the fiberglass mat. *The **mat**, however, will not work with **epoxy resin**. It has a polyester soluble binder in it that is only dissolved by polyester resin.*

See 'The Fiberglass Repair and Construction Handbook' by Jack Wiley (TAB books) for some excellent information on polyester and epoxy fiberglassing. It has a lot of info on cloth, mat, resins, and standard fiberglassing techniques.

*The technique:* For a mother mold, you do not have to worry about a gel coat or anything like that. For a polyester mother mold, purchase a good quality, general purpose, polyester resin. This type of resin has wax in it, which aids in the fiberglass curing *tack free*. For epoxy, get the type that's made for laminating. Follow the manufacturer's instructions very carefully for mixing.

Whether using polyester or epoxy, it would be best to mix up some test batches and get used to working with the material first. See how long it takes to set up and get used to brushing resin into the cloth or mat. Remember, polyester will work with mat or cloth. Epoxy will only work with fiberglass cloth.

*CAUTION!: **Whether using epoxy or polyester use plenty of ventilation and a NIOSH approved mask specifically made to be used with these type of resins. Read and follow all of the safety precautions on the Material Safety Data Sheets for the resin and catalyst you will be using! You will also need some gloves that are chemical resistant or the polyester will eat through them.***

*If using mat:* cut it into 3" to 6" squares, depending on the size of the mold. Fiberglass mat is easier to use if you lay it on a flat surface (inside a polyethylene tray or tub works well) and saturate it with catalyzed polyester resin first. Set out two pieces of the squares you cut, and spread some of the catalyzed resin onto both pieces. Let them sit undisturbed for about 30 seconds, or until they get somewhat limp. You can pick the pieces up with gloved hands. Lay a piece on the latex mold and use the brush with a little additional resin to saturate the mat if necessary. The photos show mat being used to make the mother mold.

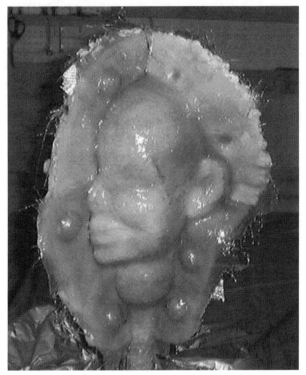

**Section of mold front covered with one layer of mat**

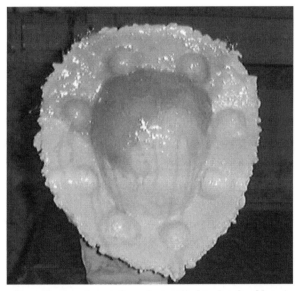

**Two pieces of mat & resin applied to back of head**

*If using cloth:* Cut a piece of cloth large enough to cover the whole first section of the mold (latex and clay wall). Put some catalyzed resin on the mold first with a disposable bristle brush, and then lay the cloth on the mold. Follow with the brush and a little more resin until you saturate the cloth. You will see the cloth kind of disappear as it gets wet with resin. That's the clue that you have applied enough resin. It's kind of tricky to get the cloth to go around all the contours of the mold.

*Whether using cloth or mat:* Use a dabbing motion with the brush to work out any bubbles or air pockets and to get the reinforcement material to conform to the contours of the mold. Use only enough resin to saturate the cloth (or mat), otherwise you will have puddles of resin in places. Resin without cloth or mat is brittle and does not have the strength that resin with the reinforcement will have. So puddles or thick spots of resin alone will be weak spots in the mother mold shell (or a fiberglass casting, for that matter). Do one complete layer at a time.

With mat, overlap the edges of each piece by *at least* 1/2" or more, as opposed to putting them edge to edge. This will make a stronger mother mold. For the second layer

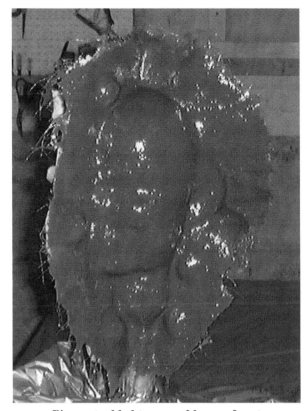

**Pigment added to second layer of mat**

Sometimes with cloth, it is necessary to make a cut with a pair on scissors in certain spots, to get it to conform around a certain contour on the mold. This is best done before you lay it in the wet resin (so you don't ruin a good pair of scissors). Four to six layers will probably be sufficient, depending on the weight of cloth that you purchased. You could do a test with some resin and small pieces of fiberglass cloth to see how many layers you need to get the thickness and strength desired.

These are the basic steps for laminating with fiberglass cloth (or mat) and resin. The same process is used for all sections of the mother mold. When the first section of fiberglass has hardened, you can remove the temporary clay wall sections. Take care when

you may wish to add a little pigment to color the resin (ask your resin supplier about a suitable coloring agent). This helps in seeing where you have been and that you haven't missed any spots. (See photo this page, top left photo) Two layers will be all that is needed with 1.5 ounce mat.

With cloth, you can take another pre-cut piece and just lay it right over the the first layer. Some of the resin that's in the first layer of cloth will ever so slightly start to saturate this new piece of cloth. Dab on more resin with your brush, being careful to add only as much as is needed to saturate the cloth. Again you will see the cloth kind of turn invisible as it becomes saturated. You are then ready to add another piece of cloth.

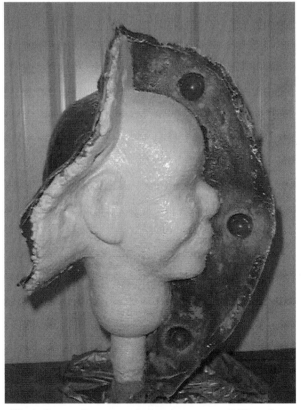

**First clay wall removed showing exposed fiberglass**

working next to the first section of fiberglass. The little strands of cloth or mat that now have resin in them are very sharp. You may want to trim some of this off with a Dremel Moto Tool® before continuing, so as to make the mold safer to work with. Take care not to use too much force in doing this, so as not to dislodge the first section of the mother mold from the latex mold.

The other sections of the mother mold can now be made. One additional section of clay will have to be formed first. Make a clay wall similar to the first clay wall. This one only needs to go along the side of the neck, as well as just under the ear and behind the ear a little (see photo below). When this clay wall is complete, coat the latex, clay wall, and exposed fiberglass flange with Vaseline® the

same as before. This area can now be fiberglassed, the same as the first half was done. When completed, remove the clay wall in preparation for glassing the last section.

The back of the neck is the only remaining area that needs to be fiberglassed (see photo below). Remember to apply Vaseline® to the latex and exposed flange areas of the first and second half of the front mother mold pieces. Some smaller pieces of mat or cloth can make it easier to fiberglass this area.

**Back of neck ready for glassing**

Being a professional style mother mold, this was taken a step further, but certainly not necessary. A metal frame was constructed and bonded to this last piece of the mother mold. The metal frame (which could be made of other materials as well) makes it so the mold can stand upright for certain casting techniques. Making a fiberglass casting or pressing wood dough or other modeling compounds can be easier to do with the mold in an upright position. These techniques can certainly still be done without such a frame. It just makes the mold easier to work with.

The metal frame was temporarily glued in place with some 5-minute epoxy (available at

**Second clay wall - ready for more glassing**

your local hardware store). See photo below. The frame was then permanently bonded in place using some strips of mat and polyester resin. Four layers of mat were used for extra strength. It is best to do this kind of bonding while the previously laid down fiberglass (the glassing that was just done on the neck area) is still pretty fresh. The resin will have gelled (no longer liquid) and is somewhat hard, but is not 100% cured. If you waited until the next day, it would be necessary to take some sand paper to rough up this area, before trying to bond the frame in place.

**Frame temporarily epoxied to fiberglass mother mold**

### Removing the Model

The first step is to remove the mother mold sections. Remove the trap-door section of the mother mold first. It should come off fairly easily. Then pry the back of the neck section off. You can use a screw driver or a wooden wedge (door shims from your local hardware store work well) to help pry it away from the other sections of the mother mold. Take care not to damage the latex mold underneath while doing this. Finally, pry apart the two front halves of the mother mold and carefully remove them from the latex

**Trimming latex flange area**

mold. Wipe off as much of the Vaseline® that remains on the latex as possible. Try not to get any Vaseline® on the inside of the latex mold as you do the following steps.

Take a pair of good, sharp scissors, and cut around the outside of the latex flange. Cut about a 1/4" strip of latex off of the flange, or just enough to expose the plastic shims. You can now carefully peel the trap-door section of latex off of the model. Set this inside of

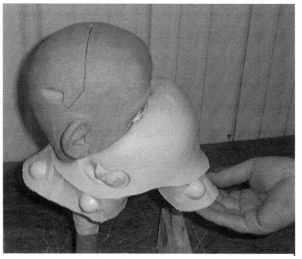

**Beginning to remove latex head mold**

the mother mold section for the trap-door area.

You can now strip the main part of the latex mold off like a rubber glove, by peeling it backwards from the open area of the mold. It is turned inside out as you pull it off of the head, and finally down off of the head stick. (See photo previous page and below)

**Latex turned right side in**

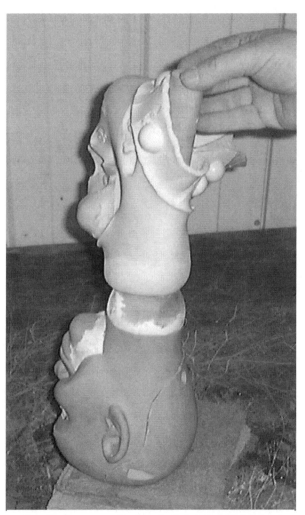

**Continuing over the head stick, latex inside out**

Be careful not to distort the latex by stretching it too much. It will still be a little *green*, so to speak, for a few days yet. While

**Mother mold pieces**

it is inside out, coat the inside with a little talcum powder (baby powder will work).

The talcum powder keeps the latex from sticking to itself. It is only necessary to do this once. A latex mold is just tacky enough after it is first made that it can stick to itself somewhat on these inside areas. It's not a big problem. Just something to be aware of. The tackiness goes away once it has had talcum powder on it.

Brush off the excess talcum powder, and then turn the mold back 'right side in'. Take the pieces of the mother mold and reassemble it with the latex mold in place. Allow the new mold (still inside its mother mold) to air out for a few days before use. You may want to run some air into the inside of the mold with a fan to speed this up a little. Make sure that the latex mold is positioned correctly inside the mother mold while it continues to cure and that it is not distorted in any way. The latex mold can be damaged if it is allowed to cure in a distorted or pinched position. If it is pinched or distorted inside the mother mold, it will retain this distortion after it fully cures. You would then have to make the latex mold and mother mold all over.

### Open Mold Advantages

An *open mold* of this type eliminates many alignment problems and seams that can be found with two-piece molds. On an open mold, the ears do not create any problems, as

*Open* latex head mold - Back view

there will be no seams there to contend with. In fact, there is no seam at all on the head, except around the trap-door area. Just a little trimming around this area after casting is all that is required. Most of this is going to be hidden by the wig anyway. This type of mold can make the *clean-up* work that is normally done after casting a lot easier.

With an open mold, you can 'hand lay up' fiberglass (lay down fiberglass cloth or mat and resin), butter on a thickened resin, or press in wood dough or epoxy putty through the *opening* in the mold. With a **two-piece mold** you have to lay up or cast each half of the mold individually and then join the two halves together, which can be a little tricky. Sometimes it is hard to get the seams to match up and get a good solid joint. On a head mold this is difficult around the ears especially. This is one reason some figure makers suggest casting the ears separately and gluing them on later. With an open mold this is not necessary. About the only disad-

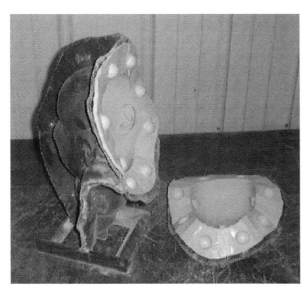
Completed mold reassembled inside mother mold

vantage is it can be a little bit tight working inside the opening in the open mold (where the trap-door is) if you are laying up fiberglass or buttering (see Chapter Six) the inside of the mold.

*Open* **latex head mold - Top view**

Once you've laid up the fiberglass or thickened resin (wood dough, epoxy putty or other suitable medium), you are pretty much done. You will have to do a separate casting of the trap-door, but that's not hard to do. Normally you would have to cut the trap door out of a two-piece mold casting anyway, so this method saves that step as well (if you did a *rotational* or *slush* casting with an open latex mold it would be necessary to cut the trap door out later).

### Latex Slit Mold for the Head

This mold style is actually quite simple to make, but its uses are pretty much limited to slush casting or rotational casting (see Chapter Six). The latex slit mold is made by first applying latex over the entire model of the head. It is built up in coats (two to three coats

per day) just as described previously. There are no shims or the like to use when making this type of mold. When the latexing is done, you make a mother mold. This can be made in one piece for the back half of the mold and one or two pieces for the front of the mold. But now, here's the secret. After you have removed the mother mold, you cut a slit in the rubber in order to remove the model (or casting for that matter). Then, any time you make a casting, you can remove the finished piece through this same slit in the mold.

You can make the slit starting at the top of the head and then going down towards the back of the neck. The slit should only be big enough to remove the model of the head and no bigger. When you reassemble the mold with the mother mold, the slit pretty much disappears. It is best however to make the slit in a spot that will not show much. With the slit going from the top of the head down to where the bottom of the trap door would normally be, the wig will be covering this area of the head.. When doing a casting it would be best to put a sheet of thin plastic (plastic sandwich wrap or similar material) between the latex and the mother mold. If you do not do this, you will get a build up of casting material inside the mother mold when doing a slush casting.

Some mold makers like to take a hole punch (as used for paper) and punch a small hole at both ends of the slit. This keeps the slit from tearing and growing larger. You probably won't need to do this, but is mentioned just in case that becomes a problem.

The advantage to this type of mold is that there are less steps and less labor than in making a *two-piece mold* or *open mold*. This type of mold works best for *rotational* or *slush casting* (see Chapter Six on casting).

Something to keep in mind when making a slit mold is that you need a place to pour your casting material in when it is completed. On a head mold you could pour casting material in where the head stick normally goes. After you make the mold and remove the model there will be an open hole where the head stick was. You can make a plug out of latex (use Vaseline® as a mold release) or silicone rubber (see Chapter Five) that fits inside the opening where the head stick hole is in the head mold.

A split mold will not work for hand laying up of fiberglass or any other type of casting techniques where you need easy access to the inside of the mold. There is no such access in a slit mold. Thus, a slit mold is limited in what one can do in the way of casting. It is, however, very handy, if you need to do a quick mold and make a few quick castings, or if you know you are only going to do roto-casting or slush casting.

### Two-Piece Mold

A standard two-piece head mold can also be done with latex rubber. You can use the *clay bed* method as described in the next chapter on *RTV Molds*. Although this technique is best done with a rigid model, it is possible, with great care, to do the same with a clay model. You would follow all of the basic instructions for building up a clay bed, to divide the model in half along the parting line. Make the clay bed wide enough to produce a good flange of latex on the finished mold.

You could then make the first half of the mold *and* mother mold (which might be a one or two-piece mother mold for the front half). The latex is of course applied one layer at a time as usual (RTV can be done in layers or done in one application). The mold is then turned over, the clay bed is removed and

Vaseline® is applied to the exposed part of the latex where the clay wall used to be. Finally, make the second half of the mold the same as you did for the first.

A two-piece mold can be easier for using some casting materials. Hand laying up of fiberglass, buttering the inside of the mold with thickened resin, or applying wood dough or an epoxy modeling compound, can all be easier to do in a two-piece mold. You have better access than with the open mold. The problem, as mentioned before, is lining up the seams of the two halves of the head (after they are cast), as well as bonding them together adequately. It can certainly be done, but be prepared for some challenges.

The exception to this would be slush casting or rotational casting in a two-piece mold. The two pieces of the mold are strapped together and the casting material can be poured in through the hole where the head-stick was. When the casting material has set up, it is an easy matter to take the mold apart and remove the casting from inside. In this case, a two-piece mold essentially works as well as an open mold. You will have more trimming where the seams are, however. A two-piece mold is also slightly easier to construct than the *open* mold described earlier. The mother mold is easier to make (less pieces and fewer clay walls to form). You have to decide which advantages are more important to you.

### One Piece Latex Mold (hand or foot)

A one-piece latex mold is the easiest mold to make for hands and feet. It is assumed that the hand or foot model is sculpted in clay and attached to a mounting board. The first step is to draw a line about 1 1/2" to 2" bigger than the wrist for a hand model, or ankle for a foot model, on the mounting board. This is where you will apply some latex onto the

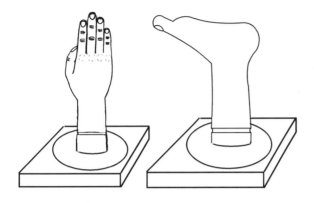

**Draw a line around model on mounting**

as thick as a head mold. In fact, it will be easier to pull the mold off the castings if the mold is not too thick. It is recommended however, not to make these any less than 1/8" inch thick. When you are finished latexing the models, you can make the mother molds. This can be made as a two piece mother mold either of fiberglass or one of the other materi-

mounting board in addition to covering the model. This will make a nice latex *flange* around the opening of the mold when completed, and is standard practice in the latex mold making industry. (See illustration and photo, this page) It also keeps this area of the mold from distorting once the mold is removed from the model as well as providing something to pull on when demolding a casting. As mentioned before, this is one of the secrets of dealing with the shrinkage of latex. Always make a nice flange around the area of the mold opening.

If you haven't already done so, seal the model with sanding sealer or clear acrylic sealer. There is no need to seal the mounting board. In fact it can help to keep the latex in place if the mounting board is not sealed. The natural porosity of the wood will allow the latex to adhere temporarily (kind of like an adhesive bandage sticking to your skin). Latex shrinks as it dries and this will help keep things in place on the mounting board.

You use the same basic latexing techniques presented earlier in this chapter (follow the latexing schedule on page 44). You can apply two to three coats per day, the same as for a head mold. The mold thickness of a hand or foot model can be about 1/8" thick. Hand and feet molds do not need to be

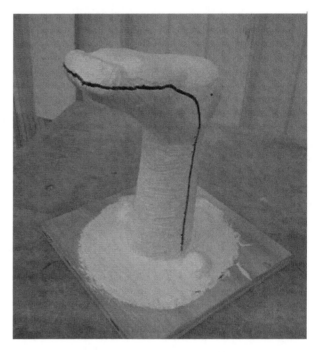

**Foot model latexed and parting line marked**

**Latex foot molds with fiberglass shells completed**
Note: the latex is slit in the flange and back of the mold

als described shortly (plaster and urethane paste). See next section (Making a Plaster 'mother mold') for a description of parting lines and clay walls. A hand mold is illustrated there.

After the mother mold is complete you can remove the mother mold pieces and then carefully pull the latex from the models. You will most likely have to make a slit in the latex to do this. You do not want to over stretch the latex when you remove it from the models. The shape of feet and hand models is such that the latex mold will usually not pull over itself (stripping it off 'inside out' like a rubber glove) easily.

On a foot model, cut a slit through the flange going up the back of the ankle, just far enough to remove the mold from the model. On a hand model, cut a slit through the flange going up the side of the wrist just long enough to remove the hand model easily. It's usually best to cut the slit on the 'pinky' (little finger) side of the hand.

### Making a Plaster mother mold'

A plaster mother mold gives one the option of working with less toxic substances when making a mother mold. Polyester, epoxy, or urethane resins can be worked with safely, but have the potential for damaging one's health if safety precautions are not taken. *There are still some health warnings to be aware of when working with plaster or gypsum products (plaster, Hydrocal, Hydrostone, etc., are all gypsum products). The biggest one is not breathing in the plaster dust. Use an approved dust mask when working with these products.*

Leave the latex rubber mold on the model while making the mother mold. First determine the parting line (see Chapter Three) or lines (if you need a *three-piece* mother mold

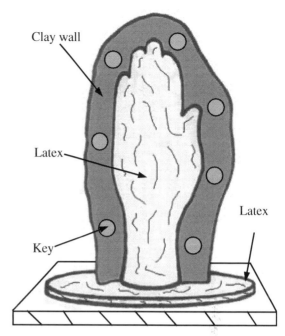

**Clay wall on latex hand mold**

for some reason) where the mother mold will separate and draw a line on the latex mold with a permanent marker. See photo previous page. On a hand mold, generally the parting line would be along the sides, with the mother mold separating from front to back.

Take some oil based clay and roll out some strips of clay 1" or 2" wide by 3/4" thick. Start laying a strip of clay around the latex mold to one side of the parting line. Begin forming a clay wall all around the mold. This is just a temporary wall that helps in making the first half of the mother mold. Chances are, the clay will not want to adhere very well to the latex mold. A little patience and persistence is needed. Feathering the clay (squishing the edges of the clay tightly) against the latex will help. Also, starting near the base of the mold can help. In general, it is not a good idea to have oil-based clays in contact with latex as has been mentioned. However, it is usually not a problem for the length of time it takes to make the first half of the mother mold.

Take an old spoon and rotate it in the clay wall to make some half sphere shapes. This will make **keys** in the clay. Be careful not to knock the clay wall loose from the latex while doing this. The keys will align the two halves of the mother mold when completed. (See illustration, previous page)

In Chapter Three, the plaster was mixed by sprinkling it into the water slowly. This is the traditional way of mixing plaster. It can be critical to mix it this way if you are looking to get the best absorptive qualities and consistent results in hardness in the final plaster casting. For a mother mold, this is neither desirable nor necessary.

***Read all of the safety precautions from the manufacturer prior to working with plaster or other gypsum products!*** Here's a different approach to mixing plaster that I learned from a professional plasterer. It is easier and faster to mix a nice thick batch of plaster this way, like what is needed for making a mother mold. Take a clean mixing container and add about 2 cups of dry plaster. Now take some water and add to the dry plaster. Mix quickly, adding more if necessary. You want a very thick but workable consistency (like sour cream).

The water has to be added somewhat slowly, as it is very easy to add too much. If that does happen, you can add more plaster to thicken the mix. Add just enough water to make the mixture workable, but thick enough to *stay put* on a vertical surface. It will take a little practice to get the mix just right. A batch of plaster mixed this way will be ready to use immediately. It will thicken some more and begin to set up as you start making the mother mold, so you have to work quickly.

For a harder, more durable plaster mother mold, you can mix in some Hydrostone (another type of plaster or gypsum product, which is very hard) with the plaster. Hydrocal will work in place of Hydrostone, as it is also a harder type of plaster. Ordinary casting plaster has better *body* to it and thus is easier to form or shape the way you want it when it is mixed thick. Hydrostone (or Hydrocal) all by itself does not have much body at all, no matter how thick you try to mix it, but it is extremely hard. So, by mixing the two together, you get the best of both worlds. You can usually get Hydrostone or Hydrocal at the same place you get your casting plaster. (See suppliers list) Mix the casting plaster 50:50 with the Hydrostone or other harder plaster, before adding the water to the mix.

Begin applying some plaster (or Hydrostone and plaster mixture) where you want the first half of the mother mold to be. You can start by using a combination of your hand and a 1" putty knife. Use disposable latex gloves to keep the plaster mix from drying out your

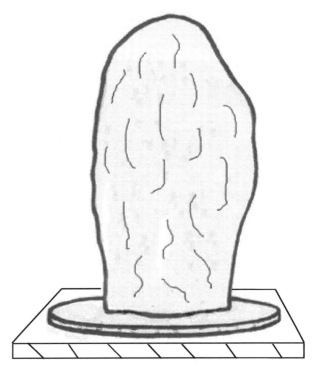

**Plaster covers the latex and clay wall completely**

hands. Apply this first layer as evenly as possible. Mix up another batch immediately and apply it evenly over the first coat.

Some mold makers like to add some hemp (hemp is sisal fiber, which also available from A-R Products), or burlap strips in with the plaster mixture for the remaining coats. These act as reinforcement and will make the mother mold stronger, and much less likely to break. This is what many of the special effects shops in Hollywood do to make a quick, strong, mother mold. So, it is a tried and true method.

If you use hemp, mix it in with thickened plaster mix as you apply the subsequent coats over the first coat. If you use burlap strips, you will probably need to use a little more water when you make your plaster mix. If the plaster mix is too stiff it won't soak into the burlap sufficiently. Apply some wet plaster over the first coat. Dip a burlap strip in the mixing bowl, and then put the plaster soaked burlap onto the mold. Use as many strips as it takes to cover completely with one layer. Keep adding plaster and plaster soaked burlap (or hemp) until you achieve a 1/2" to 3/4" thickness.

In would be best to do smaller batches of plaster and build the mother mold up in layers, as opposed to mixing up one big batch. If you mix too much at one time you risk having the plaster set up in the mixing bowl before you finish getting all the layers on. You will have to take some care not to accidentally dislodge the clay wall while applying the plaster and reinforcement.

After the first half hardens sufficiently, remove the clay wall. You will need to apply some mold release where the exposed plaster is. Rub some paste wax (automotive paste wax will work) onto the plaster where the

clay wall was previously. After that, apply some Vaseline® over the paste wax. This will help the two halves of the mother mold separate when you are all done. There is another method that works well if you have some latex on hand. Just simply paint some latex rubber on the plaster where the clay wall was previously and let the latex cure. Try not to get the coat of latex too thick. Apply a layer of Vaseline® over the latex to be sure things will separate easily.

If you want to make it easier to separate the mother mold halves when complete, here's a little trick for doing that: make some small squares out of oil-based clay (1/2" by 1/2" by 1/8" thick) and affix them to the plaster (where the clay wall was), near the edge about 3" to 4 " apart. Put these on before applying the Vaseline®. The small clay squares will give you little access channels of sorts. When the mother mold is complete, the channels that the clay leaves can be used to pry the mold apart with a screwdriver.

After you have added the little clay squares and mold release, you are ready to make the second half of the mother mold. Mix more plaster and build up the second half the same way as you did the first half. When both halves are completely cured, you can separate the two halves. Carefully scrape out the small clay squares and use a screwdriver to begin prying the mold halves apart. You can use small wooden wedges to finish prying them apart if necessary.

Plaster bandages (see suppliers list) can also be used to make a mother mold. The plaster is impregnated into the cloth bandages and only requires being dipped in water to activate the plaster. The plaster bandage roll is cut into shorter strips. After being dipped in the water, the strips of plaster bandage are draped over the mold and pressed into place with your fingers. Keep adding additional layers of plaster bandages until it is about 1/4" thick. Plaster bandages can typically make a lighter weight plaster mother mold than the other techniques.

**Urethane paste mother mold on a hand mold**

### Urethane Paste Mother Molds

"Last, but not least", as they say, a *urethane paste* mother mold has some interesting advantages over fiberglass or plaster mother molds. Because you are not dealing with reinforcement materials such as fiberglass cloth, mat, hemp or burlap, it is for the most part easier to use than the methods and materials described thus far. There are less materials to buy. The paste conforms to the contours of the mold easily, so you don't have to fight with fiberglass cloth or mat, trying to get them to stay put. It is pretty mild in terms of fumes as well. *You should still follow all of the precautions that the urethane manufacturer recommends!*

You can use all of the same setups and basic techniques as outlined for the fiberglass and plaster mother molds, described previously in this chapter. You would make clay walls the same as you did for these types of mother molds. You would, however, apply the urethane paste instead of fiberglass or plaster to the sectioned off areas. Mix the urethane paste according to the manufacturer's recommendations. It is generally done in a few coats or layers as opposed to one thick coat. After the last coat, you let the paste fully set up, remove the clay wall and then make the next section of the mother mold. Remember to apply Vaseline® to the exposed areas where the clay wall was previously. Otherwise the next section of mother mold will permanently bond to the last section made!

You may find this to be the best option in making mother molds. It's a matter of personal preference. A urethane paste mother mold is reasonably quick to make, strong, and in many ways is much less of a hassle to work with. This material is a little newer to the scene than the other materials discussed, but many mold makers have found it to be very nice to work with. Urethane pastes are available from both *Smooth-On* and *PolyTek Development Corporation*. (See suppliers list at back of book)

PolyTek's version is called **POLYGEL®** **Plastic-75**. It consists of two liquids, Part A and Part B, which after mixing one-to-one by weight or volume, immediately self-thickens and gels to a brushable or trowelable consistency. It cures at room temperature to a hard, strong RTV (room temperature vulcanizing) plastic. Polygel® Plastic-75 thickens to a paste with a three minute working time. As the liquid components of Polygel® are stirred together, the mix changes color and thickens to a buttery, non-sag paste. A shell or mother mold can be built up in two or three coats, each applied about ten minutes apart, so a mold shell can be made in less than an hour and demolded in about four hours.

*Plasti-Paste* from **Smooth-On** works similarly and consists of two components, Part A and Part B, that are mixed together. It has a working time of about ten minutes, and demolds in about four hours. 'Working time' is just like it sounds. It is the amount of time you have to work with the material before it gets too stiff to use. The longer working time of Plasti-Paste might be a little less intimidating and better to try first, if you are unsure as to which urethane paste to buy initially. Essentially, either material will make a good strong shell.

### Summary

Latex is a very versatile and easy to use material provided you follow the guidelines here and your suppliers recommendations. The main thing in working with a latex mold is making sure you use a good release agent when making a casting. It does not have the natural release properties of silicone rubber. Release agents will be covered in detail in Chapter Six. Also, a latex mold should be stored in a cool, dark place to slow down the natural aging of the rubber. If cared for properly, a latex mold can last for many years. Some casting materials, such as polyester resin, will shorten the life of a latex mold with repeated use. Do not use any type of petroleum products on the inside of the mold. The limited use of Vaseline® as a release agent when making a mother mold, does not appear to have any detrimental effects on the latex.

Although a **mother mold** does not have to be pretty, it needs to be functional. The better it is made, the longer it will last. Also, the more time you take in making a quality mother mold, the better it will serve you in making castings. An improperly made mother mold will make it hard to fit the latex mold (or other rubber molds) back inside of it. Having good flanges and keys on the latex mold, as well as the mother mold sections, helps to assure that everything will go back together easily and accurately. If everything lines up well, the better your castings will come out. This is especially important on a head mold. The accuracy of the shape of the mouth area and eye sockets depends on a quality rubber mold (whether it be latex, silicone or urethane rubber) and mother mold. It can be the difference between a mold that is a pleasure to use and one that might cause a person to curse. It can also be the difference between a mold that yields one *fair* casting (then is no longer usable), and one that yields many, many, good castings repeatedly. Take the time to do it right!

After reading Chapter Five on RTV Molds, and Chapter Six on casting techniques, you will better know which type of molds might best suit your needs. It depends on what it is you want to do. A one-time casting, production casting, or custom work will all require different types of molds. Think each process through carefully and try to determine which type of mold will work best for your application. It can also depend on what material you are casting. For example, if you want to make some neoprene castings of hands or feet, you can only use plaster type molds. Other types of molds will not work for the absorption process. It is suggested that you read all of the chapters on molds and casting techniques at least once through before deciding what type of molds and materials to use for your figure making application. Silicone molds do have some advantages over latex molds that you may or may not feel is important. It really depends on what type of projects you will be doing. Silicone molds and their uses will be covered in the next Chapter.

# CHAPTER FIVE

# *RTV MOLDS*

RTV mold-making materials cover a variety of products which can be quite useful for figure making. What is an RTV material? RTV stands for *room temperature vulcanizing*. Sound intimidating?!? All this basically means is that these materials will cure at room temperature. They do not require heat to cure as do a number of mold-making or casting materials such as injection molding plastics, polyethylene plastics, vinyl, etc.

Although this chapter focuses primarily on silicone rubber, most of the techniques described here can also be done with urethane rubber. Urethane is also an RTV compound, that cures at room temperature. The biggest difference between making a silicone and urethane mold is that making a mold from urethane requires a lot more model preparation than silicone does. Urethane rubber has adhesive qualities. If you do not prepare the model correctly and use the proper release agent, it will most likely bond to the model like glue.

***Advantages of silicone rubber are:*** Silicone rubber molds do not require a mold release agent, as nothing will stick to silicone rubber, except more silicone rubber! This is probably one of the biggest advantages to silicone rubber molds. All other types of flexible rubber molds usually require some sort of release agent (see Chapter Six) when casting most types of resin materials. If you forget to use a release agent with a latex or urethane rubber mold, for instance, and you cast some urethane plastic, it would most likely bond to the mold and ruin it. Not so

with silicone. When cured, silicone rubber has an oil-like substance in the pores of the material that gives it a natural releasing ability. A variety of materials can be cast in silicone rubber molds, such as epoxy, urethane, fiberglass (which can be either polyester or epoxy resin), wood dough, epoxy putties, etc., with no worries of accidentally ruining the mold.

Silicone rubber can also be cast in thick sections at one time, something you can not do with latex. So, it is possible to have a silicone mold done within a 24-hour period. You can pour a silicone rubber mold several inches thick, and it will still cure completely with no problem. It cures on a different principle than latex. This makes it possible to make certain types of molds that would be impossible with latex, such as blanket mold s or block molds. These mold types will be covered later in this chapter. Urethane rubber also cures well in thick sections.

Silicone rubber also has less shrinkage than latex rubber and with certain silicone compounds, no shrinkage at all. Incredible dimensional stability can be achieved with the right material. This can be very important for doing any type of production work (casting many figures in the same mold). Good dimensional stability can save one a lot of detail work. For example, let's say you had a model of a head and a jaw model for this same head, that fit really well together. If you made a silicone mold of both of these items, the parts cast in them would be very true to the original models. There would be little or no fitting of the jaw to be done when the castings of the head and jaw were made!

Silicone molds are also pretty much impervious to heat. Certain resin materials can generate a fair amount of heat when curing, which can, over time, take its toll on a latex mold. Silicones can take temperatures between 400 and 600 degrees F, depending on the variety of silicone you get. Silicone rubber molds, in general, are also more resistant to chemical degradation than a latex mold. Certain types of casting materials, however, can attack the integrity of silicone rubber, causing it to wear out prematurely. Some silicone rubber compounds (i.e., platinum base, described shortly) are pretty much inert and will not deteriorate with time the way a latex mold can. Latex can get gummy or dry out and crack with exposure to sunlight and the passage of time (especially if not properly cared for).

***Disadvantages of silicone rubber are:*** Number one is cost. Silicone rubber can cost anywhere from $75.00 to well over $200.00 per gallon, depending on the quality and the variety that you get. Number two is it's more finicky to work with when making a mold. Silicone rubber generally has to have a catalyst added to the liquid rubber, and then it has to be very carefully mixed or it will not cure properly, or will have soft spots in the finished mold.

The majority of silicones require the use of a scale to carefully weigh the components to be mixed. If you make an error in measuring these types of silicone, it will not set up correctly or will not set up at all. There are some newer varieties of silicone, however, that do not require a scale. Also, with some types of silicone you need a vacuum chamber to remove the air from the rubber after it is mixed. But if you get the right kind of silicone, this will not be necessary.

### *Types of Silicone Rubber*

"Hey, can't I just buy some silicone rubber and be done with it?!?" It is unfortunately a bit of a silicone jungle out there. There are many, many manufacturers and just as many different types of silicone it seems. Without getting too technical, some general descriptions will be given so that you can make an informed decision before purchasing product.

***Tin-Based Silicone:*** Tin-based silicone is what is called a *condensation cure* silicone and in general is much more user-friendly when making a mold. It is not affected by sulfur or other such contaminants that can cause some silicones not to cure. Tin-based silicones eventually deteriorate with time (will get crumbly or tear more easily than when first cast), or in other words, do not have a good 'library life'. It is not an inert material. It changes with time. Some tin-based silicones can produce alcohol, which can initially inhibit polyurethane castings (the urethane will not cure too well until the alcohol disappears). Tin-based silicones are generally more economical and exhibit excellent chemical resistance during polyester resin casting. So, if you were going to do a lot of polyester fiberglassing, this would be a good choice.

***Platinum-Based Silicone:*** The platinum-based silicones are called *addition cure*, and are a lot more finicky to use than the tin based silicones. There are many substances than can cause 'cure inhibition' with platinum based silicones. If that happens, the material may not cure in places or the entire mass of rubber may not cure at all. You will have a sticky mess to contend with, and waste a lot of money. You have to start over if cure inhibition takes place. There are certain things you can do to prevent this. Use a non-sulfur-based clay, for one. Also, sealing the model with the right type of sealer is the other biggest item that will help assure success with a platinum silicone. It is usually best to mix up a small amount to test that there will be no problems.

After reading the above, you may be wondering why one would want to even bother with the platinum silicones. It has to do with the advantages of this type of silicone rubber. Platinum-based is, for the most part, *inert* and will not degrade with time. This is probably the biggest reason to consider using a platinum-based silicone. In general you will get many more castings from a platinum-based silicone mold than a tin-based silicone. In terms of general durability and 'library life' (a platinum mold can sit on a shelf for years and still be quite usable), it is a superior product. Platinum silicones are more dimensionally stable than tin-based and generally

do not shrink (the shrinkage of tin-based silicones is actually pretty minimal). Also, platinum silicones do not produce alcohol, which can inhibit polyurethane castings, as previously mentioned. Platinum is particularly well-suited for polyurethane resin casting.

***Shore Durometer:*** This is a term you will hear in connection with silicone rubber compounds (both tin and platinum), so a brief explanation is in order. This term also applies to urethane rubber. The relative hardness of the cured silicone rubber has a rating of *Shore Durometer A*. The 'A' stands for a flexible rubber product as opposed to rigid plastics which are significantly harder (plastics are rated on a Shore D scale). Usually silicones will have a rating like *Shore Durometer A 30*, or just *Shore A 30*. The number at the end is usually somewhere between 10-60; the lower the number, the softer the cured rubber. Thus, a Shore A 10 silicone would be very soft and flexible. Shore A 60 is a very stiff, rigid rubber.

***Silicone Recommendations:*** The first recommendation would be to start with a tin-based (condensation cure) silicone to help assure success with your first few silicone mold-making projects. A tin-based silicone mold will probably yield quite enough castings to make it worth your while, and you will be much better acquainted with how to use silicone rubber in general. There are methods that will help make a tin-based silicone mold last longer that will be covered in Chapter Six. You can then try a platinum-based (addition cure) silicone later, if you feel you need the advantages it has.

Here's a few tin-cure silicones to consider: ***GI-1000*** from ***Silicones, Inc.*** is a very popular tin-cure silicone, used extensively in the special effects industry. ***Dow Corning's HSII*** is a popular tin-cure silicone as well. It has a very good tear resistance, which can be one of the more important properties to look for in a silicone rubber compound. This silicone can be purchased from ***Alumilite.*** (See suppliers list) ***SILPAK, INC*** in Pomona, CA, has a nice line of silicones, both tin-based and platinum-based. One of the owners, Jerry Galarneau, is very knowledgeable and can recommend the right silicone for your project. Prices are reasonable.

If you can find a good 1 to 1 ratio silicone, you can get started making silicone molds without the use of a scale. You can measure by volume instead, which is much easier. You simply measure equal amounts and mix. These types of silicones are generally much more forgiving if you are slightly off in your measurements, and will set up just fine if you are off a little. Most other silicones are usually a 10 to 1 ratio and have to be measured by weighing on an accurate scale.

When you feel you are ready to try a platinum-cure, there is a very nice 1 to 1 ratio platinum silicone available from PolyTek Development Corporation (see suppliers list). It is called PlatSil 71-20. It has a Shore A durometer of 20, so it is pretty flexible. It also has a very good tear resistance, which makes it a very durable silicone.

*Centepoise:* There is another term that can be helpful to know, which is ***cps***. You will find this listed in the spec sheets on silicone rubber. ***Cps*** means ***centepoise***, and basically is the viscosity, or how thick the liquid resin is. The higher the number, the more viscous or thick the material. In general, it is best to find a silicone in the 10,000 cps to 25,000 cps range. Getting into the higher cps ranges will pretty much require you to own a vacuum chamber for working with silicone. Otherwise you will have a lot of air entrapment and bubbles in your finished mold.

### *Weighing Silicone Rubber*

As mentioned, there are some 1 to 1 ratio silicones available that can be used without a scale. These are nice, if they have the properties you want, as you can measure by volume (by eye) without needing a scale. The majority of silicone rubber compounds, however, require that you measure the amounts needed by weight. This type usually comes as two components, which are generally the base material (liquid rubber) and the activator (which activates the rubber and causes it to set up and become a solid rubber in about 24 hours). It is very important with this type of silicone rubber to weigh the components carefully to get the rubber to set up properly. This is critical. Otherwise you can end up with a gooey mess that can not be reclaimed. Silicone rubber is not cheap! Both the base material and the activator need to be weighed accurately for good results.

A good scale, then, is a necessity for working with most silicone rubber compounds. A *gram scale* will handle most of your needs. If you get an electronic gram scale, make sure it goes down as fine as a half of a gram (0.5) for reasonable accuracy. A standard triple-beam gram scale (mechanical, as opposed to electronic) is very reliable, will last for years and has little to go wrong with it. They are also

**Triple beam scale**

less expensive than the electronic scales. They can be found used. In the larger cities, look for a shop that fixes or calibrates scales. They often have used ones available for a good price. A new one isn't that much, so that might be the best route to go. You can also purchase additional weights, so you can weigh larger amounts on the scale. Gram scales usually come standard with a 500 gram capacity. With additional weights you can weigh up to 2,000 grams. (See suppliers list in the back of the book for where to get gram scales)

If you are concerned about learning to work with grams (instead of pounds and ounces), don't be. It is, in fact, easier when once learned. For instance, try figuring out how much 10% of a pound and three ounces is one time, and you'll see why grams are much easier. Step by step instructions for working with a gram scale will be presented, to help you past any hurdles.

Weighing out the components for silicone is not hard to do, but there are a few tricks to working with a gram scale. Many silicones are mixed at a 10 to 1 ratio of base to activator (see what your supplier recommends). Or put another way, 100% base material to 10% activator by weight. So if you had 100 grams of silicone you would need 10 grams of activator (10% of 100 = 10). How does this work on a gram scale?

First make sure that the scale is zeroed out. When there is nothing on it and all the weights are on zero, the balance beam pointer should be balanced and pointing at the center line mark. If not, there should be an adjustment to get it to balance properly at zero weight.

The next thing that has to be considered is the weight of the mixing container. This is called the 'tare' weight. Set the mixing container on the scale platen (a round metal disc on the scale). Move the little weights on the balance beam until it balances at the center line once again. Add up the total of the weights. As the weights are set in different spots on the balance beams, they point to a certain number. Let's say that in this example, one weight is at 20, and another at 5 (the largest weight is still at zero). That would, of course, add up to 25. You would then write this figure down.

Next, figure out how much silicone you're going to use. For example, let's say you are going to use 200 grams of silicone base material. You would set the scale for 225 grams total at this point (200 grams base material + 25 grams *tare* weight). The scale pointer will drop down as there is nothing in the mixing container yet.

| Set scale - Base material |
|---|
| 25 *tare* weight |
| +200    base material |
| 225    scale setting |

With the mixing container on the gram scale, begin pouring the silicone base material into the container. When the pointer comes up and balances at the center line, you will have exactly 200 grams of silicone base material in the mixing container.

If you accidentally pour too much silicone you can pour some back into the original base container. The tricky part is that the balance pointer does not start to rise until you get within 5 to 10 grams of having poured in the total amount of silicone. By the time you see the pointer start to rise, you will probably have poured too much silicone into the container. *Tip:* to keep this from happening, as you are pouring push down on the platen (the place the mixing container sits on) and then let go. Keep doing this as you are pouring. You can feel when the scale is just about to balance, and back off on how fast you are pouring. This helps eliminate surprises.

Finally, in this example, you will need 10% activator to base material. You have 200 grams of base material so you will need 20 grams of activator (10% of 200 = 20). You would then set the gram scale for 245 grams total (25 grams *tare* weight + 200 grams base material + 20 grams activator). Pour in the activator very slowly, until the the pointer comes up and balances at the center line. If you accidentally pour too much activator in, there is no easy way to correct for this. You can not pour the activator back out of the mixing container once it has come in contact with the silicone. So go slowly and use the *tip* mentioned above.

| Set scale - Activator | |
|---|---|
| 225 | 'tare' & base |
| + 20 | 10% activator |
| 245 | scale setting |

Don't rely on your memory. Write these figures down as you work and double check your addition. The carpenter's rule of:

'measure twice, cut once', is very applicable when working with silicone. A wrong calculation can cause the silicone to not set up.

There are gram scales that come with a 'tare' feature that will make the scale read 'zero' with the mixing container on the platen. That way you do not have to remember any tare numbers or figure them in. These are easier to work with, but cost more than a standard gram scale. Most good electronic scales have a *tare* feature as well. Electronic scales are also typically easier to use.

### Mixing and removing entrapped air

The last item before getting into 'how' the molds are made, is the mixing and removing of trapped air when working with silicone. Silicone must be mixed correctly in order to avoid problems. If it is not mixed adequately, you can end up with parts of the mold that are uncured. This can be a serious problem, especially if those uncured spots end up on the inside of the completed mold. The same is true for urethane rubber.

First of all, always use clean mixing containers and stirring utensils. If you have previously mixed some *tin-cure* silicone in a certain mixing container, do not do any mixing of *platinum-cure* silicone in that same container. This is called 'cross contamination'. Some of the chemicals in the tin-cure silicones will contaminate and inhibit the cure of the platinum-based silicone. Even though you think you may have cleaned the container out well, traces are there and will cause you grief later on. So, keep your mixing containers and utensils separate for tin-cure and platinum-cure silicones.

Silicone can be mixed by hand (with a mixing spatula) or with a power mixer. A drill motor with a *Jiffy Mixer*™ mixing head works well (see suppliers list at the end of the book), but will introduce more air into the silicone than hand mixing does. If you do not have access to a vacuum chamber, it would be better to mix by hand.

Whether you mix by hand or with a power mixer, after a minute or two of mixing, carefully scrape the sides and bottom of the container as you mix. This helps prevent unmixed material from showing up in your mold. Some manufacturers of silicone include coloring in the activator. This aids in telling you if the silicone is well mixed or not. The color will be uniform, with no streaks, when the base and activator are thoroughly mixed. Scrape the sides and bottom of the mixing container two or three times during the mixing process to ensure that the entire mass of silicone is well mixed.

As mentioned, mixing does introduce air bubbles into the liquid silicone, which can show up in the finished mold. Ideally, the mixed silicone should be put into a vacuum chamber to pull the air out before pouring. A ready-made commercial unit can be purchased, or a home-made vacuum chamber can be fabricated. (See Appendix B) Perfectly acceptable molds can be made without the use of a vacuum chamber, but you need

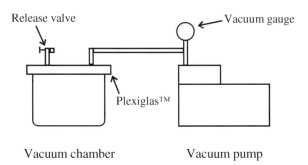

**Vacuum chamber and pump- Basic components**

to use a low viscosity silicone to be able to achieve this. Low viscosity is in the 10,000 to 25,000 cps (centepoise) range. The mold-making techniques discussed next can all be done without a vacuum chamber. If you have access to a vacuum chamber, or have the funds to get one, by all means use it. Some basic instructions for working with a vacuum chamber are also found in Appendix B.

### *How to make Silicone Molds*

Whenever your are trying a new material for the first time, it is highly recommended to do some smaller test batches to get used to working with it. It is much better to make an error on a small test batch than an important project. Although silicone rubber is not really all that difficult to work with, there are things that can go wrong. It is much less likely to happen if you've at least had a trial run with the material first.

There are several types of molds possible with silicone rubber. The *'blanket mold'*, the *'skin mold'* and the *'block mold'* are the three most useful silicone molds for figure making. As mentioned, the techniques for making and using these types of silicone molds could also be used for making *urethane rubber molds.* Urethane rubber, however, does not have the natural release properties of silicone. You *must* therefore carefully seal the models and use a release agent when making a mold (urethane rubber is a natural adhesive). You would also have to use a release agent when doing castings in a urethane rubber mold. Follow all of the manufacturer's instructions very carefully when working with urethane rubber.

The first two types of silicone molds have some similarities in how they are made and have in common what is called the *clay bed method*. Both the *skin mold* and *blanket mold* use the ***clay bed method***, so a brief description of that will be covered first.

### *Clay Bed Method*

The clay bed method is applicable to any two-piece mold that you might make (silicone, urethane or latex), for a head, hand, foot, or even a body mold. Although a clay model can be used, a rigid model is best. First draw a parting line (see Chapter Three) on the model with a permanent marker. Lay the model face up on your work table or work board, supported by clay underneath. Position the model so the parting line is pretty much parallel with the work surface.

Begin forming a bed of clay just under the parting line on the work surface next to the model. Build up the clay bed all the way up to and following the contours of the parting line. If you have a more complicated model, that has more than one parting line (see Chapter Three), position the model so that the first section you wish to make a mold of is face up on the work surface. Make a clay bed with only the first section surrounded by the clay. A foot model can be more of a challenge due to its shape, but even this can be done without too much trouble. (See photos this page)

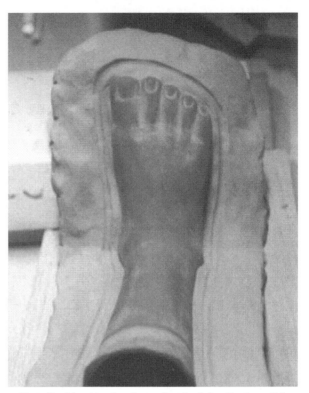

**Detail of 'gutter key' on clay bed for foot model**

The clay bed should extend 2 to 2 1/2" out from the model. It will go all the way around the model, except where the opening in the mold will be. That would be the wrist on a hand model, ankle area on a foot model, or control stick area on a head model. If the parting line is undulating (wavy), the clay should go up and down, following the parting line. The bed of clay is temporary and helps in making the first half of a two-piece mold,

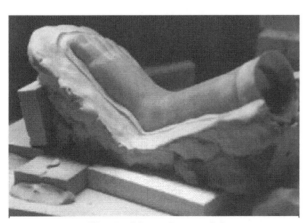

**Clay bed for a foot model**

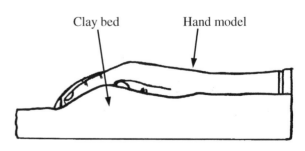

**Clay bed formed around parting line of hand**

skin mold, blanket mold or even a two-piece block mold.

Carve out a *half round* groove in the clay bed about 3/4" away from the model that is 1/4" wide by 1/4" deep approximately. Make sure the groove is well-shaped and has no undercuts (see Chapter Three). This groove should go all the way around the model. This is called a gutter key. It will not only help to align the mold halves, but it will also help to keep liquid resin from leaking out at the mold seam when doing a casting later (see Chapter Six). This can be a big help if you are planning on doing a lot of castings.

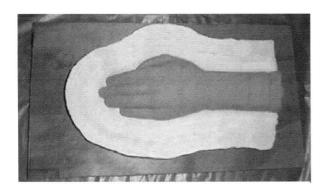

**Top view - Clay bed around hand model**

For the best alignment, you should also make some mold keys in the clay bed. You can make keys by making half-sphere shapes in the clay. By spinning the head of a spoon in the clay, you can make some nice keys. These should be placed between the gutter key and the outside edge of the clay bed, every 3" to 4" apart. After finishing the clay bed around the model, you can make either a *'skin mold'* or *'blanket mold'*. The skin mold will be covered first.

### Silicone 'skin mold'

In some ways making a skin mold is similar to making a latex mold. It is done in layers as with latex, but can be done in fewer layers, and completed in one day. With silicone, you can do one thin layer and then one or two thicker layers.

When making a skin mold, you may want to insert some plastic shims (or cardboard shims) vertically in the clay bed, just near the edge. Make sure there is enough clay to hold the shims in place securely. The shims will help the silicone stay put on the clay bed and make less of a mess as you make the skin mold. Use some Scotch™ tape between the shims to avoid leaks between the shims.

There are two choices for doing the following: you can either purchase a pre-thickened silicone or add your own thickening agent. Although you can make a skin mold without a thickened silicone, it can be frustrating and very time consuming. If you thicken your own silicone, you have more control, but a nice mold can be made with the pre-thickened variety as well. There is also less hassle in buying and using the ready-made thickened silicone.

When a silicone rubber (or any resin for that matter) is made thick like a paste, it is then called a ***thixotropic*** resin. It is no longer fluid. Traditionally, to make a silicone rubber thixotropic, you add a product called ***Cab-O-Sil*** (fumed silica). You keep adding Cab-O-Sil to the rubber until it is thick enough to no longer run off of the mixing spatula. Some manufacturers have a chemical thickening agent for their particular silicone. Cab-O-Sil works well and will make any silicone you purchase thixotropic.

***Pre-thickened silicone:*** If you buy ready-made thixotropic silicone, mix it according to the manufacturer's recommendations precisely. **Silpak, Inc.** carries a nice pre-thickened silicone. (See suppliers list) It will probably appear almost too thick to work with. Just be patient and it will work fine.

Mix a small batch (just enough to cover the clay bed and model with a thin layer) and very carefully work the silicone into all the cracks, crevices and other detail areas of the model and clay bed as best you can. This is called **wetting out**, which basically means making sure the model has been completely covered with a thin layer, taking care to eliminate any voids or bubbles. It almost goes without saying, it is easier to **wet out** a model with a thinner silicone. If a small bubble does appear in the finished mold, it is not a major deal. It will look like a small 'wart' when you cast a part, and can easily be sanded off. So it's not the end of the world, but you will have a nicer mold if you try to avoid any bubbles on the surface coat.

Let the first layer set up a little (this is called gelling). Mix up more pre-thickened silicone, a bigger batch this time. Cover over the first layer completely, trying to keep it an even thickness over the entire model and clay bed. Continue mixing up more batches and applying to the mold until the silicone is between 1/4" and 3/8" thick. This thickness will be strong enough for most applications. If any of the instructions described here vary from the manufacturer's recommendations, always follow the manufacturer's instructions.

***Cab-O-Sil thickened silicone:*** The very first layer is just slightly thickened. This is where you have more control with thickening your own silicone. Mix up a small batch of silicone (just enough to cover the clay bed and model with a thin layer), adding the catalyst and mixing per the manufacturer's directions. Cab-O-Sil is added in small quantities into the silicone mixing container, and then mixed thoroughly into the catalyzed silicone. You can tell how thick it is getting by holding up the mixing spatula and seeing how

fast the silicone runs off of it. Add just enough Cab-O-Sil to make it so the silicone does not run off of the model so easily. Of necessity, you must add the Cab-O-Sil somewhat slowly, so as to not add too much. If you get the silicone too thick, you can not make it thin again. You would have to start over with a new batch. ***Follow all of the manufacturer's cautions on working with Cab-O-Sil. Use an appropriate dust mask.***

Carefully work the Cab-O-Sil thickened silicone into all the cracks, crevices and other detail areas, 'wetting out' the model and clay bed as described previously. A 1" disposable brush will work fine for this. Let the first layer set up a little first or gel.

Mix up more Cab-O-Sil thickened silicone, a bigger batch this time. Add just enough Cab-O-Sil so the silicone will not run off of the mixing spatula. It will be more like a paste. Scoop up some Cab-O-Sil thickened silicone on the spatula and just let it hang over the mixing container. Observe whether the silicone is sagging or falling off of the spatula. If so, add just a little more Cab-O-Sil. Now you can take a spatula or putty knife and spread the silicone all over the model as evenly as possible. Cover over the first layer completely, trying to keep it an even thickness over the entire model and clay bed.

Continue mixing up more batches and applying to the mold until the silicone is between 1/4" and 3/8" thick. It can be easier to work with smaller batches until you get used to working with thickened silicone. Although freshly mixed silicone usually adheres well to previously set up silicone, it is best to apply the next layer while the previous layer still has some tack to it. The material will be well-gelled, but not tack free just yet. That's the ideal time to add another layer of freshly mixed silicone.

*Mother Mold:* After the silicone cures completely (whether pre-thickened or Cab-O-Sil thickened), you can make the first half (or section) of the mother mold as described in Chapter Four. Most silicones cure in 16-24 hours, unless they are a faster setting silicone or you have added a fast catalyst. There is no need to build any clay walls or anything of that nature. You can make a plaster, fiberglass, or urethane paste mother mold shell over the cured silicone on this first part of the skin mold.

When the mother mold shell has set up completely, take the whole assembly (model, clay bed, silicone mold and mother mold) and turn it upside down on the work table. Take care to keep it all together as you flip it over. Then you can carefully remove just the clay bed, while leaving everything else in place. Take some pieces of clay and set them under the mold to support it while working on the second half of the skin mold. Clean any remnants of clay off of the model and the now exposed flange of silicone, where the clay bed was previously. Put a thin layer of Vaseline on this silicone flange, but try not to get any on the model. *If you forget to do this, the second half of the silicone skin mold will bond to the first half of the skin mold!*

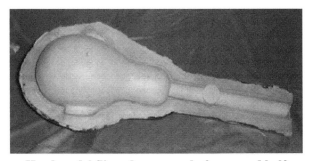
**Head model flipped over, ready for second half**

The second half (or next part) of the skin mold is made exactly the same way as the first section was made. If there are more than two sections to make, you will need to form another clay bed around this area before making the next section. Mix and apply the silicone (pre-thickened or Cab-O-Sil thickened) as described previously. When all the layers or coats of silicone are fully cured, you can make the second half (or next part) of the mother mold.

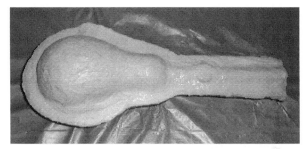
**Silicone applied to second half of skin mold**

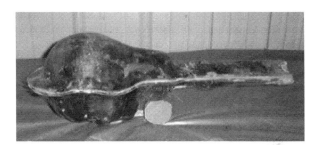
**Skin mold with fiberglass mother mold - completed**

When the mother mold shell has completely set up (and you have finished all sections), you are done making the skin mold. (See photo above) Carefully remove the mother mold pieces from the silicone mold. Then, even more carefully, remove the silicone skin mold sections from the mold. Clean any remnants of Vaseline off of the mold or mother mold. Check the manufacturer's instructions to see how soon a casting can be made in your new silicone mold. It's best to let it sit for a few days. When you are ready to do a casting, refer to Chapter Six.

It can take a lot of clay to make a clay bed for a head model. Here's a way to get around

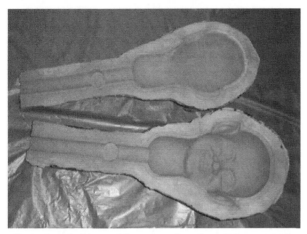

**Completed skin mold - opened and model removed**

this: take a piece of plywood and make a cutout the shape of the head. Support the head model horizontally, with some wads of clay on the work board. Set the plywood with the cutout, around the head model, and support it with some blocks of wood. The plywood board with the cutout should sit 1/4" to 1/2" lower than the lowest part of the parting line on the head model. You need to have enough depth of clay on the board to be able to make gutter keys and alignment keys. Form the clay bed on top of this blocked up piece of plywood. You can then proceed with the same basic instructions as shown on pages 72 and 73.

**Completed head that was cast in the skin mold**

***One piece silicone skin mold:*** A skin mold, can be made as a one piece mold the same way as a latex mold. The difference is you can not strip silicone off a model or a casting like a 'rubber glove' the same as latex. Silicone generally does not have the same tear strength nor will it stretch as far as latex and so it usually has to be handled with a little more care. A one-piece skin mold will most likely have to be a slit mold (see Chapter Four) for the above mentioned reasons.

For a hand or foot model you would start with the model attached to a mounting board the same as with a latex one piece mold. For a head model, you could use the jig described on page 18, to hold the head upright while applying the silicone for the skin mold. When the model is all set up, you would then make a skin mold over the entire model instead of just part of it. As previously described, build up the skin mold with as many coats as it takes to make it 1/4" to 3/8" thick.

The next step would be to make the mother mold. On a latex mold you would make a clay wall over the cured rubber. ***This will not work on a silicone mold, as the clay will not by any means stick to cured silicone.*** To get around this, you will need to lay the skin mold down temporarily on the work board or work table. The clay will not stick to the silicone skin mold, but it will stay in place on the work board. You will thus be making a temporary clay bed for making the mother mold.

First, determine the parting line on the mold. Form a clay bed around the mold, similar to what is described under ***Clay Bed Method***. The only difference is you will not need to make a ***gutter key*** in the clay, but will need to make some alignment keys in the clay with a spoon. Make the first half of the mother mold and let it set up. Turn the whole setup over, and remove the clay bed. Apply some Vaseline to the exposed part of the mother mold where the clay bed was previously. Finally, make the second half of the mother mold.

Pry the mother mold apart and off of the silicone skin mold. You can now take a utility knife or Exacto™ knife and make a slit in the skin mold. Make the slit only as big as is needed to remove the model. Use great care to keep the silicone mold from tearing unnecessarily while removing the skin mold from the model. (See Chapter Four about making a slit mold for the head)

There is less labor in making a one-piece mold this way, and you will use slightly less silicone rubber in the process. It should be stated, however, that a two-piece mold is generally nicer to work with. You have to think if the advantages of a one-piece skin mold outweighs the advantages of a two piece skin mold. On a head mold, because a one-piece skin mold will end up being a slit mold, it will pretty much only be useful for slush casting or roto casting. This is not necessarily a disadvantage on a hand or foot model, as these will most likely be slush cast anyway. (See Chapter Six)

One other possibility would be to make an **open mold** (see Chapter Four) with silicone. You would need a pretty flexible silicone rubber in order for this to work, probably about Shore A 20. It will be a little trickier demolding the castings, as you really could not turn the silicone mold 'inside out' like you can a latex mold. It would have to be carefully slid off of the model or casting, wriggling and pulling, until you get past the widest parts of the head. Also, you would have to get creative to make the clay walls for making a mother mold, as the clay will not stick to the silicone. A two-piece **skin**

**mold** or **blanket mold** can work for most of what you need, so you might want to try that first. Again, you have to decide if the advantages of an open mold justify the extra work.

### Silicone Blanket Mold

Another way to make a two piece silicone mold, is what is called a 'blanket mold'. The end result is similar to a skin mold, but in some ways is easier to make. You do not have to use pre-thickened silicone or Cab-O-Sil thickened silicone with this method. It is more of a mix and pour method, when once set up. The downside is that there is a little more initial setup than with a skin mold.

With a blanket mold the mother mold is actually made first and then the liquid silicone rubber is poured in between the model and the mother mold. This may seem like a backwards approach, but is an old mold maker's trick, and the reasons for doing it this way will become obvious as you read through the description.

For the sake of illustration let's use a hand model again. The principles would apply to other models as well (head, body, feet, etc.). The first step is to set the hand model on the a work board or work surface, supported by some clay so the parting line (Chapter Three) is on a horizontal plane. Then build up a clay bed around the model all the way around the

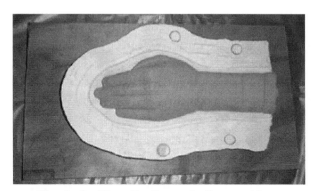

**Clay bed with gutter key and alignment keys**

parting line, as described earlier in this chapter (see *'Clay Bed Method'*). Make a *gutter key* and *alignment keys* in the clay bed.

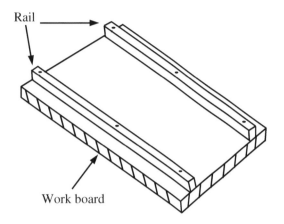

**Jig for rolling out a blanket of clay**

The second step is to make a clay blanket to lay over the hand model temporarily. A very simple jig will help in making the blanket. Fasten two 1/4" or 3/8" thick rails to a work board about 12" apart. Now you can use a rolling pin, a thick piece of PVC pipe or a wood dowel (which rolls on top of the rails that are fastened to the work board) to roll out a blanket of oil-based clay the same thickness as the rails.

Take the blanket of clay that you rolled out and carefully drape it over the hand model

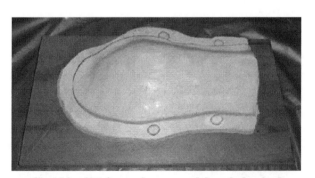

**Clay blanket formed over model and clay bed**

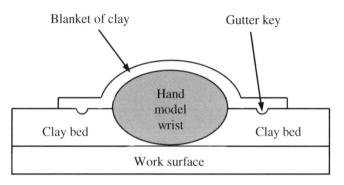

**Cross section: blanket of clay on model**

and clay bed. Trim the blanket of clay so that it overlaps the gutter key (see Chapter Four) by approximately 1/2". The alignment keys should not be covered by the blanket of clay. These will align the mother mold when completed. (See photos and illustrations this page and next)

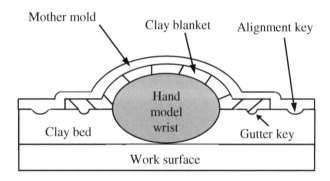

**Cross section of Blanket Mold**

Make the first half of the mother mold (as described in Chapter Four) out of plaster, fiberglass or urethane paste, according to your preference, over the blanket of clay and clay bed. The mother mold should cover over the entire blanket of clay as well as the exposed clay bed that has the alignment keys.

After the first half of the mother mold has set up, carefully lift it off of the blanket of clay and clay bed, trying not to mess up the

**Mother mold shell (urethane paste) for first half**

alignment keys in the clay bed. Then, in turn, carefully remove the blanket of clay from the model and clay bed. Save the clay blanket for later estimating the amount of silicone needed. Make sure that the gutter keys in the clay bed still look good and did not get damaged when you removed the blanket of clay. Reshape as necessary.

This may not all make sense just yet, but it will shortly. It will be necessary to drill some holes in this first half of the mother mold before putting it back in place over the clay bed. The holes should be at the high points along the top of the mother mold, 2" to 3" apart. The hole at the highest point will be used for pouring the silicone in (this one should be about an inch in diameter) and the others let the air escape as the silicone is poured in (these could be a half inch or less in diameter). See diagram at right.

After the holes have been drilled in this first half of the mother mold, put it back in place over the model and the clay bed (the alignment keys in the clay bed will help position it correctly). It will then be necessary to strap the mother mold down against the clay bed. An adjustable banding strap works well for this. Not too tight, not too loose, just snug. This will keep the mother mold from rising as the silicone is poured in place. You'll note a space where the blanket

of clay was previously. When the silicone rubber is poured in, it will take up this space and take the exact shape of the clay blanket.

Before you get ready to actually pour the silicone in place, it will be necessary to put an additional bead of clay where the mother mold meets the clay bed. Press this bead of clay firmly in place and smooth it over nicely. You will also need to put a small dam or wall of clay over the opening near where the wrist of the model is. (See illustration below) Take care to seal this area *really well* as liquid silicone rubber will leak through the smallest crack or crevice, and you will have quite the mess to clean up!

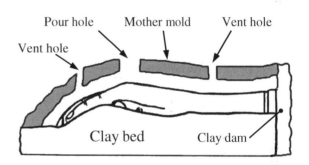

**Pour hole and vent holes in mother mold**

***Estimating the amount of silicone:*** The final step for completing the first half of the blanket mold is to mix some silicone rubber and pour it into the opening in the mother mold. How much silicone will you need? Remember the blanket of clay you saved? This is the volume of silicone rubber that is needed. Take the blanket of clay, wad it up, and put it temporarily into the mixing container. If you have used clay with sulfur in it for some reason, it would be best to line the cup with plastic wrap or aluminum foil to avoid contamination. See how high it comes up inside the container and make a mark with a permanent marker on the inside. Take the clay out of the mixing container and make sure there are no clay remnants left inside.

If you haven't done so already, weigh the mixing container to determine the tare weight. ***This would be a little hard to do after you poured silicone in it!*** After weighing the container and writing it down, you can pour silicone rubber into the mixing container up to the mark that you made. Put the container on the scale and move the little weights on the gram scale around until the scale balances. Note the total and write it down. Subtract the tare weight from this total and that is the weight of the silicone base material. Let's say the total was 260 grams and the tare weight was 25 grams. The amount of base material would be 235 grams because 260 - 25 = 235.

Take the amount of base material and figure what 10% of that would be. In this case you would need 23.5 grams of activator (10% of 235 = 23.5). Add 23.5 to the total (260) and set the scale for this amount (23.5 + 260 = 283.5). A common mistake is to add the 23.5 to the total weight of the base material (235 + 23.5 = 238.5) and set that as the total on the scale. But if you did this you would come up short on the weight of the activator. The tare weight *always has to be figured in!* Again, write everything down as you go and double check all of your math before actually pouring and mixing in the activator. In this example, you would set the scale to 283.5, and add activator until the scale balances. You can then mix the silicone.

***First half of blanket mold:*** Mix the silicone and activator thoroughly as described earlier in the chapter. If you have used a high viscosity silicone for some reason, remove air bub-

bles with a vacuum pump if necessary. (See ***Appendix B***) Pour the silicone slowly into the 1" diameter hole in the top of the mother mold. Pouring slowly will help to avoid entrapping air which will create more bubbles. Eventually the silicone will rise to the level of the lowest 1/2" holes on the mother mold. As the silicone just starts to overflow from these, cover them over tightly with clay, so the silicone can not leak out. Continue pouring and plugging holes as necessary until the silicone comes up as high as the 1" diameter hole. The 1" whole should be filled level full. It is not necessary to plug this hole with any clay.

**Pouring silicone (note: strap removed for clarity)**

It would be best to keep an eye on the mold for awhile to make sure that no leaks develop. At a certain point, the silicone will gel, after which you do not need to worry about leaks. How soon the material will gel depends on the working time of the silicone. Let the silicone set up without disturbance for 24 hours or according to the manufacturer's recommended cure time.

***Second half of blanket mold:*** While keeping the first half of the blanket mold intact (keep the model inside the silicone and the silicone inside the mother mold), flip the whole thing over and remove the clay bed. Support this first half with some clay underneath the mother mold to keep it level. The other side of the model is now exposed and ready for the second half of the blanket mold to be made.

Follow the directions for the first half of the blanket mold and make a second clay blanket similar to the one that you did for the first half. You will not need a clay bed as the first half of the silicone mold and mother mold will take its place. When you are making the second half of the mother mold, don't forget to put some Vaseline on the first half as a mold release. Also, you can use some small clay squares to help with separating the mother mold later (see *Mold Making Tip* page 61). After the second half of the mother mold is completely cured, it is removed the same as you did with the first half. Then remove the clay blanket and save it for estimating how much silicone will be needed for this second half.

Coat the first half of the exposed silicone blanket mold with Vaseline *or it will bond to the second half of the mold.* Estimate the amount of silicone needed as before (see page 79, *Estimating the amount of silicone*) using the clay blanket as a guide. Mix and pour to complete the mold. After the silicone has fully cured, carefully pry the mother mold halves apart and off of the silicone blanket mold. Finally, separate the silicone blanket mold at the parting line, and gently peel the two halves away from the model. You are not trying to turn the halves inside out as you go. It is only necessary to pull or stretch the silicone just enough to release it from the model. Set the model aside, and reassemble the blanket mold and mother

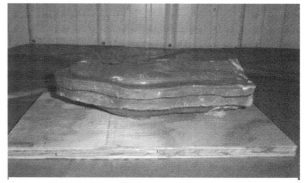

**Both halves of blanket mold completed**

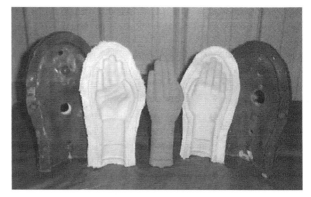

**Blanket mold pieces and hand model**

mold. Let the mold cure the recommended amount of time per the manufacturer, prior to making any castings (see Chapter Six).

### Silicone Block Mold

A silicone block mold has a few uses in figure making, so it is presented here as well. It can make a nice mold for the jaw (see Chapter Six for info on making jaw models), an eyeball mold or other such parts. A block mold takes a lot less time and energy than the other types of molds we have discussed thus far (silicone or latex). It is a fairly easy way to make a silicone mold, but can cost more in materials.

Block molds could possibly work well for hand or feet molds, but would require two to three times the amount of silicone that a skin mold or blanket mold would take. So you would have to weigh the extra expense of the silicone against the possible labor saved. A block mold of a head or body model would be prohibitive in cost and would not be recommended.

To make a block mold, you start out with the model secured to a mounting board in an upright position, either with screws, glue or whatever will hold it securely in place. In this example a jaw model will be used. (See Chapter Six for ideas on making a jaw model) If you are using a clay model make sure the armature is securely fastened to the mounting board. The idea here is that you do not want the model to start floating upwards after you start pouring the silicone, which can sometimes happen when making a block mold.

**Jaw model on work board**

The next item would be to make a form to go around the model. This could be a box shape or a cylinder shape (like a coffee can). The important thing is that the form be strong enough to hold the weight of the silicone and not leak when it is poured into the form. Ideally you want this form to be about 1/2" to

1" away from the model on all sides and 1" higher then the model. Block molds are usually thick enough when completed that they do not need to have a mother mold.

Here's a way to make a box form. Pick up some scrap 'laminated counter top' (usually available at the larger *home improvement centers*). Cut the pieces as illustrated to make four 'L'-shaped forms (the laminate should be on the inside of the forms). The forms are clamped together with four 'C' clamps. You can adjust the size of the mold box, by loosening the 'C' clamps and then sliding the board forms to make it larger or smaller. Use banding straps or twine to hold the form down in place on the mounting board around

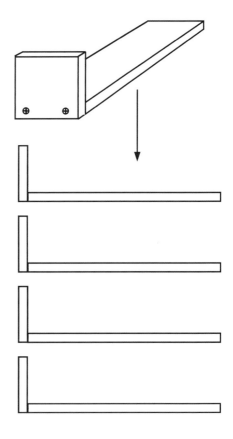

**Make four mold forms**

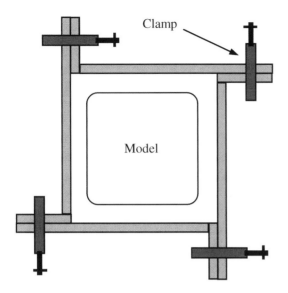

**Top View - mold form clamped together**

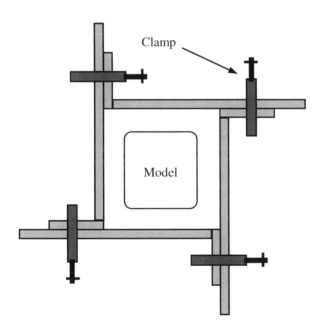

**Top View - mold form easily adjusts to different**

the model. If you do not do this, it is quite likely that silicone will leak from the bottom of the form.

Roll out some beads of clay about 1/4" in diameter, and carefully seal the joints of the form. Push the clay bead firmly against the

joint, squishing it tightly against the mold form. Do this inside and out on the vertical seams of the mold box as well as around the bottom of the form. Silicone can leak through the smallest cracks very easily!

Estimating the amount of silicone you need will have to be done the best you can by eye in this case. Try to estimate how much silicone it will take to fill the form up over the top of the model by 3/4" to 1". Add catalyst and mix per the manufacturer's instructions. Pour the silicone into the lowest part inside of the mold form, as opposed to pouring it directly on the model. The idea here is to let the silicone rise slowly up and over the model as you pour it in. Doing it this way will help keep air from getting trapped, which can cause bubbles in the finished mold. If your guess was less than the amount you needed to cover the model by 3/4", immediately mix up a little more silicone and pour it into the form. It will blend just fine, as the first batch should still be quite liquid.

If the model is fairly complex (lots of detail, cracks and crevices for the rubber to flow into), here's a trick some mold makers use to help ensure the elimination of bubbles near the surface of the model. After you have mixed up your batch of silicone, pour just a small amount in the mold form at first. In this case you can pour it directly on the model. Now take the work board (which has the model and mold form secured to it with banding straps hopefully), and rotate in several directions. What you are trying to do is *wet out,* or coat, the entire model with a thin layer of silicone, prior to pouring the whole batch into the mold form. You can also assist this process by using a brush to help *wet out* the entire model.

After the model looks well-coated, set the work board back on the table, and pour the remainder of the silicone into the mold form. As described previously, pour the silicone into the lowest part inside of the mold form, as opposed to pouring it directly on the model. Let the silicone rise slowly up and over the model, to help avoid introducing any unwanted air into the mold rubber. This should produce a very nice mold.

After 24 hours (or whatever amount of time the manufacturer recommends) the silicone should be fully set. Remove the forms from around the cast silicone block. On a jaw mold, you can probably remove the mold from the model without making a slit in the mold. On a a hand or foot mold, you would probably have to cut a slit in the mold. As was done with the one-piece skin mold, take a sharp knife or razor blade and cut a slit on one side of the mold. Cut the slit just long enough to be able to remove the model.

**Block mold of jaw**

Cut the slit in a *zig zag* fashion, as opposed to a straight slit to act as a key of sorts. This way the edges of the the slit will align better when you use the mold for casting. In some cases it may be necessary to make more than one slit due to the shape of the model. Keep

in mind, however, the fewer slits or cuts you have to make the easier it will be to use the mold for casting later. If at all possible, try not to make a slit in a block mold. By using a softer silicone (Shore A 20) with good tear resistance, you might be surprised at what models can be removed without a slit.

In general you do not need to worry too much about undercuts and draft when making a block mold. Silicone is a flexible material and in most cases can handle undercuts with no problem. It is best to use a silicone with a Shore A durometer between 20 and 30 for good flexibility and easy removal of the model (or casting). A good, strong, Shore A 20 is ideal. Make sure the silicone you purchase has good tear resistance.

Although undercuts and draft are not a big worry with a block mold, there is a situation you need to be aware of. Some models, due to their shape, will be prone to trapping air. If air is trapped, silicone will not flow into this area and you will end up with a bubble or void in the finished mold. Needless to say, the castings you make in this mold will come out with a bubble as well. If the void or bubble is big enough, you may have to make the mold over.

Note the illustration on the next page. As you start pouring silicone into the form, and the level of silicone starts to rise up to the top of the undercut, air would get trapped in the pocket there.

One solution would be to turn the model upside down or sideways. This would eliminate the problem. If that's not possible, another solution would be to set the model at an angle on the mounting board until the air pocket is no longer present. You have to picture in your mind how the liquid silicone will rise and flow around the model. In this

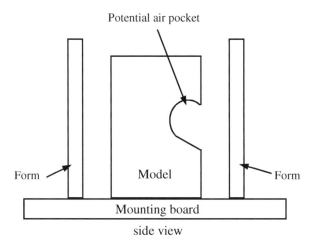

**Look for undercuts that can trap air**

way you will be able to spot potential problems like these and then be able to come up with a viable solution before pouring the liquid silicone rubber. For some models, the location of undercuts or other such potential places to trap air is so severe, it would be best to make a skin mold.

***Two-piece block molds:*** In some cases a two-piece block mold would be the best way to go, depending on what the ***undercuts***, ***draft*** or ***parting lines*** tell you (see Chapter Three). Take the example of an eyeball mold. The model, an eyeball, is basically a sphere. There is no easy way to make a one-piece block mold with this type of model. A two-piece mold will be the easiest. It will have a parting line exactly halfway across the middle of the model. Making a skin mold or blanket mold is just too much work for this small of a mold. A two-piece block mold is relatively easy to make in comparison.

Make a temporary clay bed around the eyeball model. The eyeball should be facing in such a way so that the area for the ***iris*** is pointing upwards. This is an important prin-

ciple. Anytime you pour silicone to a make a mold over a model, the areas of the model that have the most important detail should be facing up. That way air bubbles will rise up and away from the surface of the model, helping to make a perfect mold.

You can make a small gutter key if you will be casting a lot of eyes. This will help keep the mold from leaking when doing castings. At the very least, you will need to make some alignment keys. A spoon will probably be too big. You can use some small marbles or other such item to press some ***half sphere*** shapes into the clay bed.

Build a small box form around the eyeball model and clay bed, and seal well with beads of clay. Estimate the amount of silicone needed. Mix up the silicone and pour it into the lowest part of the form, and let it slowly rise up and over the eyeball model. Pour to approximately 1/2" or so higher than the top of model. Let the silicone completely cure.

Remove the form and temporary clay bed without disturbing the silicone. Flip the mold over so the other side of the eyeball model is exposed, ready to make the second half of the mold. Apply some Vaseline® to the exposed area of silicone where the clay bed was previously. Do not put any Vaseline® on the eyeball itself. Put the box form back around the mold. Mix up more silicone and pour it into the mold form, the same as you did for the first half. After it has completely set up, remove the mold form. Carefully pull each half of the freshly cast block mold pieces away from the model.

You can either slush cast (see Chapter Six) a hollow eyeball or cast it solid. For a slush casting, it is not necessary to have an opening or pour hole in the mold. The casting material can be poured in prior to closing the

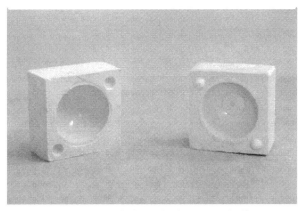

Two-piece block mold for an eye ball

mold. For making a solid casting, it will be necessary to make an opening in one half of the mold. Take an Exacto Knife® or other similar sharp cutting tool, and very carefully cut a 1/2" hole in the mold, or just big enough to pour your resin in.

### *Summary on Silicone Molds*

Between the chapters on plaster molds (which includes undercuts, draft and parting lines), latex molds, and this one on silicone molds, you will have learned some good, solid mold-making principles. These principles, when once learned, can be applied to other materials as well. These certainly are not the only ways to work with these materials. There are some more advanced techniques that could be learned, but these are beyond the scope of this book. The idea here is to give both the novice figure maker and the more seasoned figure makers, a good, solid mold-making foundation to work from.

There is always more to be learned, but that can be part of the fun. New ideas and better methods are developed all the time by first time mold makers and seasoned mold makers alike. What has been presented here are proven methods that work. But don't stop

there. Use your imagination. Who knows where it will take you? Read all the information you can on making molds or attend a mold-making seminar if possible. The **Internet** is also a great resource for finding mold-making information.

Be prepared to make mistakes along the way, both in mold-making and other aspects related to figure making. But don't be too hard on yourself. Mistakes are most definitely part of the learning process. If you're not making some mistakes, you are probably not learning much. Ironic but true. One of the greatest inventors of the last century, Thomas Edison, once said, *"Results! Why, man, I have gotten a lot of results. I know several thousand things that won't work!"* What he was trying to indicate was, that he was successful because he wasn't afraid to try things. He wasn't afraid of making mistakes. He had many so-called 'failures' along the way. But from them, he found out what did work. And you will too.

Read this chapter carefully to see which type of mold would be best for your first attempts with silicone. You might want to try a very small block mold as your first project, to 'get your feet wet'. This will help you get familiar with measuring and mixing silicone. You will also see how it sets up and behaves compared to latex or other mold-making materials. Again, there are some **one to one** ratio silicones available that can make this process a whole lot easier. When in doubt, start there. Silicone is a slightly more advanced material to work with and will 'keep you on your toes', so to speak. But don't be intimidated or afraid to try it. It is a fascinating mold-making compound that can make some very nice molds for figure making.

# CHAPTER SIX

# *CASTING TECHNIQUES*

Now that you have made molds (of plaster, latex, silicone or urethane) from the models, you may very well be asking, "Now what?!?" Casting is the answer. For some, this is the most exciting part of the process. Casting parts in molds that you made yourself! This is where you really start to see the fruits of your labor. There are a variety of materials and techniques that can be used in the casting process. The ones we will focus on here are those that are the most useful for figure making. Before we get too far into casting techniques, here's a little background information that can be helpful

A word that you will often hear used in connection with vent figures is *composition*. What does this term really mean? Originally the word composition referred to a wood chip and glue material that was used to make old doll's heads and some older vent figure toy products. This type of composition material was very susceptible to moisture. Over time, as castings made from this material started to take on moisture, they would swell up and even start to peel. If they got too wet, they would just fall apart, as the glue used to make this composition material was water based.

Here is where the confusion sets in. Some early figures began to be made from Plastic Wood®. Some very famous figures were made from this material. Howdy Doody, the first Mortimer Snerd (later copies were made of fiberglass), and of course the majority of the famous McElroy brothers figures were all made of Plastic Wood®. In time, other so-called composition materials came in to use. Today these include, but are not limited to, fiberglass (using polyester or epoxy resin), rigid latex, rigid neoprene, urethane resin, and epoxy modeling compounds. So, when someone says that a figure is a composition figure, it could easily be any one of a number of materials. Typically, today, when you hear the word *composition* in relation to vent figures, it loosely refers to any figure that is not made of basswood (the original, traditional figure making material).

The most interesting challenge that new figure makers come against in making a composition or cast figure, is that in general, most of the parts to be made need to be hollow. Not only hollow, but durable as well. For the most part it is much easier to cast an object solid (just pour the casting material in the mold and fill it full) than to try to make it hollow. However, this would make a very heavy casting for one, and on a head casting, you would have nowhere to install the mechanics (moving eyes, mouth, etc.)

So most of the casting techniques that will be presented in this chapter are for making hollow cast parts. This can be especially challenging when making a head casting. This is where most beginners get hung up or get frustrated. To help avoid frustration, it is recommended to start with one of the easier casting techniques first, such as pressing epoxy putty in a mold or using this same material using a *moldless* technique.

This really is a progressive book that does not leave you with only one method for making a cast vent figure. A lot of information has been put into this one volume, not to boggle the mind, but so that you will have many different options. You can start with the easier methods first, and at a later point in time, try some of the other casting techniques that might be a little more advanced. For this reason, you will probably find this publication a handy reference for years to come. Some figure makers find a technique they like and pretty much stick with it. Others experiment all the time, enjoying all of the challenges along the way. You have to find what works best for you.

### Control stick considerations

Before getting too far into the casting techniques you need to give some advance consideration to where the control stick will be attached when doing head castings, no matter what casting material is used. The easiest thing to do is make a latex or silicone plug (see Chapters Four and Five for information on working with these materials) the size of the control stick (the diameter of the control stick and maybe two to three inches long).

The completed rubber plug is temporarily put inside the mold where the control stick would be. When you do a casting of the head the casting materials will be pressed in around, flow around or be laminated (fiberglassed) around this rubber control

Silicone plug for control stick area of head mold

stick plug. When the casting has cured and the plug is removed there will be a nice strong cast 'flange' inside the neck for you to glue in a control stick later. By doing this, it will be very easy to glue the head stick in straight. Use of this rubber plug will be described in different parts of this chapter.

### Epoxy Putties ('Magic Sculp')

This really is the easiest place to start if you have never made a cast figure before. An epoxy putty is a two-part compound that is mixed together. The mixed putty will set up into a hard plastic of sorts.

There are many different epoxy putties or epoxy modeling compounds that have been introduced on the market in recent years. Many of these can be found at hobby shops or taxidermy supply shops. The one that seems to be the easiest to use and has the best working qualities is **'Magic Sculp'** (that is the correct spelling!). This product was first introduced to the author by figure maker Rick Price. Having tried several of the other brands of epoxy putties since then, Magic Sculp still comes out as the winner, as the one that's the nicest to use and produces the best results.

***Preparing the molds:*** If you are using a silicone mold, there is usually no further preparation necessary. An exception would be an older silicone mold. As silicone molds are used over and over again, they lose some of their natural self-releasing ability. In either case it would be good to do a small test. Mix up a small batch of Magic Sculp and press it onto a non-critical part of the mold (on the mold flange can be a good spot). After this test piece has set up and hardened, see how easily it peels away from the mold. If there is much in the way of sticking, you must use a mold release. If you are going to do a lot of castings, a coat of mold release sprayed into the mold prior to casting is a good idea, to prolong the life of the mold.

If you use a mold release, a spray mold release such as Ease Release 2300 (available from A-R Products or Smooth-On, Inc.) is a good choice. Sometimes a little talcum powder (baby powder) is all that is needed. In some cases, both talcum powder and spray release is a good idea, especially if you are having a lot of trouble with sticking. Use the spray release first, and then dust the inside of the mold with talcum powder over the spray release. Any time you use talcum powder, use a clean brush to gently spread it around making sure all parts of the inside of the mold are well covered. Shake out or brush out excess talcum powder before continuing.

In general you have to be more careful with a urethane or latex mold. You have to make sure you have the mold release adequately applied before pressing Magic Sculp into the mold. Again, do a small test to see if you need to use just talcum powder or a combination of spray release and talcum powder. A mold can be ruined or seriously damaged if Magic Sculp or other such casting material bonds to it.

A plaster waste mold needs to be thoroughly dry and sealed with a few coats of sanding sealer first. Then apply a spray mold release (Ease Release 2300 or other suitable release recommended by your supplier), or a thin layer of Vaseline. Do a test with a small amount of mixed Magic Sculp, pressed into a non-critical part of the mold. Let it set up completely and see if it will release from the plaster mold with no problems. It should be noted, that even if it releases well, there is a likelihood that you will have to break the waste mold to remove the casting. (See Chapter Three)

When doing a head casting, the rubber plug mentioned under *'Control stick considerations'* should be put into the mold before proceeding. On an 'open' mold, it is treated with mold release as mentioned above, and inserted into the hole in the bottom of the mold where the neck is. In a two-piece head mold it can be placed in one half of the mold, the half that will be cast first. If necessary you could make two of these rubber plugs, one for each half of the head mold. That way

Silicone plug

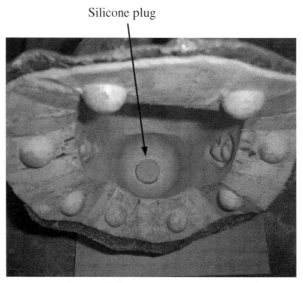

Top View - Silicone plug in an open mold

you could make both halves at the same time, without having to wait for one half to cure first. An **open** mold or a two-piece head mold work best for doing a Magic Sculp casting. A 'slit' mold just isn't designed to work with this process. (See **slush casting** in this Chapter)

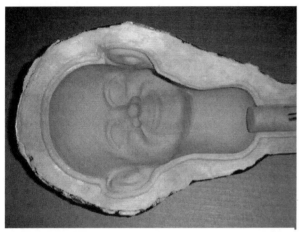

Silicone plug placed in one half of two-piece mold

***Mixing the Magic Sculp:*** The description here will be be for Magic Sculp. However most of the other epoxy putty compounds work similarly. It comes in two parts, the **'Resin'** and the **'Hardener'**. Take equal amounts of each out of the containers. If either the resin or the hardener compound seems too stiff, heat it to 100° F to soften. Put the material in a resealable bag and seal tightly. Put it in a microwave oven on high for 5 to 10 seconds. Go slowly and don't heat it up too much (it will burn your fingers!). It doesn't take long to heat up the material. To have a longer working time, let the material cool back down to room temperature before mixing. It will still stay soft for weeks after being heated this way, even after cooling. Magic Sculp does not mix well if the material is too stiff.

Only mix small amounts at a time, especially when you are first learning to work with Magic Sculp. You can use a couple drops of water on your fingers or a little talcum powder to make it less sticky to work with. Neither will hurt the Magic Sculp. Some like to work with disposable latex or nitrile gloves when working with it and some figure makers work with their bare hands. It washes off with soap and water, which is nice! Although the Magic Sculp containers when first opened have reasonably strong odor, this dissipates shortly. Magic Sculp in general has very low odor and is very pleasant to work with. ***You should still read and follow all of the manufacturer's safety precautions.***

Mix equal amounts by volume (not by weight) of resin and hardener. *Tip:* If you roll into a ball, it makes it easier to see if you have equal amounts of each. Mix very thoroughly until it is one homogenous color with no streaks. It is now ready to use. In general you will have a few hours of working time. As you get closer to the end of the working time, it will become somewhat stiff and harder to squish and shape. Again, it is better to work with smaller amounts, mixing up several small batches as opposed to one big batch of material.

Take a small piece of the mixed Magic Sculp and press it into the shape of a small pancake. It should be about an inch or two in diameter, and about 1/16" thick approximately. Press it into the mold firmly, making sure to work out all irregularities in the putty. Take another small piece of mixed material and do the same. Press it in right next to the first piece you pressed in. Overlap the edge of the second piece over the first piece by about 1/4". Around these seams you need to be especially thorough in pressing the Magic

Sculp against the mold. The more meticulous you are in doing this, the less patching you will have to do on the finished casting.

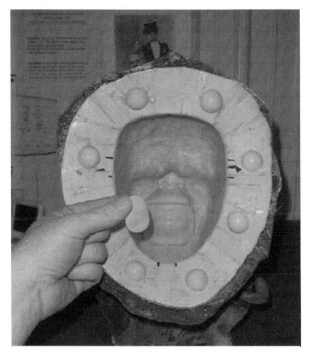

Magic Sculp pressed into an 'open' latex head mold

Keep taking small amounts and pressing it into the mold as described above. Mix up more Magic Sculp as necessary. When doing the ears in a head mold, you can press these full of Magic Sculp for some extra strength. It won't hurt to have the ears cast solid. If working with an 'open' head mold, keep going until the main part of the mold is completely done, one really thin layer. You can then do the same for the separate trap door part of the mold. For a two-piece head mold, hand mold or foot mold, do both halves of the mold complete with one thin layer.

When doing the next layer, no matter what kind of mold is being used (head, hand, or foot), it will be necessary to add some reinforcement. The simplest way to do this is to purchase some fiberglass mesh that is used for plaster work. Cut it up into smaller pieces, 2-4 inches in length. Gauze bandage or other similar materials could also be used for reinforcement. Fiberglass mesh, however, is a much stronger material.

Fiberglass mesh used to strengthen Magic Sculp

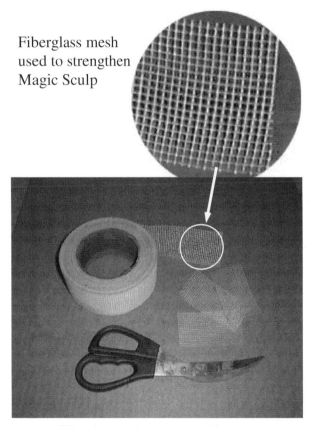

Fiberglass mesh cut in to small pieces

Place one of the cut fiberglass mesh pieces into the mold. Take some freshly mixed Magic Sculp and press it right over the fiberglass mesh, covering it with a thin layer. So you are essentially making a Magic Sculp and fiberglass mesh sandwich, with the fiberglass mesh in the middle. Again, as you press the Magic Sculp in place, you want to press it in firmly so it will not only adhere to the fiberglass mesh, but the previous layer of

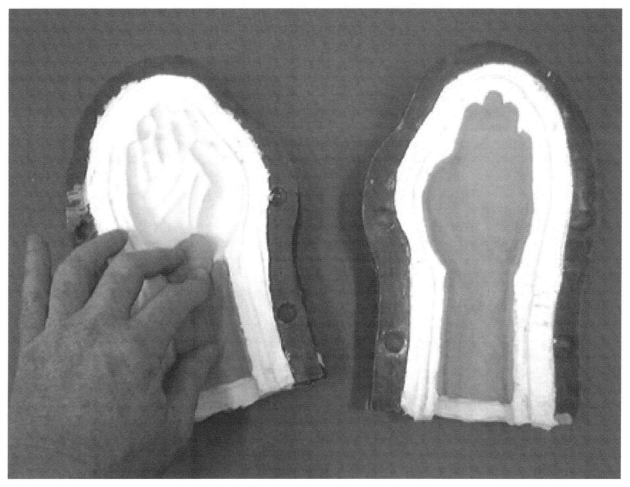

Magic Sculp pressed into silicone hand mold

Magic Sculp as well. As you do this, you also want to make sure there is some overlapping of the individual pieces of fiberglass mesh, for strength.

Going this route, your finished casting should be about 1/16" thick or just slightly more. This will make a nice, lightweight casting that's reasonably strong. If you went a full 1/8" thick on a Magic Sculp casting, it probably would not need to reinforce it, but it couldn't hurt. This will be a heavier casting, but quite strong. Magic Sculp is a very strong and durable material, but it can be brittle when cast too thinly. Every 1/32" that you add builds strength. Figure maker Rick Price

adds a layer of fiberglass cloth and polyester resin on the inside of the casting for strength. ***Polyester resin can be quite nasty to work with, so if you went this route, it is imperative that you follow all of the safety precautions when working with these materials.***

If you have been working in an 'open' latex mold, as soon as your casting fully sets up, you can carefully remove it from the mold. If you've been working in a two-piece mold let the two halves fully set up before doing the next step.

Remove the two cast halves from the two-piece mold. For a head mold, make a cutout for the trap door before proceeding. Take a

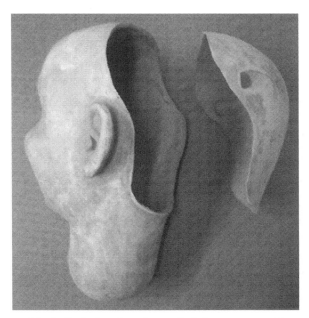

Magic Sculp head casting pulled from open mold

Seven, page 123, and Appendix A, for more information on jaw model castings)

For a hand or foot casting, again take the two halves out of the mold first. Mix some more Magic Sculp and form four to six contact points (see photo next page) near the inside edge of each half of the casting (actually these contact points could be

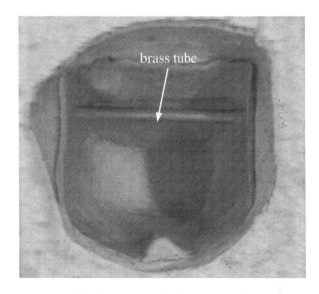

brass tube

Magic Sculp jaw inside latex mold

look at the photo above to get an idea of the size the trap-door should be. Take some large rubber bands and strap the two halves of the head together temporarily.

Take some freshly mixed Magic Sculp, reinforcement material (gauze bandage or nylon mesh), and press them firmly into place all around the seam, the same as you did for the second layer when making the castings. Make sure the seam is well covered, about 1" to 1 1/2" wide. If some Magic Sculp squishes out the other side of the seam, take some water on your finger tips and smooth all along the seam. Magic Sculp smoothes very easily with just water. In fact, with the water, you can smooth and blend until the seam is pretty much invisible.

When doing a jaw casting, if the mold is set up to do so, you can set a brass tube pivot in place prior to making the casting. This way you can form the Magic Sculp around the tube and it gets bonded in place automatically when the casting cures. (See Chapter

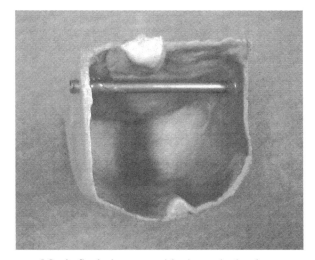

Magic Sculp jaw cast with pivot tube in place

formed when making the casting initially). Let these set up fully before doing the next step. Mix some additional Magic Sculp and place some on each contact point. Use enough so that some Magic Sculp will squish out between the contact points when you press the two cast halves together. An alternative way to do this would be to roll out a bead of mixed Magic Sculp, place it all along the seam and then press the two halves together tightly. Which ever way you choose to go, bind the two halves tightly together with twine, banding straps or large rubber bands while the Magic Sculp sets up. Finish the seams up with more material, and smooth with wet fingers.

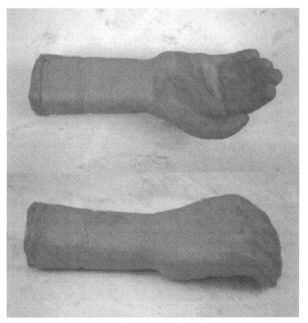

Magic Sculp hand casting

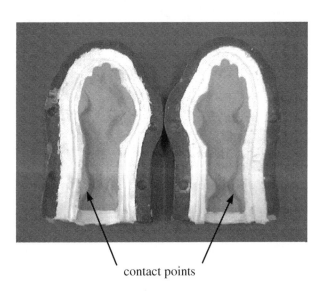

contact points

Contact points - Magic Sculp hand

Magic Sculp will normally harden after several hours or overnight. You can speed this up a little with some heat. A temperature of about 120° F is warm enough to speed the cure by quite a bit. You can make a 'hot box' for this process, if you will be doing a lot of Magic Sculp work, and would like it to set up a lot quicker.

To build a hot box, build a plywood box big enough to hold your molds. Inside this box you will need to put a few receptacles for some 60 to 100 watt light bulbs. The exact number of light bulbs and wattage depends on how well the plywood box is insulated. *The light bulbs should not touch the wood or the molds, of course. If you are not familiar with hooking up electrical devices, have a professional make this 'hot box' for you. You don't want to start any fires!* Use a thermometer inside the 'hot box' to check the temperature. It would be best if the temperature did not go over 120° F. Be sure that the mold materials can take this heat as well before placing them in the hot box.

*Moldless castings:* You can make a moldless casting with Magic Sculp. This particular method was popularized by William Anderson many years ago, using Wood Dough, and is still a viable method for making a figure. Magic Sculp is, however, much easier to work with, making this method worth giving some serious consideration. This can be a good way to go if you don't want all the hassle of making a mold first.

The basic concept: First make a sculpture, let's say for a head, that is about 1/8" or so smaller in all dimensions than you want the final casting to be. This can be done in oil-base clay. The features of this rough sculpture of the head do not have to be very well defined. Put some talcum powder on the clay sculpture to act as a mold release. If you can, put the sculpture in the refrigerator for several hours, prior to doing the next step. This will make the clay harder and stiffer than normal.

Mix up some Magic Sculp and press little 'pancakes', a few inches in diameter, on the outside of the clay sculpt of the head. Overlap these 'pancake' pieces by about 1/4" to 1/2" for strength. Give special attention to these areas where the Magic Sculp is overlapped and make sure the pieces are joined together well. Press and squish until you are satisfied that they are well joined. Go pretty thin on this first layer.

Some like to make the so-called Magic Sculp 'pancakes' bigger in size than just 1" or 2" in diameter. That way there are less seams to join together. It's a matter of personal preference, and you will have to find out what works best for you. Keep going until the entire head is covered. You can cut the head into two halves later or make a seam as you put the Magic Sculp in place over the clay. If the Magic Sculp is still somewhat pliable you can cut a seam with a knife before it sets up.

Do rough features first, and fine detailing later. Try not to add too much material when doing the rough features on the face. You can always add more Magic Sculp later when

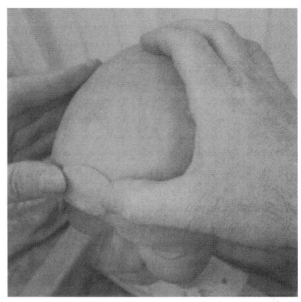

Magic Sculp pressed over rough clay head

detailing. It is much easier to add more later than to carve or sand it away when you have put too much on. Work on details of only one feature area at a time, say for instance the nose area. Mix up only enough Magic Sculp to do the nose. When that's done, do the right cheek. When that's done do the left cheek, etc. This way you should have enough working time to finish detailing these individual areas quite nicely, before the material becomes unworkable.

When the head has completely cured, remove the two halves off of the clay understructure. Carefully remove any excess clay from the inside of the casting. You can then bond the two halves together as previously described in this chapter.

An alternative to making a two-piece head casting that has to be bonded together later is this: Apply the Magic Sculp over all of the head and then make a cut for the trap-door. This cut can be done with a knife if the material has not fully set up. After the Magic

Sculp has hardened, you can first remove the trap-door and then scoop out the clay from the inside of the head. Depending on how you set up your armature for the clay (see Chapter Two), you may have to cut that out too. A simpler armature of wadded up newspaper and masking tape would be better in this instance. In any case, going this route saves you the trouble of having to bond the head halves together later.

These are the basic principles of doing a moldless casting. The same thing could be done for hands or feet, but it can be a little harder to do these parts. The hard part is getting the clay out from the inside of the casting, unless you do it in two halves as you did for the head casting. You would then have to bond the two halves together when completed, which is more work.

Magic Sculp is a fascinating material and can get you started making a figure or two right away. It is pretty user friendly and has some advantages in ease of use over other materials and processes. A big 'thank you' is in order to Rick Price for helping to introduce this interesting material to the figure making community!

### Plastic Wood  (Wood Dough):

Plastic Wood or Wood Dough has been used a lot in the past. It is unfortunately not the same formulation as it was in years ago, and the quality has changed as well. Some figure makers report that they have still been able to use these newer formulations with success. Most have reported that they like the 'Dap® Wood Dough' best. Many wood dough products on the shelves these days contain some harsh chemicals, and have to be handled accordingly. *Read all of the safety precautions on the container and follow closely!*

Plastic Wood or Wood Dough is a one part compound that requires no mixing and is generally used straight out of the can. Apart from that, the process for both Wood Dough and Magic Sculp is very similar. The basic instructions previously described for using Magic Sculp can be used for pressing Wood Dough into a mold. Be sure to read carefully about using mold release prior to casting and do a test as described. It would be best to also use some reinforcement in the process, the same as with the Magic Sculp. Wood Dough can also be quite brittle. There have been more than a few vent figure heads made from this that have dropped on the ground and shattered like a light bulb. With all the hard work that has to be put in to build a figure, you want to make sure it is going to be reasonably durable and last for awhile.

### Paper Maché

Paper Maché, although considered to be 'low-tech' compared to some of the newer methods available, is still quite viable, and can produce a good strong casting that will work for figure making. It is a little time consuming and requires some patience. The finished castings can also be somewhat susceptible to moisture, but much that can be pretty much countered by using a good sealer inside and out.

Since there are many books and such on paper maché already available, mostly some tips and suggestions will be provided for those wanting to try this age old process. The two most important aspects of getting a good paper maché casting is the type of paper used and the type of glue or bonding agent that is used. This can dramatically affect the final results.

*Type of paper:* Those in the puppet making industry who have had years and years of experience using this process highly recommend **Red Rosin Sheathing Paper**. This can be found at the larger building supply emporiums like Home Base, Home Depot, Menards, etc. It was originally created for the roofing industry, but puppeteers have known of its usefulness for puppet making for some time. It is the paper of choice because of its workability and strength in the finished cast piece. The structure of the fibers has greater length than other paper products (such as newspaper) and therefore make a better bond when mixed with a bonding agent. Paper maché works much like fiberglass in that respect. The paper is like the fiberglass cloth and the bonding agent is like the polyester or epoxy resin.

The 'Red Rosin Sheathing Paper' is softened by putting it in hot water. The paper is only immersed in the hot water long enough to soften it to the point of desired workability. This can range anywhere from 3 to 10 minutes depending on how hot the water is. If it soaks too long, the paper will turn to mush! The idea is to heat and soak it just long enough to make it more like a putty that can be formed and shaped. When it is ready, take it out of the water and use some towels to blot up the excess moisture. The paper should be damp and workable, but not sopping wet prior to adding the bonding agent.

**Bonding agent:** One mixture that seems to work quite well is a 50/50 mixture of Elmer's wood glue and wood cellulose wallpaper paste (available at your local home improvement center). Mix the wood cellulose wallpaper paste according to the manufacturer's directions. Then add an equal amount of Elmer's wood glue to the mix.

The other bonding agent that seems to work well is 'Aqua Resin' (see suppliers list). This is an acrylic type of resin, reportedly non-toxic, and dries very hard. This may be more expensive than the other bonding agent mentioned above, but a little goes a long way.

**Basic process:** Apply a release agent prior to applying paper maché to the inside of the mold. A thin layer of Vaseline can work well for this. Whichever bonding agent you decide to use, the basic process is the same. Damp pieces of the 'Red Rosin Sheathing Paper' are saturated with the bonding agent, and the excess is squeezed off with your fingers. The piece of paper, now rich with bonding agent, is applied inside a mold. Press it in place with your fingers. Keep saturating more paper with bonding agent and apply to the inside of the mold, overlapping the previous pieces as you go. Keep going until you have one complete layer applied. Use a hair dryer to dry this first layer of paper maché. When this is dry, apply the next layer the same as the first. Again, use a hair dryer to facilitate drying between layers. It will take anywhere from 3-5 layers to get a nice strong casting.

When the last layer is completely dry and the casting seems strong enough, remove it from the mold. If you have cast a head in a two piece mold, making each half separately, you will need to bond the two halves together. Make a cutout for the trap-door on the back of the head. You can then use more paper maché to bond the two halves of the head together on the inside of the casting. (See the *'Magic Sculp'* heading for more details).

The paper maché casting should then be sealed inside and out to be fully protected from moisture. A good lacquer sealer is recommended. ***Use with plenty of ventilation and follow all of the manufacturer's safety*** *precautions!* The paper maché casting will soak up the lacquer sealer, further strengthening the piece. Use some Wood Dough or Spackle® to smooth out any surface irregularities on the outside of the casting. When this has dried, you can sand the finished casting to further smooth it out.

These are the basics only. You will learn much by doing. The best part is, all of the components for making paper maché are non-toxic (depending on what you end up using of course). So for those with health problems and such, this may be the best way to go. Paper maché done the right way can be very strong and last a long time.

### Urethane resins

Basically, urethane resin is a two-component liquid plastic that sets up quickly compared to most other resins. There are some slower setting varieties, but most set up very quickly. The majority of urethane resins pour like water or a very thin syrup. There are some special formulations that are heavily filled and are more like a paste.

*Mixing urethane resins:* Urethane resin comes as an 'A' component and a 'B' component. The majority of urethane resins are mixed to a *one to one* ratio or equal amounts of the 'A' and 'B' components. There are exceptions to this, so read the manufacturer's instructions carefully. Some are mixed by weight and some are mixed by volume (some can be mixed either way). Mixing by volume is of course easier. If you are going to mix by volume, purchase some clear or translucent plastic disposable cups from the grocery store to use for measuring. These will make it easy to see if you have equal amounts of a 'A' and 'B' parts of the resin.

If you have a urethane resin that should be mixed by weight, use a gram scale (see Chapter Five) for accurate weighing of the 'A' and 'B' components. Because urethane resin is so thin, it is sometimes difficult to pour from the original container. Pour it into a smaller cup first and then pour from this cup into your measuring cup on the scale. This will make it much easier to pour small amounts. Always use clean measuring cups for this. ***Wear rubber gloves to protect your hands and arms. Safety goggles are a must! Wear a NIOSH approved filter mask. Follow all of the manufacturer's safety precautions carefully. Thoroughly read all of the Material Safety Data Sheets.***

Weighing urethane on a gram scale

Use one clean cup for the 'A' component and one for the 'B' component. After you have measured out the correct amounts, pour the 'A' component into the 'B' cup and mix per the manufacturer's instructions.

*Preparing the molds:* For latex molds, spray Ease Release 2300 (or other recommended release agent from your supplier) inside the mold, the mold flange, and other areas where resin could possibly leak out accidentally.

Although silicone molds do not require a release agent, using it will prolong the life of the mold. Whether using latex or silicone molds, you can follow this with a dusting of talcum powder (baby powder) inside the mold. Shake out or brush out the excess talcum powder. The talc will make the castings more paintable after removed from the mold. The type of release agent used can also affect the paintability of the castings when complete. Ask your supplier for a mold release that is compatible with painting.

It is best to turn a one-piece or open mold 'inside out' before applying mold release, to ensure adequate coverage. What you have to watch for is when you turn the mold 'right side in', that you do not touch or accidentally wipe off any of the mold release. You may end up with a spot where the casting sticks to the mold. Urethane has adhesive qualities and latex has no natural release qualities like silicone rubber does. So be sure that all parts of the inside of the mold get treated adequately with mold release.

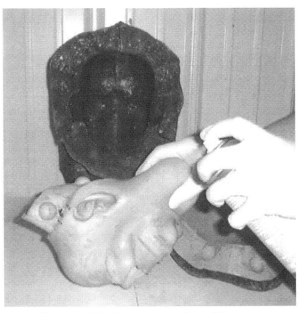

Head mold inside out to apply mold release

Hand mold ready with mold release and talc

If you have made a urethane rubber mold, follow the same basic instruction for treating a latex mold with mold release. Some urethane rubbers can be very tricky to cast urethane resin (plastic) in. Even with mold release you can sometimes have problems. If you are going to cast urethane resin into a urethane rubber mold, get a very specific recommendation from the manufacturer or supplier. Have them recommend which mold making rubber, casting resin, and mold release are compatible and would work best without problems. You can save yourself a lot of heartache if you do.

A plaster waste mold needs to be thoroughly dry and sealed with a few coats of sanding sealer first. Then apply a spray mold release (Ease Release 2300 or other suitable release recommended by your supplier), or a thin layer of Vaseline. It is very important with urethane resin to have the plaster be well sealed and do a very thorough job in applying the mold release. After applying mold release, do a test with a small amount of mixed urethane resin onto a non-critical part of the mold. Let it set up completely and see if it will release from the plaster mold with no problems. It should be noted, that even if it releases well, there is a good likelihood that you will have to break the plaster waste mold to remove the casting.

***Barrier coat or prepainting a casting:*** A barrier coat inside a mold further protects it from the chemicals in the casting resins. The barrier coat is applied over the mold release in a latex mold. In a silicone mold you do not need to use mold release for this process. There are commercial preparations specifically called 'barrier coat'. However, many paints will work just as well. You can spray primer as the barrier coat. Let this dry before continuing. You then make a urethane casting inside the mold. The primer or barrier coat will **bond** to the urethane and actually become part of the surface of the cast piece.

Going this route, your castings will come out of the mold pre-primed ready for hand painting of the flesh tones later. (See Chapter Eight) If you have some flesh tone paint, you could paint this inside the mold instead of the primer, and the part would come right out of the mold, painted flesh color. You would then only need to do the detail work, such as cheeks, eye brows, lips, etc., afterwards. If you have made a good mold with just the right texture on the inside, this is the texture the paint will have on the finished casting. So it doesn't matter how rough you paint it into the mold prior to casting. The surface will still come out nicely. Another old mold maker's trick!

**'Buttering' with filled resin:**  Buttering a mold is another technique that allows one to make a hollow object with a casting material. It basically involves troweling or brushing a thickened resin into a mold. The term 'buttering' comes from the fact that the resin used is about the consistency of soft butter,

and can be spread like butter as well, inside a mold. After it sets up, it makes a nice, rigid, durable, hollow casting. It is applied one layer at a time or in some cases, applied in one thick layer. It is usually easier though, to obtain a more even thickness by doing 2 to 3 thinner layers.

As previously mentioned, most urethane resins are very thin in viscosity (like water or a very thin syrup). These are nice for slush casting (explained later in this chapter) or other similar casting processes, but are much too thin for 'buttering' a mold. You can either purchase a urethane product that is already thixotropic (a paste and not a flow-able liquid resin), or try to thicken the resin yourself. It is much easier, to buy the ready made product.

Most urethane resins set up too quickly to have time to add the needed fillers and have enough working time to spread the mixture in side the mold. Many urethanes have a one to three minute working time, with the average resin starting to set up in about two minutes! This is not much time to do anything. You only have time to mix up the resin and use it immediately. So, in order to try to thicken the resin yourself, you would need to find some urethane resin that has a longer working time, probably in the 5 to 15 minute working time range. Most urethane supplier carry urethane resins with longer working times. (See suppliers list) You can add Cab-O-Sil (see Chapter Five) or microballoons, available from many resin suppliers to thicken the resin.

Cab-O-Sil will only thicken the resin, microballoons will also make it lighter in weight. Microballoons are very tiny glass micro spheres and can be used to make just about any resin lightweight. There are also other lightweight fillers available for resins.

Ask your resin supplier for a recommendation and proper mixing instructions for adding such fillers to the urethane resin.

Ready made 'urethane pastes' are a much easier way to go. These were originally formulated for making mother molds, but they can be used to make castings and can work well for buttering a mold. Both **PolyTek Development Corporation** and **Smooth-On, Inc.**, make a 'urethane paste' that would work for this process. (See suppliers list) Noted figure maker Ray Guyll recommends a urethane product called 'Light Cast', which can be troweled or buttered into a mold as it thickens. (See suppliers list at end of book)

PolyTek's version is called **POLYGEL®
Plastic-75.** It consists of two liquids, Part A and Part B, which after mixing one to one by weight or volume, immediately self-thickens and gels to a brushable or trowelable consistency. It cures at room temperature to a hard, strong RTV (room temperature vulcanizing) plastic. Polygel® Plastic-75 thickens to a paste with a 3-minute working time. As the liquid components of Polygel® are stirred together, the mix changes color and thickens to a buttery, non-sag paste. A shell or mother mold can be built up in two or three coats, each applied about ten minutes apart, so a mold shell can be made in less than an hour and demolded in about 4 hours.

***Plasti-Paste*** from ***Smooth-On*** works similarly and consists of two components, Part A and Part B that are mixed together. It has a working time of about 10 minutes, and demolds in about 4 hours. 'Working time' is just like it sounds. It is the amount of time you have to work with the material before it gets too stiff to use. The longer working time of Plasti-Paste might be a little less intimidat-

ing and better to try first, if you are unsure as to which urethane paste to buy initially. Essentially either material will make a good strong casting.

Follow all of the directions supplied by the manufacturer when mixing and applying the urethane paste to the inside of a mold. Don't forget to apply mold release. Build up the thickness of the casting to about 1/8" thick or so, depending on the material used and the manufacturer's recommendations.

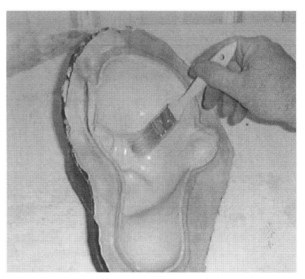

Brushing urethane paste inside one half of head mold

If buttering an ***open*** head mold, do the main part of the mold and then the separate trap-door piece separately. Let these castings fully set up before removing them from the mold. For a two-piece head mold, you ***butter*** each half of the head separately. After the material has fully set up you can remove the two halves from the mold and cut out the trap-door area for the back half of the head. You will now need to bond the two halves of the head together. The trap door piece you cut out does not get bonded.

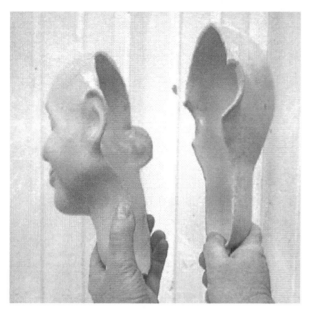

Front and back half of buttered head casting

You can usually use the same urethane paste to bond the two halves of the head together. Bind the cast head halves together temporarily with twine or large rubber bands (you can make some large rubber bands by cutting up some old tire inner tubes), and apply the urethane paste on the inside seam. A little masking tape on the outside of the seam can help keep the paste from squishing out and making a mess.

There are some urethanes that do not bond well to previously cured material. It is best to always purchase urethane that **knits** or **bonds** well to itself. Otherwise you will have to find some type of adhesive to bond the two cast head pieces together, such as a two part *high strength* epoxy (hardware store) or one of the newer super glues.

Some of the *super glues* available at the hobby stores have two-part systems that have some great advantages. It has the **glue** and **activator**. You first spread the glue around the seam or joint. Bind the two halves to-

gether temporarily. The activator is then sprayed along the seam, which 'kicks off' the glue and makes it set up rather quickly. This makes it much easier to assemble the two halves together accurately, get the glue where you want it and get a very good glue joint.

The 'buttering' process could likewise be used for hand or foot molds. It would be necessary to have two-piece molds in order to do this. A one-piece latex mold would not work. It is also possible to do a cast body using this technique. It would be best to have an 'open' style body mold (similar in design to an 'open' head mold; Chapter Four) to make it easy to apply the urethane paste and not have the hassle of trying to bond the two halves together later.

### Slush casting with urethane:

Slush casting is another way to make a hollow casting. This can be done with a slit mold, a two-piece mold, an open head mold, a one-piece latex mold, a small block mold, etc. Although you can slush cast polyester or epoxy resins, the cast parts would be extremely brittle. Drop the cast part once and it will shatter like glass! Polyester and epoxy resin get their strength from the glass cloth or mat (see Fiberglassing, 'Epoxy & Polyester resin' in this chapter). Without some type of reinforcement polyester and epoxy resin are pretty much useless to cast parts for figures.

Rigid urethane plastic (the regular liquid resin or non-paste variety), however, can be slush cast without any type of reinforcement and has very good durability. Not to say that it cannot break, but compared to polyester and epoxy castings without reinforcement, urethane is very resistant to breaking from impact. This is especially true if you use a good quality urethane resin. There are urethane resins that can be dropped from several feet off the ground onto concrete and suffer no damage. Pretty tough stuff!

***'Slush casting' basics:*** Prepare the mold with mold release as previously described. Assemble the mold together with the mother mold. On an *open* head mold (see Chapter Four), strap or clamp the trap-door part of the mold to the main part of the mold. On a two-piece head, hand or foot mold, close the mold and strap it together.

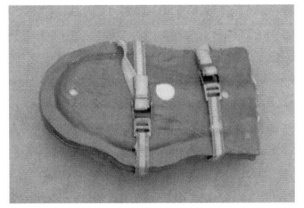

Hand mold secured with banding straps

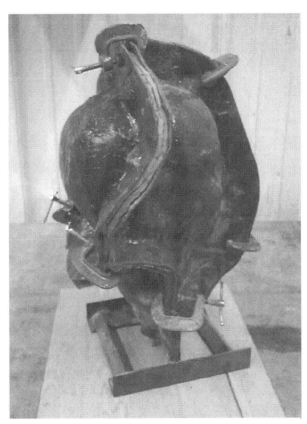

Open head mold clamped together for slush casting

Whether you are using a plaster waste mold, latex mold, urethane or silicone mold, the procedure for slush casting urethane (plastic) resin is the same. The first step would be to mix up a small batch of urethane resin. You want just enough to coat the inside of the mold with a very thin coating.

You can pour the material in an opening in the mold. On a head mold, this can be the hole where the control stick is located, on the bottom of the neck. After pouring the urethane resin in the head mold, you can plug the opening (see control stick considerations on page 88). On a hand or foot mold there is an opening at the wrist or ankle area where the material can be poured in.

After pouring the mixed urethane into the mold, you begin by tilting the mold at different angles and rotating it at the same time. This is the ***slushing*** part. The idea is to keep the mold moving (tilting and rotating) while the material sets up. At first it will be very liquid. As it starts to set up a little, it will move more slowly inside the mold. Finally it will barely move at all as you tilt or rotate the mold. You can then slow down the speed at which you are rotating the mold as the material moves slower. At a certain point, the mixed urethane will not move at all as you tip or tilt the mold. This means the material has gelled.

The idea is to try to get as even a coating on the inside of the mold as possible. This takes a little practice, so don't get discouraged if your first casting is not perfect. After the first coat has gelled, you can ***slush*** in a few more coats of mixed urethane resin right on top of the previous coatings until you get the thickness desired. On a hand or foot casting that could be about 1/16" thick or so. On a head mold, you would want it about 1/8" minimum thickness (this is approximately one pound of material on an average size head). It is always best to slush the next coat immediately after the last coat had gelled, for the best adhesion between coats. You can pre-measure the correct amounts of 'A' and 'B' of the urethane in separate mixing containers, ready for the next coat.

With the right urethane, 1/8" is plenty strong. You can make it thicker, but it will start to get very heavy. You could add some lightweight filler, but you need to keep in mind that some fillers make the resin thicker, even in the so-called fluid stage, and may not flow so well in the mold when slush casting. Some figure makers like thinner castings, some like thicker castings resembling a carved basswood head. You have to use a fair amount of lightweight filler to have a head this thick and not weigh too much when completed. Some experimentation with different amounts of filler would be needed.

Ideally, it is best to *slush* two to four really thin coats (one after the other) to get the final thickness that you want. If you try to slush just one thick coat all at once, you will most likely have parts of the casting that are way too thick and parts that are way too thin. Or, you will end up with most of the urethane as a big 'blob' of hardened material somewhere inside the mold.

Urethane resins **exotherm** (generate heat) as they cure. The more resin you put into the mold at one time, the more heat there will be, and a greater likelihood that a large mass will set up somewhere inside the mold. When this happens, you will undoubtedly have *bare*

spots in the mold where you will see no resin, or it will be paper thin. The key with slush casting is to use smaller batches and build up the thickness of the casting slowly and evenly. Some urethanes will bond well to previously cured material, some will not. So check with your supplier to make sure, prior to purchasing the urethane.

Rotating hand mold to slush cast urethane

It would also be best to start with a hand mold or a mold of the jaw, something small at first. With a hand mold, for example, the wrist area is open and you can see what is happening during the slush casting process. Carefully watch the resin as you tilt and rotate the mold. **Wear safety glasses and other protective equipment. If urethane resin is splashed into your eyes it can possibly cause permanent damage!** You have to be careful or the resin will spill out of the opening onto the floor. Let the mixed resin come close to the end of the mold as you tilt it. Rotate the mold, and then tilt it back the other way. You should be able to pretty much see which areas are getting coated and which ones are not. Rotate and tilt the mold in such a way that the inside of the mold gets evenly coated throughout. (See photo above)

Watch what happens as the urethane resin goes through its various stages, from very liquid, to a thicker and thicker liquid, until it

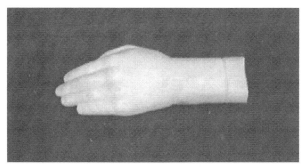

Slush cast hand (hollow)

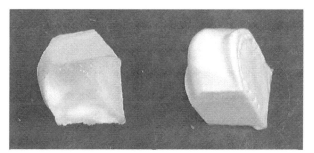

Rear view              Top view

Slush cast jaw - showing inside and outside of casting

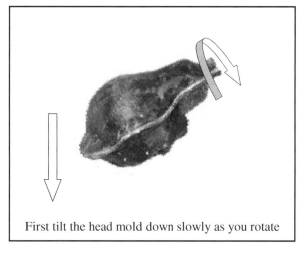

First tilt the head mold down slowly as you rotate

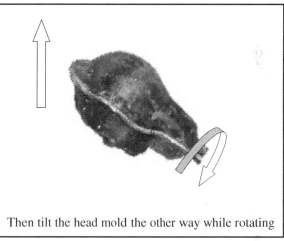

Then tilt the head mold the other way while rotating

finally gels completely and will not move anymore. Do the additional coats the same as the first. Remove the casting from the mold when it has cured enough to pull it without distortion.

Successfully slush casting a head mold takes a fair amount of practice. There are a lot of **peaks** and **valleys** on the inside of a head mold, and a lot more surface area to cover, making it much more challenging to get a good coating of resin throughout. You also cannot really see what is going on inside

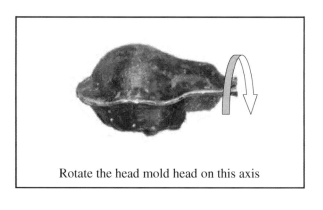

Rotate the head mold head on this axis

the mold as you slush cast. Again, 3 or 4 thin coats will work better than 1 or 2 thicker coats on a head casting. Also, pay attention to how you rotate and tilt the mold while slushing the material.

For a head mold, try rotating the mold on the shorter axis and do the tilting back and forth slowly (like a slow moving *see-saw*) on the longer axis. (See photos this page) It will take some experimentation to find the best speed for the rotation and tilting. It should be noted that slush casting urethane can be hit an miss when it comes to a head casting in particular. It is best done on a true roto casting machine (a unit that rotates a mold on two axis at the same time; see page 118) rather than by hand. This is not to say that it cannot be done by hand. It's just that getting the inside of a head mold evenly coated with the resin by hand will be fairly challenging.

Slush cast urethane head

After enough time has passed and you are sure that the material has gelled on the first coat, set the mold down for a few minutes. Depending on the speed of the resin you purchased and the ambient room temperature, you should be able to pull out the plug from the bottom of the neck area within about 5-10 minutes. There will be a point where the urethane resin is starting to get hard, but can still be cut easily with an Exacto Knife®. Cut a hole in the curing urethane resin through the neck hole in the mold (if the resin is not rigid enough, wait a few more minutes). The hole should be just big enough to be able to pour in more resin for the next batch.

Mix up another small batch of urethane resin. If you think a pound of material is the correct amount for your casting, you could mix up 1/4 lb. of resin for each pour or coat. That would be 1/8 lb. of the 'A' part of the material, and 1/8 lb. of the 'B' part of the material for each of the four coats that you slush. Mix up the next batch and pour it into the hole in the neck area. Apply more release agent to the plug if necessary. Reinsert the plug and slush this batch the same as the first. Continue this way until all four batches (or however many you determine to do) have been slush cast. Read the manufacturer's instructions to see how soon the casting can be taken out of the mold. Do not pull it out of the mold too soon or it will distort!

After the head casting has set up pretty well, you can cut out the area for the trapdoor (see pages 40 and 93 for the approximate size of the trap-door area). You can then hold the head up to a light and see how well you did. If you find some thin spots, don't panic. There's a couple of ways to fix this.

You can mix up some very small amounts of urethane and do what's called *painting in* the thin spots. Take a gloved finger and dab

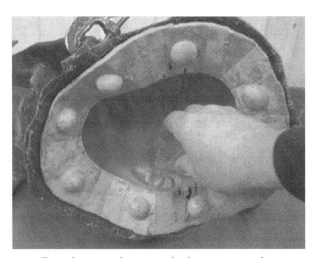

Pouring urethane resin into ear cavity

the resin on the thin areas. As the resin starts to set a little, it will thicken, and you can then get a layer of urethane placed over the thin spot on the casting. You have to work quickly as the resin sets up fast. Do as many layers as it takes to cover the thin spots adequately. This works better with some resins than others. Some bond well to previously cured resin and some do not. Do a test to be sure.

Instead of using urethane resin, some figure makers fill in the thin spots with Magic Sculp or other two part epoxy modeling compounds. It may be necessary to roughen the area a little first with a medium grit sandpaper if possible.

If you have trouble with the ear areas, you can cast the ears first. You can cast up enough urethane resin to fill one ear and cast it solid. When this has gelled sufficiently, you can mix up more resin and cast the other ear solid. Leave the cast ears in place and then slush cast the remainder of the head as normal. It is best to slush cast as soon as possible after the ear areas have gelled. This technique works best in an open mold, as you have easy access. It can be done in a two-piece head mold by pouring the resin into the opening in the neck, and then positioning the mold so the resin goes into the ear cavity. Repeat for the other ear. This is a little trickier to do this way, but can be done.

***Urethane resin recommendations:*** When selecting a urethane resin for slush casting it is best to get one of the faster setting resins. When slush casting, you want the material to set up reasonably quick. Otherwise you will get quite worn out, rotating and tilting the mold, especially if the mold has some weight to it. A 15-minute working time may not seem that long, but it can feel like an eternity when slush casting. A 3-minute working time is much better. If you get one that sets too fast, that can cause problems, too.

Some urethane resins are better for 'thin wall' castings (such as hollow parts for vent figures) than others. There are some brands or varieties that do not cure quite hard enough in thin sections. The resulting castings will not be quite durable enough for a good quality vent figure. Some urethanes also take paint better than others. There are a lot of different urethane manufacturers and just as many if not more formulations for different types of urethane plastic. It can be quite the confusing jungle out there, so some recommendations are in order.

***BJB Enterprises*** has some very nice urethane resins as well as other mold making and casting supplies. (See suppliers list) The ***TC-808*** Rigid Urethane available from them works well for slushing and makes some tough, thin wall, castings. It is also more readily paintable than a lot of urethanes. You can also get their products from Burman Industries (See suppliers list).

Spraying 'Extend-It' inside urethane container

*Alumilite* carries a very tough resin as well. (See suppliers list) It can make some very strong, thin wall castings. It seems to be a little touchier to work with than some resins, but overall of the very highest quality. It sometimes has more problems with pinholes or small bubbles in the surface of the casting, which seems to be more of a problem the longer the container has been opened. Alumilite has recommendations for preventing these types of problems in their literature. A little more patience might be required, but you can get a very nice casting.

*Smooth Cast 300* from Smooth-On, Inc. (see suppliers list) is a nice urethane resin to work with and is somewhat user friendly. It tends to have a little *flex* in the cured castings compared to the BJB TC-808 or Alumilite urethane castings. This is more noticeable in a larger casting such as a head casting. In some ways that can make a casting less brittle and less prone to breakage if dropped. However, the other two resins cure to a very durable cast piece as well.

The shelf life of *all urethane resins* is usually shortened after the container has been opened. Air and moisture can contaminate the material (moisture causes urethanes to foam) and cause it to eventually go bad. Some are more susceptible to this than others. In any case, it is best to use up urethane resins as soon as possible after opening the containers. You can greatly extend the shelf life by spraying 'dry nitrogen' into the container before closing it. Many resin suppliers carry this product, with such names as *Belch* (seriously!) or *Xtend-It*. (See suppliers list) *Use as directed and follow all safety precautions!* The 'dry nitrogen' forms a blanket over the urethane, protecting it from air and moisture.

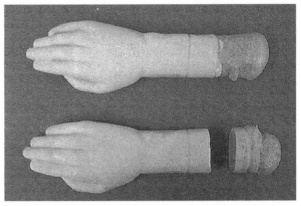

Hand casting with foam core (and then trimmed)

*Backing with rigid urethane foam:* Here is a little trick that works great for hand or foot castings. Slush cast one or two thin coatings inside a hand or foot mold. This makes a very thin shell inside the mold. After the material has gelled, you follow by pouring in a rigid urethane foam. When fully cured you can trim the casting with a hack saw, coping saw, band saw, etc. (See photo above)

Rigid urethane foam is mixed similar to regular urethane resin. It is a two-part system with an 'A' component and a 'B' component. When mixed and then poured into the mold, after a short time the material begins to foam and rise. When cured, it turns into a dense, rigid foam, and bonds to the thin shell you first slushed. You can get foams that are as strong as a good hardwood.

Rigid urethane foam comes in different densities and is rated in pounds. A two-pound density is like packing foam and not that strong. It is recommended to get a minimum of *ten-pound density* of rigid urethane foam. BJB Enterprises has a nice foam that compliments the TC-808 rigid urethane. The *TC-300 #10* (the 10 stands for 10-pound density) works well. If you go higher on the density, say a 15-pound foam, it will of course weigh a little more than the 10 pound density foam. The 10-pound foam is just fine in most cases. You can get urethane foams from other suppliers as well. (See suppliers list)

When everything has fully set up, the rigid urethane foam supports the thin urethane shell. The outside shell looks nice and will look good when painted later. A hand or foot cast this way will be strong, lightweight, and more like a carved wood part. The outside shell can be cast slightly thinner than when making just a hollow casting with the standard rigid urethane by itself. It is a simple method that works quite well.

It is possible to cast just the foam by itself without first slushing a thin rigid shell. Some foams are *self-skinning*. They create an outer surface that's better than the foams that are not self-skinning. In general, however, the foam will not take as good of detail from the mold as the regular rigid urethane will. So it is usually best to slush a thin shell or skin first and follow with the rigid foam, as described above.

### Fiberglassing with epoxy and polyester

Fiberglassing is the process of laying up resin and glass cloth (or mat) together to make a strong, thin, rigid casting or shell. Thus, one more way to make a hollow object. Usually a gel coat (a thicker resin) is painted into the mold first, then layers of glass cloth and resin are applied directly over the gel coat (and bond to the gel coat). Sometimes a finishing layer is applied as a final coat on the inside of the casting.

The number of layers and the thickness of glass cloth or mat determine how thick the final shell or casting will be. The gel coat provides the smooth outer surface of the casting so the glass fibers do not show through or otherwise have a rough surface. A

well done gel coat followed by good laminations (fiberglass) will save you hours of patching work later. That is really the only purpose of the gel coat. Otherwise you could laminate or fiberglass without it. Fiberglassing can be done with polyester or epoxy resin. The process of fiberglassing with polyester or epoxy is pretty much the same, however there are a few differences.

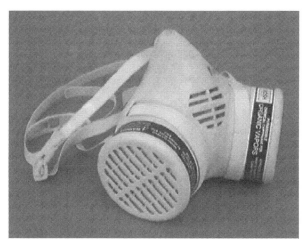

NIOSH approved respirator with organic filters

***Polyester resins for fiberglassing:*** Polyester resin has a very strong odor and exposure to these fumes can definitely be a health risk. **Use of a NIOSH approved respirator (make sure it is rated for this type of use; they are not all the same) is mandatory when working with polyester. Carefully read and follow all of the safety precautions concerning the resin and catalyst prior to use. Failure to do so can lead to serious health problems.**

Polyester can be used at different air temperatures fairly easily by altering the amount of catalyst used. There is also a larger 'working window' of time with polyester as far as how long you can go between coats and still have a good bond between layers than with epoxy. There are certain types of polyester fiberglassing resin that contain no wax, and will stay tacky for many hours after it has gelled and even partially cured. This allows you to walk away from the project for awhile and still be able to add additional layers later. Polyester is also much cheaper than epoxy (not necessarily a good reason to choose it over epoxy, but it can be a factor).

***Epoxy resin for fiberglassing:*** Epoxy does not have a very strong odor, and in general is much more pleasant to work with, but it still has potential health risks. ***All safety precautions need to be faithfully followed with epoxy as well!*** Epoxy 'gel coats' are more forgiving and easier to apply, trouble free. Epoxy is very temperature sensitive, however, and will not work well below 75-80 degrees F (actually it will sometimes not work at all with cooler temperatures). There is a smaller 'working window' of time with epoxy as far as how long you can go between coats and still have a good bond between layers. Once you have applied the last layer and it has set up, you cannot add additional layers and have it bond well without some extra work. Epoxy is quite the adhesive, so molds have to be well prepared with mold release. Although the above can sound fairly negative, epoxy can still be the better choice of resin to start with, if directions are followed carefully.

***Preparing the molds:*** Whether using polyester or epoxy for fiberglassing, the first step is to prepare the mold as described under ***'Urethane resins'*** (*preparing the molds*) on page 98. The only thing that needs to be noted, is that polyester can be inhibited by latex rubber. What that means is if you do a fiberglass casting with polyester resin in a latex mold, the latex can cause the outer surface of the casting not to fully cure and

will remain tacky. The best solution is to apply a barrier coat to the inside of the mold. A barrier coat is just like it sounds. It is a coating that provides a barrier between the polyester and the latex mold.

A simple barrier coat can be a thin layer of Vaseline brushed into the mold. Sometimes this is all that is needed. For a finer cast surface, you can spray mold release, and then spray some paint or primer inside the mold. This will also act as a barrier coat between the latex and the polyester resin. In addition to this, the paint will adhere to the casting and the part will come out prepainted! (See sub-heading ***'Barrier coat or prepainting a casting'***, page 100).There are also commercially produced barrier coats that one can buy from resin suppliers. PVA is a common barrier coating used in the fiberglassing industry and can be obtained from your fiberglass materials supplier.

***Gel coat application:*** After the mold has been properly prepared, the next step is to apply the gel coat. With polyester you can purchase a pre-made gel coat, ready to apply (after catalyst has been added and mixed into the gel coat resin). With epoxy you take general purpose casting epoxy and make your own gel coat by adding a thickening agent to make it thixotropic (see suppliers list). Check with your supplier, they may have a pre-made epoxy gel coat available or will have a filler that they recommend for that particular brand of epoxy. Whether using epoxy or polyester, follow the manufacturer's instructions for adding the correct amount of catalyst or hardener.

***Wear chemical resistant rubber gloves to protect your hands and arms. Safety glasses are also recommended. Follow all of the manufacturer's safety precautions carefully. A NIOSH approved respirator with***

*organic vapor cartridges is typically recommended when working with these materials.*

After the gel coat material has been catalyzed, take a disposable bristle brush and apply a thin layer of gel coat to the inside of the mold. With polyester resin gel coat, it is best if sprayed, but most hobbyists are not set up for this. If going this route, 2 to 3 light coats are better than one heavy coat. A brush can do a satisfactory job if done with care. You may only need one or two coats if using a brush. Epoxy gel coat is best done with a brush and *not* sprayed.

Gel coats are usually quite thin. You do not want to get it too thick, as the gel coat is not a reinforced layer. A gel coat should be less than 1/32" thick. Resin suppliers usually say the preferred thickness is .010" to .020" thick. A coating less than .005" thick can cause wrinkles in the gel coat. This is especially true when brush marks are present. Use a better quality brush when applying polyester gel coat and apply carefully. You can also check the thickness using a gel coat 'thickness gauge' available from fiberglass suppliers. (See suppliers list)

A wrinkle can also occur if the gel coat is not cured enough prior to lay-up. Before doing any laminations, you should check the surface of the gel coat to see if it is tacky. It should be sticky but should not be wet enough to transfer to your finger. Use a gloved finger to test.

*Ear cavities:* The ear areas of the mold can be one big cavity with a lot of detail therein, depending on the type of head mold you made (*open* mold for instance). This type of cavity inside a mold is very difficult to lay up or laminate fiberglass in. It can be much easier to cast them solid. Use some filler with the resin for strength and help control

*exotherm* (heat generation). Some chopped strand (from your fiberglass supplier) can work fine. Mix a little in with the resin, and fill one ear cavity solid. Let the material gel. Do the other ear the same as the first.

With epoxy, after the second ear has gelled, you should start fiberglassing the rest of the head right away. As long as you can still dent it with your finger nail, you should be okay. If it is a gel or like a hard rubber, it hasn't gone through the final stages of cure yet and will bond fine. If it has fully hardened it would be best to prepare the surface before continuing. Wash this area with clean water and an abrasive pad (Scotch-brite™ 7447) to remove the amine blush (wax-like film on cured epoxy). Dry with a paper towel to remove the dissolved blush before it dries on the surface. If there are any remaining glossy areas, sand with 80 grit sandpaper.

*Fiberglassing with epoxy & polyester:* The next step is to do the actual fiberglassing or laminating. This involves adding resin and fiberglass cloth (or mat) to the gel coat, a layer at a time. For epoxy use laminating epoxy resin.

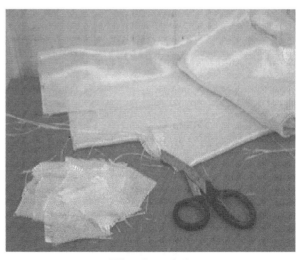

Fiberglass cloth

For polyester you have two basic choices: (**1.**) There are general purpose polyester resins that have wax in them. The wax goes to the surface shutting out the air and aids in curing the resin tack free. (**2.**) Polyester laminating resin remains tacky (it is naturally inhibited by contact with air) for a long time after it has been applied to the inside of the mold. This is a better choice for laminating or fiberglassing as you can take your time making a fiberglass casting. But then you will have to follow with a finishing resin (an extra step and extra material to buy) in order for the last layer to fully set up tack free. Which way is easier? If you are just starting out learning fiberglassing techniques, it would probably be best to go with laminating resin and follow with finishing resin. This will give you more time and will be a more forgiving process overall.

General purpose polyester resin does not require a finishing resin. It will cure tack free in a short period of time (how much time depends on the amount of catalyst used). So you have to make sure that the general pur-

pose resin doesn't cure *too much* between layers or it will not bond well.

Fiberglass cloth comes in a variety of weaving patterns, but for most figure casting work a plain weave will do just fine. Cloth also comes in various weights (which refers to the thickness of the cloth) per square yard and is rated in ounces. Start with cloth in the six to ten 'ounce' range. It goes without saying that the thicker the cloth the less layers you will need to achieve the desired thickness. Keep in mind, however, that the heavier (thicker) the cloth, the harder it is to get it to conform around the curves on the inside of the mold when fiberglassing.

Resin dabbed onto fiberglass cloth inside head mold

Glass fiber mat (referred to as 'mat') is glass fibers in a random pattern (as opposed to cloth which is woven in a specific pattern) and is sold in weights per square foot rather than per square yard. Two layers of 3/4 ounce should be about the right thickness for a head casting. Mat in general will probably be easier to work with than cloth when doing a casting. *The **mat**, however, will not work with **epoxy resin**. It has a polyester soluble*

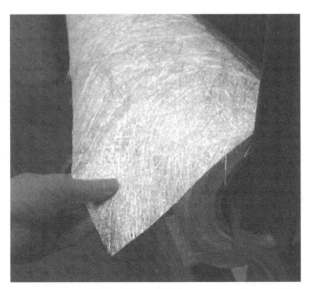

Fiberglass mat (on a roll)

*binder in it that is only dissolved by polyester resin.*

Fiberglass mat is easier to use if you lay it on a flat surface (inside a polyethylene tray or tub works well) and saturate it with resin first. Then you can lay it inside the mold (which already has the gel coat applied and is partially set, but still tacky) and use the brush with a little additional resin to saturate the mat and get it to conform to the contours. With fiberglass cloth, put some resin on the mold first (over the gel coat) and then carefully lay the cloth inside the mold. Follow with a brush and a little resin to saturate the cloth. Whether using cloth or mat, use a dabbing motion to work out any bubbles or air pockets.

Keep adding resin and pieces of cloth (see photo previous page). Use only enough resin to saturate the cloth (or mat), otherwise you will have puddles of resin in places. Overlap the edges of the cloth or mat by *at least* 1/4" to 1/2" as opposed to putting them edge to edge. This will make a stronger casting. If necessary cut some smaller square pieces (of cloth or mat) to go around the contours. Whether you use mat or cloth, cover the entire area completely with one layer.

With polyester laminating resin it is okay to let the first layer gel (the resin is no longer a liquid, but not hard yet; kind of like gelatin, but still tacky), and even wait anywhere from a few hours to a couple of days, before applying the second coat. With epoxy, you can also let the resin gel before doing additional layers, but you cannot wait very long or you will have to sand or wash the inside of the casting first. It would be best with epoxy to keep going until all the layers are done. Apply additional layers of resin and cloth (or

Fiberglass head casting bonded together from inside

mat) until you achieve the thickness desired. A thickness of 1/16" to 3/32" is usually adequate for a fiberglass casting if done properly.

When you start laying the cloth or mat inside the mold, it is okay for it to go past the outside edge of the mold. After the casting has cured, you can pull it from the mold and trim off the excess with a cutting disc on a Dremel Moto Tool. It helps if you mark where in needs to be cut with a permanent marker, prior to pulling it out of the mold.

***Bonding the head casting together:*** If you have used polyester laminating resin, it will still be tacky and ready for the next step. General purpose polyester resin, if it has not

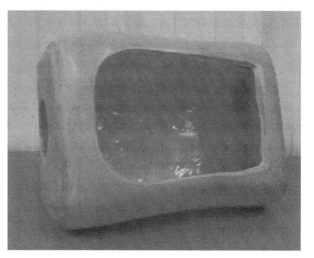

Cast fiberglass body - back side

Fiberglass head casting from open mold

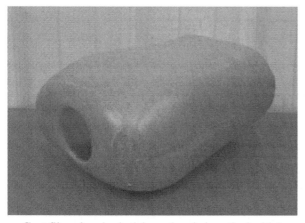

Cast fiberglass body (pieces bonded on the inside)

With epoxy it is best to wash this area with clean water and an abrasive pad (Scotch-brite™ 7447) to remove the amine blush (wax-like film on cured epoxy). Dry with a paper towel to remove the dissolved blush before it dries on the surface. If there are any remaining glossy areas, sand with 80 grit sandpaper.

If you have done a two-piece mold, after laying up all the pieces of the mold with fiberglass, the next thing to do is to join the cast pieces. Remove the castings and trim as necessary. Do a cutout for the trap-door. Bind the head together temporarily with tape. Use more cloth (or mat) and resin and cover the inside seam. Two layers of 3/4 oz. mat or equivalent thickness of cloth should be used for enough strength on the seam area. Use a *finishing resin* for the last layer, and coat the entire inside of the head with this, if it's still tacky. Let set up fully, and then remove the tape that was holding the two halves together. Use Magic Sculp or other suitable patching compound to fill in any gaps on the outside of the seam area. If you have used an *open* mold to cast a head, this step is not necessary.

sat too long, will be okay. When in doubt, sand the inside of the casting along the seam to help make a good 'mechanical bond'.

The same basic steps for bonding the two halves of a fiberglass head casting can also be done with a body casting. After the halves have set up adequately they can be removed from the mold. On a body casting you would do the bonding through the cutout in the back piece. Do the joining the same way as described for the head. Fill any gaps in the seam with Spackle or Magic Sculp.

One of the biggest secrets in learning to do fiberglassing successfully is practicing with smaller test batches and getting familiar with the process. This book does not and can not be a thorough treatise of all the aspects of fiberglassing. The purpose is to give you a basic understanding of fiberglassing techniques and specifically how it applies to figure making. See 'The Fiberglass Repair and Construction Handbook by Jack Wiley (TAB books) for some excellent information on polyester and epoxy fiberglassing. A lot of well researched info on cloth, mat, resins and standard fiberglassing techniques. The Fiberglast Corp. has a good beginning video on basic fiberglassing techniques. It is specifically for working with epoxy, but the principles apply to fiberglassing with polyester as well. (See suppliers list)

### Absorption casting - Liquid Neoprene

Neoprene is an interesting material as it can make a hollow object easily without too much work on your part. Some find it more flexible than they would like for a rigid casting material. For this reason it can work well for hands or feet (where rigidity is not important), but is difficult to use for making a head or body (where rigidity can be very important). It takes a little longer to sand out any imperfections as it is more like sanding a hard rubber than wood or plastic. But it will sand, and sand smooth enough for figure making.

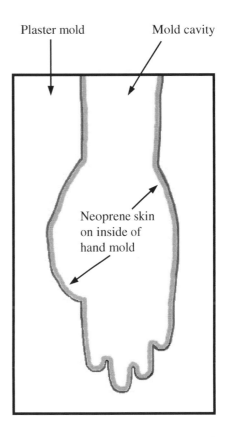

Plaster mold      Mold cavity

Neoprene skin on inside of hand mold

Liquid neoprene leaves a 'skin' on inside of mold

Another material that can be cast in plaster molds with the absorption process is *rigid latex*. The technique is essentially the same as doing a neoprene casting. Rigid latex is, however, an organic material and will eventually deteriorate with age and become very brittle and crumbly. Neoprene is not really susceptible to those types of problems, however it can turn soft when exposed to too much heat. Each material has its advantages and disadvantages.

A clean, uncontaminated, plaster waste mold could be used to make a neoprene casting or two, but will not hold up very well to repeated use. If you want to produce many castings or do anything that resembles production work, it would be best to make some higher quality *block* style plaster molds. The type that is needed is the same used for *slip casting* as is used for making dolls or slip cast pottery. There is a great book on this subject called, "Plaster Mold and Model Making", by Charles Chaney and Stanley Skee (out of print, but still can be found). It takes you step-by-step through all of the processes involved in making production style slip casting plaster molds.

Generally, No. 1 Pottery Plaster (a USG product, see suppliers list) is used for absorption casting. Adding some Hydrocal (another USG product) to the No. 1 Pottery Plaster, 50/50, will greatly improve the durability of your molds. The molds will eventually deteriorate in any case, as repeatedly casting neoprene is hard on the molds. It is just the nature of the material.

Cured rigid neoprene appears to be somewhere between a plastic and a rubber. It is slightly flexible, but mostly rigid when fully cured. Neoprene generally shrinks 10% after curing. Liquid neoprene can only be cast in plaster molds. It is very important that the plaster mold be free of grease, dirt, oil or any other type of contamination. The plaster absorbs the liquid from the neoprene leaving the solids behind to cure, forming a 'skin' on the inside wall of the mold. If the mold is contaminated, the absorption process will not work properly or not at all in some cases.

As soon as you pour liquid neoprene into a plaster mold, the process of drawing moisture out of the neoprene begins. A thin coating of solids, begins forming a *skin* on the inside of the mold where the plaster comes into contact with the neoprene. This coating or skin continues to get thicker and thicker the longer you leave the neoprene in the mold. When the neoprene skin gets to the desired thickness, you pour out the remaining liquid. You let this skin or coating cure overnight. You would then open the mold,

remove the finished casting and let it fully cure. That's how it works in a nutshell. A more detailed description of working with liquid neoprene follows.

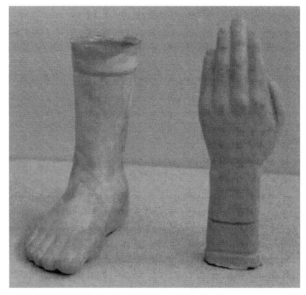

Neoprene hand and foot castings (ready to trim)

If the plaster molds are completely dry, dunk them in a tub of water for a few seconds. The absorption process with neoprene works best in slightly damp molds. Put the mold together and band it with large rubber bands (you can cut bands out of an old car tire inner tube), banding straps, or twine. Roll out some beads of clay and firmly press these into the seams of the mold. Put the mold in a polyethylene tub in case you spring a leak. **Wear rubber gloves to protect your hands and arms. Safety glasses are also strongly recommended. Neoprene can cause blindness if it splashes into your eyes. Follow all of the manufacturer's safety precautions carefully.** Tilt the mold at a slight angle and slowly pour in the liquid neoprene. This will help prevent bubbles from forming.

When the mold is nearly full, slowly tilt the mold back upright. Keep pouring. After the mold is completely full carefully check for leaks. Use more clay to seal the leaks if necessary. After several minutes you won't need to worry about the neoprene leaking, as a thin coating of solids begins forming within the seams. After you are sure that the mold is no longer leaking anywhere, let it sit undisturbed. Check the level of the neoprene every 15 to 30 minutes or however often is necessary. As the plaster draws the moisture out, the level of the liquid neoprene will go down. Pour in more neoprene and keep topping it off as needed.

As you are periodically checking the level of the neoprene, you can also check and see how thick the coating or skin is that will be forming. It is easiest to check this when the level has gone down. For most castings, 1/16" to 3/32" is usually thick enough. A casting 1/8" thick would probably be as thick as you would ever need to go.

When the neoprene coating or skin on the inside of the mold is the right thickness, pour out the remaining liquid into a holding container. Some have found that the shelf life of their neoprene will be longer if they do not pour it back into the original container. When you make the next casting, pour neoprene from the second *holding container* first (material that has already been used once), and then if you need more, complete the pour with fresh neoprene from your original container.

Let the neoprene cast remain in the mold for several hours (overnight is usually sufficient) undisturbed. You do not want to pull it out of the mold too soon as you will distort the casting. On the other hand, sometimes it is easier to pull a neoprene casting that has not cured 100%. You will learn to recognize the best time to pull the casting out of the

mold. After removing it from the mold, let the casting continue to cure for a few days before sanding, trimming, or painting.

### Casting techniques summary

There is one technique for urethane that was not covered here, as it could be the subject for a whole book all by itself! It is, however, actually one of the best ways to use urethane and is utilized in the toy making industry and other similar manufacturing situations. It is called core molding. It basically involves making an inner mold (or core) that fits inside of a regular mold. With this setup, the inside of the casting is molded at the same time as the outside of the casting. You pour thin viscosity urethane resin into the mold, and it automatically produces a hollow casting within 5-30 minutes (depending on the resin you use).

A core mold can be set up so that the eye and mouth openings are already done for you (no cutting or trimming). You can also it set it up so that there will be places molded on the inside that are ready to receive the mechanics. Using it is fairly easy and quick, but needless to say, there is a lot involved in making such a mold and a lot of mold making and casting experience is needed to make one successfully. It is an advanced technique and might possibly be covered in a future volume if enough interest warrants it.

If you have come this far, and made some castings already, it is probably starting to get pretty exciting at this point. After all these years, I still get tickled when I pull a quality casting out of a mold. It's hard to explain. It is really a piece of art that has gone from a concept, to clay, to a mold, and finally a cast piece. When that cast piece comes out of the the mold and resembles your original concept, it can be very exciting to say the least!

There are certainly a variety of ways to make castings for making a professional style ventriloquist figure. It seems that everyone likes something different. That's why a number of techniques were presented in this chapter. Some methods and materials are easier to work with than others. The bottom line, however, is to be able to make a cast figure that will last for many, many years.

The focus has been on methods and materials that will produce those results. There are other ways castings can be produced, and there are certainly some that would produce a figure that would last for a short while. But if you are going to go to all the trouble of making a figure, why not make one that will be long lasting?!? So, take your time and always strive to do quality work!

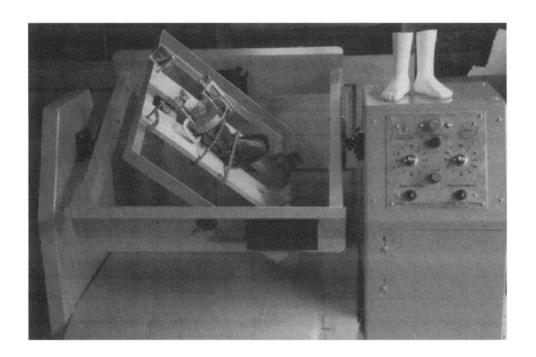

One of the author's favorite toys! A professional roto casting machine makes quick work of casting hollow parts

# CHAPTER SEVEN

# MECHANICS & ANIMATIONS

For many people installing the mechanics and controls that help animate your figure is one of the most exciting parts of figure making and for others, the most scary part. However, if you have taken on the challenge of sculpting, making molds and castings, there is no reason you cannot do the mechanics and controls as well. It is mostly a matter of having a positive attitude and not being afraid to experiment a little.

One note of caution: Many newer vents and beginning figure makers get caught up with all the possible movements that can be installed in a vent figure. The truth of the matter is that each extra feature that you add creates that much more of a challenge in operating your figure. For most beginning vents just having ball and socket neck movement, moving mouth and moving eyes is plenty to keep track of at first. You would be surprised how much adding just one extra feature can add to the difficulty of manipulation. You can always learn to work with a more complicated figure at a later date.

It should be noted that many famous ventriloquists have done, and still do, an amazing amount of manipulation with just a few animations. Edgar Bergen, Paul Winchell, Jimmy Nelson, Jeff Dunham, to name a few, have brought so much life to their figures with just a limited number of animations. You can add as many animations to your

figure as you wish, but remember that it is not required to bring a figure to life. One word of advice: Start simply and progress to more difficult projects later on. Many would like to start with a figure that has all the bells and whistles (moving mouth, eyes, eyebrows, winkers, flapping ears, etc.). Learn how to do a less complex figure first, and learn how to do that well. Then add another animation in the next figure that you build, and so on. You will learn tons from each level of mechanics that you try.

There is no standardization for the mechanics and controls on vent figures. The main goal here will be to give you enough ideas and principles for you to come up with a suitable way to animate your figure. Many of these ideas are tried and true methods used for years. Others are some newer ideas, some even experimental. As with all the other aspects of figure making, there is no one right way to do the mechanics and controls. Your ideas may be better than what is presented here. Don't be afraid to experiment and see what you can come up with on your own.

One thing that is somewhat standardized is the use of brass mechanics inside the head. These are typically found at a good **hobby shop.** Brass rods and tubes of various diameters (specific sizes will be outlined later) and brass flat stock are most commonly used in figure making. Brass holds up well to the rigors of time, is easily cut and worked to make up the various controls, levers, etc.

One general note of caution on mechanics: Certain designs of mechanics may not be compatible with some other designs. For example, let's say you wanted a tongue that sticks out and one of your other effects was a 'rod' style control for the eyes (both in this chapter). In some cases, depending on how you set it up, the rod for the eye mechanism would go right through the middle of the tongue mechanism.

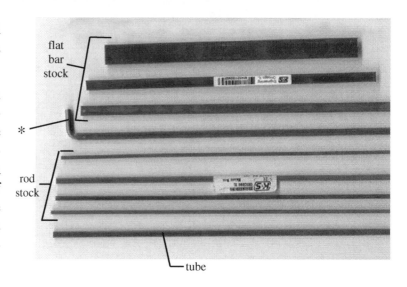

Brass rods, tubes, and flat bar stock
* Brass rod inside brass tube. End is bent in 'L' shape.

What can be done? A different type of control for the eyes would be one way to solve the problem. It would be much better to know about these types of problems before you get too far. When you are in the planning stages you will need to look carefully at all the mechanisms you are thinking of installing. Try to see things ***three dimensionally*** and verify ahead of time that they will all be compatible with each other. If not, you will have to find another way to go about it. You can save yourself a lot of grief by planning ahead.

One last note: Not all materials that heads are cast of are necessarily compatible with all glues, adhesives, or epoxy putties mentioned throughout this chapter. Some will bond to certain materials better than others. When in doubt always do a test first. In this chapter it is not assumed that you have made your head casting out of any one material, as many choices were given for this in Chapter Six. *That being the case, you must consider certain recommendations of glue or epoxy putty in this chapter to be a general guideline*

*only! You must determine the suitability of a particular adhesive through testing.*

The various animations will be presented individually, kind of a-la-carte style. That way you can pick and choose which animations you would like to install. Specific things that are important for a particular animation will be discussed under that heading.

### Control stick & trap-door considerations

You will probably have to read this chapter through a few times to decide what animations you will have and how the controls will be set up on the head stick (control stick or control post). Different sections in this chapter will show various ways to make a control that actuates a particular animation. After you have decided what animations and what controls you will have, you can then install the various levers and controls on the control stick. It is usually much easier to prepare the control stick ahead of time, prior to bonding it to the head casting. Doing cutouts, slots, drilling holes, etc., is easier to do on the control stick when it has not yet been attached to the head.

First you need to figure out what you are going to make the control stick out of. Hard wood dowels from the hardware store work well and are probably the most commonly used material for this. A control stick anywhere from 1" to 1 1/2" in diameter is a good size (I have a personal preference for a 1 1/8" diameter wood dowel). You could also make a custom control stick out of wood on a lathe. A piece of hollow PVC plastic pipe, also available from the hardware store, is yet another option. Several prominent figures have used this with good success. It is best to use the thicker walled PVC pipe for strength. Regular PVC pipe is just not strong enough and can crack.

After you have decided on what to make the control stick out of and what controls will be attached to it, you will need do a little custom work on it. You should make any notches, cutouts, drill out any holes, etc.

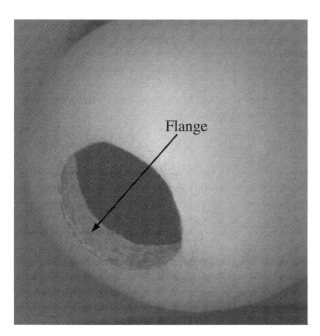

Detail - neck flange that control stick will be glued to

(described throughout the chapter) that will be necessary for installation of the controls on the control stick. Attach any levers or other controls according to what you decide upon after reading this chapter. Make sure all such controls are working smoothly at this point. If they do not work smoothly before you hook up the mechanics inside the head, they will certainly not work smoothly after they are hooked up. Take your time and do quality work. This is not to say you cannot install levers, etc., after gluing the control stick to the head, it's just a lot easier to do so before it is attached.

After the controls are all installed on the control stick and working smoothly, you can bond it to the head casting. If you have made a nice flange inside the neck area when you made the head casting, this should be fairly easy to do. (See photo bottom left) First, wrap the control stick with some *plastic wrap* to protect it from any drips or spills.

Here's one way to get good vertical alignment on the control stick as you glue it in place. Set the head casting temporarily back inside the head mold. A little mold release at the bottom of the neck area of the mold would be a good idea. Do not get any mold release on the flange inside the neck or on the control stick. Take some two-part epoxy (syringe type from the hardware store) and mix it well. Coat the flange inside the neck hole in the head casting and the end of the control stick with the epoxy. Spin the control stick slowly as you set it in the neck opening. If you've set your mold up correctly, it will help hold the control stick in good alignment while the epoxy sets up.

If you can't use the mold to do this, you will have to set the angle of the control stick by eye. You can temporarily prop the head casting and control stick in place on the work bench with some lumps of clay while the epoxy sets up.

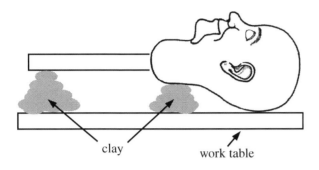

clay          work table

Supporting head and control stick for bonding

If the epoxy is too thin and wants to run all over everywhere, you can thicken it with Cab-O-Sil as described in Chapter Five. There are also some thicker two-part epoxies available at many hardware stores. After the control post is set in place and the epoxy has dried, see if it appears secure enough. If the flange on the inside of the neck was not very big or very strong, you can add some additional strength to this joint by putting some Magic Sculp (or other epoxy putty from the hardware store) around the control stick inside the head.

If you are afraid of bonding the control post to the head just yet (because of not being absolutely sure of all the control positions on the control stick for some reason), you can usually temporarily mount the control stick in place with some shims. Take a business card and tear it in half or quarters. Put these pieces of business card just inside the hole in the neck. Wedge the control stick against these and the flange inside the neck hole. Make sure it's reasonably tight and will not fall out on you (don't want the head falling on the floor accidentally). You can then work on the rest of the mechanics inside the head.

When you are sure everything seems right, you can bond the control stick to the head as outlined above.

***Cutting out the trap-door:*** If you have not already done so you will need to cut out the trap-door for the head. If you have used a molding technique that casts a separate trap-door (see Chapters Four, Five and Six), you can skip this step.

As you probably know, the trap-door gives you accessibility to do adjustments or repairs on the mechanics inside the head as well as the initial installation of them. The actual size of the trap-door can be a matter of personal preference. You do, however, want it to be big enough to have good accessibility to the inside of the head.

Mark an outline where you want the trap-door to be. Drill some small holes on the line you just marked, until you have enough of an opening to get a small saw blade in. You can find some small hand saws at a hobby shop or better equipped hardware store, or use a coping saw. Sometimes you can use just the blade with it held in a pair Vicegrips® or good pliers. Carefully cut on the outline until the trap-door is free. You can use a little Magic Sculp to fill in any gaps left from cutting out the trap-door. After the trap-door is cut out and patched up, you can set it aside for the time being.

### Mouth mechanisms

A moving mouth is the first animation that will be described. It is undoubtedly one of the most important features on your figure, so take your time and do a good job! The first step is to do the cut-out of the mouth area on the head casting.

***Cutting out the mouth area:*** If you have scribed the outline of the mouth area on your original clay model, these lines will be inside the head mold, and in turn on your head casting already. If not, don't panic! An accurate way of doing this will be described next.

The most important thing in cutting the opening in the head for the mouth piece is that the vertical cuts (on the sides of the mouth) be straight and parallel to each other. First, the control stick must be attached to the head to do the next step (see control stick considerations in this chapter). Make a jig that will hold the head in a vertical position (see pages 18 and 19) with the face pointing towards you. Set up a board (a straight piece of plywood can work well) that is parallel to the control stick (this is assuming that the control stick is glued in straight!), next to the side of the head. The last thing that is needed is a small jig that will slide along this vertical board. (See illustration this page) Two holes are drilled in this jig that you can put a pencil or fine tip marker through.

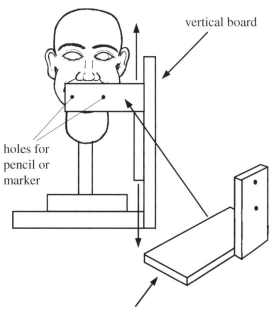

vertical board

holes for pencil or marker

Build a jig like this that slides up and down on the vertical board

Accurate way to make parallel lines for mouth cut-out

By sliding the jig up or down, you can accurately draw vertical lines from the corners of the mouth to the neck area, about 1/4" onto the neck. *For a clay model,* you are not trying to 'draw' a line, but rather, make a scribed line. Make the lines deep enough to show up well. You can do minor smoothing with your fingers. Now, when you make a mold of your clay head, these lines will be permanently on the inside of the mold. Each time you make a casting, the vertical lines for the sides of the mouth will already be accurately marked ready to cut.

After you have drawn the above lines on the face, you can cut this area out of the head casting. Drill some small holes near the lines until you can get a small saw blade in to make the cuts. Use a method similar to what is described for cutting out the trap-door to cut out the mouth area. Use a file or some sandpaper to clean up the sawn edges on the head casting. Gluing sand paper to a paint stick helps keep it straight.. The amount of care you take when doing the cutout can depend on whether or not you are going to use the cutout mouth piece or not. (See photo next page) This will be discussed next.

*Making a separate 'mouth piece':* the first step is to make the front of the mouth or jaw piece. You can do this one of two ways:

The first way is to use the *cutout* portion of the mouth area from the head casting, as described in the last section. This part of the head has to be cut out anyway. This piece can be used for the front of the mouth piece or jaw.

The other way is to make a casting of just this part of the head. There are two easy ways of doing this: **1.)** Slush cast some urethane for just the mouth area inside the head mold (see Chapter Six). In a latex mold, you could

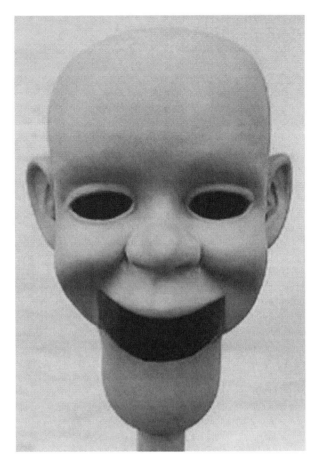

Mouth area cutout on head casting

silicone mold, as the clay will not adhere at all to silicone rubber. **2.)** Press some Magic Sculp (also in Chapter Six) into the mouth area of the head mold and let set up. With either urethane or Magic Sculp, make the mouth casting about 1/8" thick for adequate strength. Use some mold release as necessary (see Chapter Six).

After you have the front part of the mouth made or cut out, you will need to fabricate some sides for the mouth or jaw piece. (See illustration below) These can be made of plastic sheet stock (available from hobby shops or plastic suppliers in your area) that is about 1/16" to 1/8" thick. This will be more dimensionally stable than wood pieces, as they are not affected by changes in humidity. Cut pieces to fit as illustrated and glue to the front part of the mouth with the thick style or *gel* type of super glue.

You will also need to make a top piece for the jaw. This can also be made from the plastic sheet stock. Glue it in about 1/8" to 1/4" of an inch under the top of the side pieces so you have room to sculpt some teeth

Cutout *mouth piece* from head casting

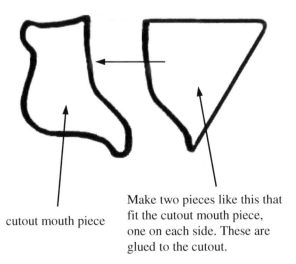

cutout mouth piece

Make two pieces like this that fit the cutout mouth piece, one on each side. These are glued to the cutout.

Making a jaw for the cast head

make a little clay wall or dam to help keep the urethane in the mouth area while you are slushing it around. You cannot do that with a and possibly a representation of a tongue. (See illustration below) You can use Magic Sculp or other two-part epoxy modeling compound to do this.

You can also use one of the clays you bake, like Sculpey III® or Fimo®. Follow the manufacturer's instructions for using these products. The sculpted pieces have to be baked separately (on a piece of cardboard or something that won't melt in the oven) and then glue them onto the mouth piece with a super glue later. Magic Sculp does not have to be baked, but Sculpey® or other similar products give you more time to sculpt. It's a matter of personal preference. If you are going to be making a mold of the jaw, you can use oil base clay instead of a material that hardens. It can be nice, though, to have a permanent model on hand at times.

The jaw or mouth piece will need some areas to attach a cord and a spring. One easy and quick way to do this is to bond some 'screw eyes' to the inside of the mouth piece

with some epoxy putty (Magic Sculp or other suitable epoxy putty from hardware store). You need one just under the back of the top piece (where the back of the tongue would be), and one on the inside near the very bottom of the jaw piece. (See illustration below) You do not necessarily want these in a straight line with each other vertically. You will have better clearance with the spring and mouth cord (to be described shortly) if that is not the case.

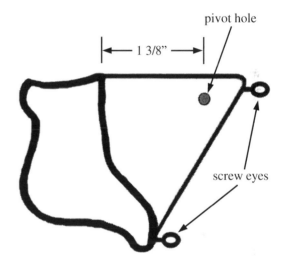

Attach screw eyes for actuating mouth mechanism
Pivot on this mouth is 1 1/2" from corner of mouth

Next, you need to determine where the pivot rod will go through the mouth piece. On an average size head (for a 38-40" figure) with a fairly normal shaped mouth or jaw, a good place to start would be about 1 1/2" from the front corner of the mouth to the pivot. This is not a hard and fast rule by any means. This is merely a place to start and greatly depends on the shape of the jaw. Also see *Appendix A*.

The pivot will be about 1/4" from the top of the mouth. This is also a place to start and is by no means any type of standard measurement either! Depending on how you have

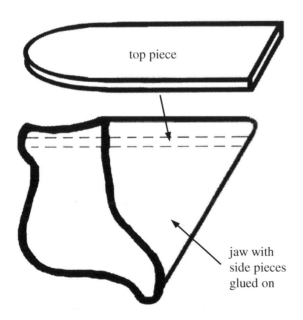

A top piece is bonded into the jaw assembly

designed the head and mouth on your figure, this could vary quite a bit. It may take some trial and error to find the best spot, depending on what you have done.

One general principle that might be helpful, is to look at your own jaw or someone else's jaw movement. See where the jaw hinges on a real person. That is typically where the jaw on a vent figure should be hinged as well. There are exceptions to this, of course. The rules in figure making are: 'there are NO rules!'

*Hinge principle:* A good working principle in the mechanics of figure making can be that of the *hinge principle*, and is very applicable to the mouth mechanism. Sometime look at an ordinary door hinge and study why it is a strong and long wearing unit. It is for the most part trouble free. It has an axle (hinge pin) and surrounding tube shaped pieces (the end of the hinge plates) that rotate around the axle. A very simple device, but extremely effective. The mouth gets the biggest workout of all the animations on a vent figure, and so it is best to have a long wearing axle.

This is why many figure makers use a brass rod and brass hollow tube for the mouth and (some other animations as well use this setup). Use a 1/8" brass rod and corresponding brass tube that fits around the rod snugly but can still rotate easily. Set the rod aside for now. Cut a length of the tube that is 1/4" wider than the jaw piece (can use fiberglass cutting wheel on a Dremel Moto Tool). Drill holes in the jaw piece and set the piece of tube in place with 1/8" inch sticking out on either side. Use two-part epoxy (syringe type from the hardware store) to bond the tube to the inside of the jaw or a small amount of epoxy putty. Do not get any epoxy inside the tube! Let it fully set up. The mouth or jaw piece is now ready for installation.

Prior to installing the jaw, you might want to consider making a mold of this separate jaw piece first. Make sure that it is sanded down and detailed nicely before doing this. It should also fit nicely in the head casting (as outlined in the next section). If everything looks good, you can set it up on a work board and make a mold as outlined in Chapter Four or Five (one-piece latex or silicone block mold both can work for this). See Appendix A before proceeding with this.

You could put a small amount of clay temporarily inside the ends of the brass tube to keep the mold making material out. The mold can go around the brass tube, but should not cover the ends of it. That way when you use the mold to make a casting, you can put a brass tube in the opening of the mold (made by the original brass tube) and make your casting right around it. The casting material will usually bond to the brass tube when set up. With this setup it is very easy to make as many jaw castings as you need, for each head casting that you make.

### Installing the mouth

Fit the mouth inside the head casting very carefully. Trim the mouth opening in the head with a file or sandpaper paddle and test the fit of the mouth piece. You don't want a

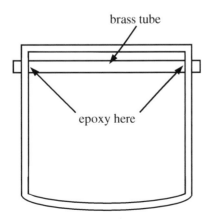

Brass tube placement inside jaw piece

very big gap between these two parts. At the same time you don't want the parts to rub when the mouth goes up and down. Take your time.

Find the axle rod and cut it short enough to fit where it will go inside the head. Take the separate mouth piece with the axle rod and hold it in place inside the head. Note where the axle rod lines up on the sides of the inside of the head when the mouth is positioned correctly. Take some coarse sandpaper and rough up this area, about 3/4" or 1" in diameter. You may also want to take a Dremel Moto Tool and cut some shallow depressions with a grinding bit, where the axle rod will be placed. The sanding will help the two-part epoxy putty adhere properly, and the depressions will make undercuts (see Chapter Three) of sorts that will help to mechanically lock things in place. This is one way you can actually use undercuts to your advantage.

Cut some shorter lengths of brass tube (1/4" to 3/8" long) and slide them onto the ends of the 1/8" brass rod that is protruding from both sides of the jaw piece. These will be used later to keep the jaw piece centered in the mouth opening. (See illustration this page)

Set the jaw inside the head and hold it temporarily in place by wedging some pieces of clay or 'Fun Tack' (*craft store* item) between the jaw and the mouth opening in the head. Mix up some epoxy putty and mold it around the ends of the brass rod and against the inside of the head. Double check that the jaw is aligned properly. Check to see that the jaw piece is parallel with the cutout in the head casting and the top and bottom of mouth is fitting as it should as well. Be careful not to bond the shorter lengths of brass tube in place just yet. They should rotate freely for now. Let the epoxy putty

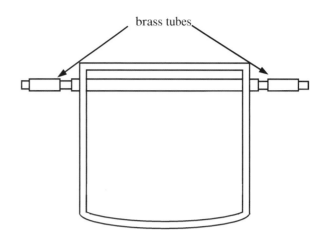

Additional brass tube pieces placed on pivot rod

bonding the brass axle rod in place fully setup before doing the next step.

You can now mix up more epoxy putty and bond the short pieces of tubing in place. They should be pushed up against the portion of tube that is protruding from the jaw piece. Form the putty around the outside ends of the shorter tubes and around the axle rod. Use enough putty to stretch over to the hardened epoxy putty holding the axle rod in place. Take care not to get any putty where the short

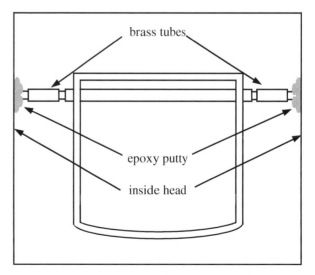

Epoxy putty used to bonds pivot rod inside head

tubes touch the longer tube in the jaw or you'll have problems later. If you stuff a business card in on both sides of the mouth slots, this will help hold the jaw piece in a centered position while the epoxy putty sets up. Let it set up overnight before proceeding.

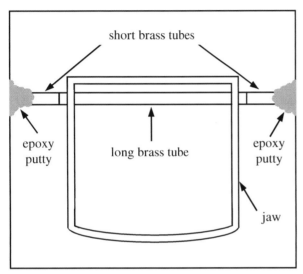

Short brass tubes held in place with epoxy putty

Check the fit of the jaw while it opens and closes. Depending on how well it was fit tested before bonding things in place, you should not have too much to do. A little sanding can take care of any rubbing that might occur as the mouth moves. If there are any unsightly gaps, you can do a little filling with wood dough, Spackle, or epoxy putty if appropriate. For additional information on fitting of the jaw piece, particularly in regard to the gap under the chin, and a better fit for same, see Appendix A.

### Mouth Animation and Controls

There are a lot of different ways to hook up the mouth mechanisms and related controls. We will cover a few possibilities here.

Something that all of these have in common is where the spring connects. On con-

temporary figures, the spring is usually attached to the top, back part of the mouth piece and then secured down on the back of the neck area on the inside. One easy way to hook up the spring is to attach a *screw eye* in the top of the control stick, inside the neck. Then the spring can run from this screw eye up to the top, back part of the jaw piece through its screw eye. The spring should have enough tension, but not too much. How much is too much? Personal preference comes into play here. Too little tension and the mouth will not be reliable. Too much tension and you will not only wear your thumb or finger out opening and closing the mouth, but you will also have a mouth mechanism that will wear out quicker.

Springs can be found at most good hardware stores and hobby shops. If the spring you get is about the right tension, but is a

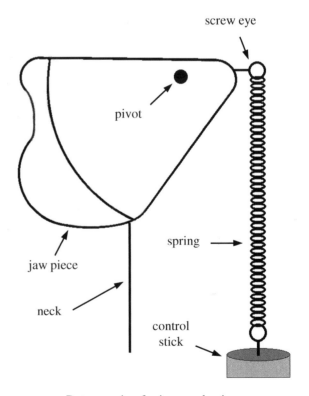

Return spring for jaw mechanism

little too short, you can attach a piece of strong wire (piano wire works well) between the screw eye and the the spring to get some more length. A spring that is a little too long can often times be cut shorter. If you cut it, you will have to bend a similar shape on the end that was there before it was cut for hooking onto the screw eye. The spring does not have to be connected to the control stick. It can also be attached to the inside of the back or front of the neck.

***Cord and pulley:*** The first setup is with a cord or string to actuate the mouth. The cord goes over a pulley to eliminate friction, and then down to a lever control on the control stick. Simple, but very effective and can last for many years. In general this is actually much easier to make and have work well than any type of rod actuated mouth mechanism. The latter takes more skill, time and patience to make work effectively and more importantly, quietly.

The secret to this setup is the pulley. This creates a mechanical advantage for a smoothness of operation that is hard to beat. Finding a pulley of just the right size can be a little challenging however. Try all of the bigger hardware stores or home building supply centers in your area and possibly the hobby shops. All you really need from the pulley is the grooved wheel part of it. It needs to have a groove big enough to handle 1/8" cord. Braided nylon cord or Dacron fishing line (120-130 test) or good quality kite line can work well.

A brass rod (pivot rod), which is bonded inside the head casting goes through the pulley wheel. The brass rod is bonded in place the same way as the mouth pivot was done. You can also make a wire frame guide to help keep the cord from coming off of the

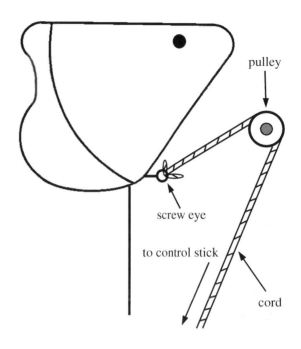

Pulley actuated jaw mechanism
Note: return spring not shown in this diagram

pulley wheel. This can be made of piano wire or copper wire. This wire frame should also be bonded to the brass pivot rod with some epoxy putty or 5-minute epoxy. Be careful not to accidentally bond the pulley wheel to the pivot rod! (See illustration below)

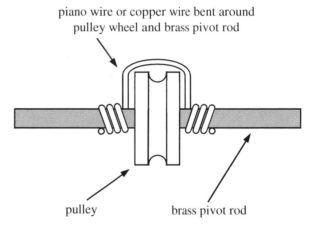

Wire guide to help keep the cord on the pulley

***Pulley tip:*** If you find a good size of pulley that works well, you can reproduce your own pulley wheel. You can make a quick silicone block mold. Set the grooved pulley wheel on a work board flat on its side. You may need to use double-backed tape to keep it held in place on the board. Build a small clay wall around to make a retaining wall. Pour catalyzed silicone inside the clay wall form, until it comes up over the pulley wheel by 3/8" minimum. When the silicone has set up, remove the model. You can make castings by pouring a strong urethane resin in the mold. (See Chapters Five and Six)

***Rocker style:*** Another way to actuate the mouth mechanism is with a rocker linkage. This works basically like a 'teeter-totter'. When one end is pulled down the other end goes up and vice versa. The rocker can be made out of brass stock. Drill a hole in the center for a pivot (use a pivot rod, bonded in place, same as was done for the jaw itself), and a hole on either end for connecting the

cord and linkage. Make sure to file the holes that you drill in the brass stock carefully. Otherwise the sharp edges from drilling will cut into the cord and cause you grief later on.

Pulling on the cord from the control stick pulls down on one end of the rocker, which pulls the other end up, thus causing the mouth to open. Depending on where you put the pivot (on center or slightly off center), you can gain some mechanical advantage, so the mouth opens quicker with less of a pull on the trigger on the control stick.

***Lever controls for the mouth:*** On the control stick itself, there are a number of ways to hook up levers to actuate the mouth. Here are a couple of popular ways of doing that:

The simplest way is to cut out a lever from some brass stock (a few inches long is all that is needed). Drill a hole in one end (for the pivot screw to go through) and one a little ways from the other end (for the cord to go through). A bend in the end where your

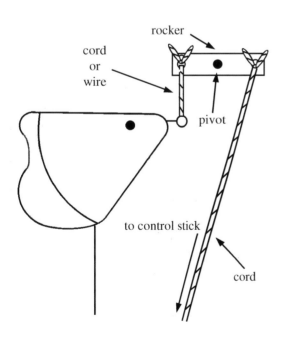

Rocker actuated jaw mechanism
Note: return spring not shown in this diagram

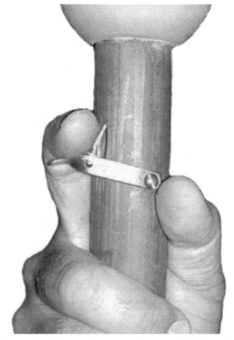

Brass stock mouth control lever - right handed

finger will use the control can make it more comfortable to use. (See photo previous page) You could also take some epoxy putty and form a comfortable shape on the end.

Another way is to set a trigger into a slot in the control stick. First make a slot in the control stick. This can be done by drilling some holes (the same width as the slot you need) and then cleaning it up with a chisel. You could also route a slot with a router table. You need to make a jig that will hold the control stick dowel steady as this is done. The slot should be about 1/2" in depth.

After a suitable slot is made in the control stick, you will need to drill some pivot holes for a pivot rod to go through. This is easiest if you have a jig to keep the drill on track. (See illustration below) Use at least 1/8" brass rod stock for the pivot. If you use a

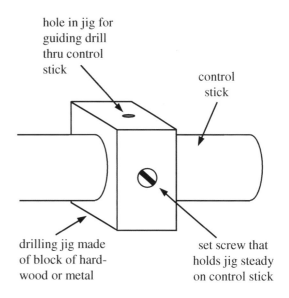

hole in jig for guiding drill thru control stick

control stick

drilling jig made of block of hard-wood or metal

set screw that holds jig steady on control stick

Drilling jig for control stick

smaller size, it can bend too easily. The pivot hole in the control stick needs to be slightly undersized so the pivot rod won't wiggle out of place later. The hole in the brass trigger that you make should be a clearance hole only, but reasonable snug. If the clearance hole is too big, it will create noise as the trigger is operated.

With both the simple brass lever on the outside of the control stick and the trigger mounted in a slot, the cord is run through a hole drilled into the control stick, up to the actuating mechanism inside the head. You will note that the hole for the cord is well below the ball part of the neck. This keeps the cord well out of the way for all possible neck movement as the figure's head is manipulated, and is a sign of quality work. (See photo on page 130 and drawing below)

*Cord knots:* When tying the cords both inside the head and on the control stick you need to have a little insurance to keep them from coming undone later. After the cord is

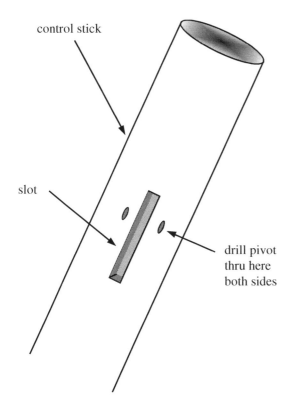

control stick

slot

drill pivot thru here both sides

Slot in control stick for mouth lever

tied snugly in place, it needs to be secured by burning the knot a little (soldering iron or a lighter can work), which forms a little **ball** on the cord. After it cools you can put a little super glue on the knot for added insurance. Note: The burning of the knot is for nylon and Dacron cord only. For other types of cord, use only the super glue.

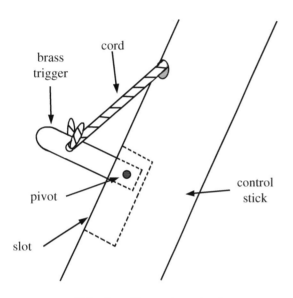

Side view: Brass trigger in slot

### Eye Mechanisms

Moving eyes are a feature many vents would like to have for their figure. You can start out with a pretty basic or simple eye mechanism and move up to a more complicated set up later on.

Before getting too far, you should make the cutouts for the eyes in the head casting. Use a technique similar to what was done for the mouth and trap-door.

A simple eye can be made with a ping pong ball or a wood ball from a hobby or hardware store. An eyeball 1 1/2" in diameter is a good place to start if you are not sure what size of eyes to make.

One of the first things to do is drill an accurate pivot hole for the eyeball to rotate on. If it does not rotate correctly, it will look a bit strange and/or get hung up on the eye socket as the eyes are turned from side to side. Making a jig for this helps quite a bit. A 'drilling box' can be made fairly easily. Construct a small box out of wood or plastic that the eyeball just fits into. Then by finding the exact centers on the outside of the box, you can see where you need to drill.

You can use this to drill the pivot hole as well as the center for the iris or the eye post on the rear of the eyeball. Clamp the box to your workbench or drill press table while drilling. A drill press vise also works nicely for holding the jig safely. The eyeball is set inside the box and the end cap is clamped or screwed in place. A 'set screw' can be put on one of the drill box sides to keep the eyeball from spinning while drilling. There are also jigs for drilling spheres commercially available from woodworking supply houses.

After drilling the pivot hole in the eyeball, you can glue in a brass tube (which will make a brass sleeve) into the pivot hole. This is not

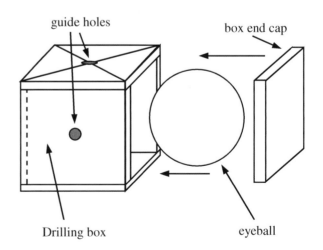

'Drill box' for eyes

absolutely necessary, but will make for a longer lasting eye mechanism. Use a brass tube that will work for a 1/8" brass rod or whatever you end up using for the pivot. Brass machine screws can work fine as well.

***Eye post:*** On the back of each eyeball you will need a post that will be used later to connect the eyes together and have them be able to move in synchronization. A wood or plastic dowel is one way to go. You can also use an 'L' screw (hardware store) or a piece of brass rod bent into an 'L' shape. (See illustration below)

Top view - eyeball with post cast in place.

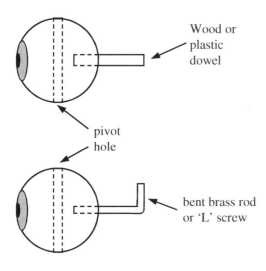

Side View

Eye posts attached to back of eyeballs

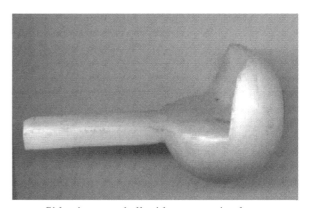
Side view - eyeball with post cast in place.

Another option is to have the eye post molded on the back of a cast eye. If you make an eye model with a post on the back of the eyeball, the castings fresh out of the mold will have a post automatically cast on each eyeball. A top quality resin has to be used or the post can break off easily! There are dozens of ways of making an eye post or other suitable arrangement for connecting the eyes to move in synchronization (to be explained later in the chapter).

***Irises:*** Making the eyeball itself is not too hard. It's the center of the eye, that is, the iris, that is the difficult part to achieve. A nice-looking iris can be one of the most challenging aspects of making a vent figure. For the most part, there are not ready made eyeballs that you can purchase in the 1 1/2" diameter range. Most are much smaller. An eyeball about 1 1/4" (32mm) can sometimes be found from doll suppliers, but are not that easy to find usually. Sometimes you can only find them in glass, which is VERY difficult to work with. The other thing that is often encountered is that the cornea or iris part of the manufactured eyeballs are made with a sizable bulge. The iris sticks out so far that it interferes with the movement of the eyes in the eye sockets of the head or with the winkers (to be described later).

Here are a few possibilities for making a suitable iris for eyeballs that you make yourself:

**1.)** You used to be able to get plastic teddy bear or owl irises quite easily from a craft or hobby store that were suitable. These can be embedded into a wooden eyeball without too much trouble. The problem is these are getting very hard to find, especially the nice ones that have a low profile (are not really domed or do not bulge out quite a ways when installed), and are of good quality. Some are just poorly made and do not resemble a human iris at all. Sometimes if you can find them from a supplier, the minimum order is so high as to be unfeasible for the average figure maker. A few suppliers are listed in the back of the book.

**2.)** If you can get some manufactured acrylic eyeballs where the iris is about the right size, you can remove the iris from the eyeball and glue it into a wood eyeball. These are available from doll making suppliers. The same thing can be done with glass eyeballs, but it is very difficult to cut and/or grind the white part of the eye away without getting glass splinters! *Extreme caution is advised.*

**3.)** You can take photographs of irises (from real eyes, pictures on the Internet or scanned from a book) on a computer, resize them and print them out on a color printer. Cut the irises out of the printed page. These can be inset into a wooden eyeball. Drill a very shallow flat bottom hole (use a Forstner style bit), in the front of the wood eyeball and glue the printed iris in place. Coat the iris and eyeball with a clear resin (hardware store, home improvement center or resin supplier). The downside to this method is the possibility of the colors eventually fading as can happen with inkjet inks.

**4.)** A variation on #3: Drill a shallow flat bottom hole. Drill one additional hole in the center of the first hole, the size you want the pupil of the eye to be. Hand paint the iris colors within the area of the flat bottom hole. Example: for a blue colored iris, paint a slightly darker blue first going all the way out to the edge of the shallow flat bottomed hole. Then paint lighter shades of blue, using more than one color, as in a real iris (pulling the brush out toward the edge as you apply paint). Refer to some actual photos of eyes. Use black paint to paint the inside of the smaller hole that you drilled, to simulate the pupil. Use oil paints or acrylics. Let the paint dry completely. Coat the iris and eyeball with a clear resin as mentioned above (hardware store, home improvement center or resin supplier).

**5.)** With a ping pong ball, you can first cut out a circle (with a very sharp Exacto knife) the size that you want the iris to be. Take this cut piece, and paint an iris (as described in #4) on the back side of the cut out piece. When the paint is dry, this piece is glued back into the ping pong ball (concave side out or the side you painted on). Fill in the concave iris with clear resin. A variation on this would be to glue in a printed iris as in #3, instead of painting an iris.

**6.)** You could also just paint an iris with round stencils as a guide on either a wood eyeball or a ping pong ball. Without doing any cutting or drilling, you would lay a stencil or template over the eye ball where you wanted the iris to be. Start with a hole in a stencil the complete diameter of the iris. For a blue colored iris, paint a slightly darker blue first going all the way out to the edge. Let dry. A second stencil with a hole about 1/16" smaller all the way around is used as a guide to paint with lighter shades of blue, using a few different shades of blue as in a real iris. Let dry. Finally use another stencil with a hole the right size for the pupil. Take some black paint and paint the pupil area. Let dry. Finish with a good clear sealer, semi-gloss. Needless to say, you have to be careful not to glob on too much paint with this method.

One thing to keep in mind is that having a very realistic iris is not necessarily always the goal. Some people who will see your vent figure will be given the *creeps* by a figure that is too realistic. If you've ever seen a ventriloquist figure with very realistic glass eyes (like are used for people who have lost an eye), it can be very creepy to say the least. So sometimes, a figure with eyes that are obviously puppet eyes can have a wider appeal. Sometimes somewhere in between realistic and outright puppet eyes is a good compromise. Food for thought at any rate.

*Eye mounts:* There are numerous ways that eyes can be mounted in the head. A few different ideas will be presented here.

*Eye tray:* Using an eye tray works well if the eye sockets in the head are on the same plane and not *cock-eyed* in relation to each other. If the latter is true, you will have to use one of the other methods described below. An eye tray can be made of wood, plastic or metal. Basically the eyes are mounted on the tray the correct distance from each other, and then the tray is bonded to the inside of the head.

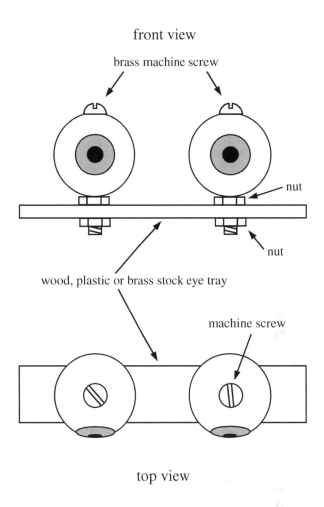

front view

brass machine screw

nut

nut

wood, plastic or brass stock eye tray

machine screw

top view

Eyes mounted on eye tray

You need to measure the distance the center of the eye sockets in the head are from each other. Sometimes it takes a little trial and error to find the precise distance they need to be. The eye balls could be attached to the eye tray with machine screws or with brass rods. (See illustrations this page and next)

After the eyes are securely mounted to the eye tray, the eye tray can in turn be mounted inside the head. A two-part epoxy compound can work well for this. As was done with installing the mouth, rough up the insides of the head where the tray will be bonded in place. You can also take a Dremel Moto Tool

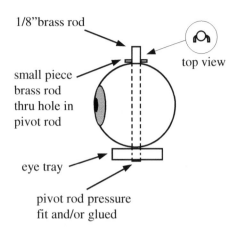

Eyes mounted on eye tray with brass rod pivot

(with a grinding bit) and make some slight indentions on the inside of the cast head. That will help lock things in place when the epoxy putty sets up.

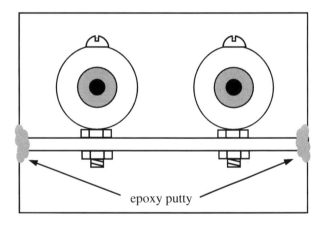

Using epoxy putty to bond eye tray inside head

**_Individual eye mounts:_** If the eye sockets in the head are not evenly lined up or have any angles that will not permit using an eye tray easily, it's best to do individual eye mounts.

You can use brass rod stock or threaded rod for the eye pivots on individual eye mounts. You can also use wood dowels. Wood is, of course, not as stable as metal parts. There is the possibility of the wood

shrinking or swelling with changes in humidity. This can create sticking on a humid day or rattling (noise) on a dry day possibly.

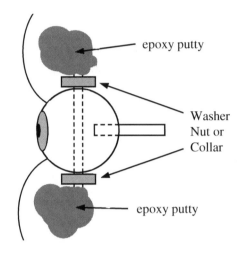

Side View

Individual eye mount with epoxy putty

One of the easiest ways to do an individual eye mount is with epoxy putty. The eyeball is set on a brass rod or threaded rod and is bonded to the inside of the head with epoxy putty. (See illustration above) Nuts or washers are used as stops for how high or low the eye can ride up and down on the pivot rod. A collar with a set screw could also be made if you wanted to get a little high tech.

**_Synchro linkage:_** Synchro linkage? Well, that's just a fancy name for connecting the eyes to move together at the same time. There are certainly many, many ways to do this.

The easiest way is to make a small bar to connect the posts on the back of the eye. This synchro bar could be made of wood, plastic or brass stock. When connecting to wood or

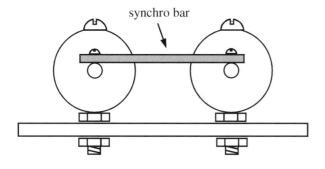

Synchro bar attached to eye posts - Rear View

plastic posts on the back of the eyes, you can simply use some small wood screws that go through clearance holes on the syncro bar into the posts. On 'L' style posts, drill some clearance holes in the syncro bar. You can then epoxy some metal nuts in place, or drill some very tiny holes in the 'L' posts and put a loop of piano wire to help keep the syncro bar in place. (See illustration above and below) Another simple way would be to use a brass rod that goes through clearance holes on the eye posts (see illustration at right).

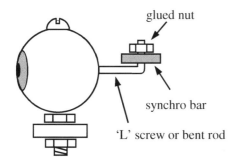

Synchro bar with 'L' style post on back of eye

The distance between the holes on the synchro bar depends on the **gaze** you want for the figure. Making the holes far apart will make your figure slightly cross-eyed. Likewise, having the holes closer together will make the eyes almost look in two different directions or kind of wall-eyed. Some figure makers purposely go one way or the other (as opposed to having the eyes perfectly aligned looking straight ahead) trying to keep the figure from looking like it has a blank stare. It's a matter of personal preference of course as to what to do on this.

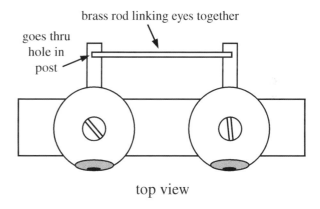

top view

Synchro rod attached to eye posts

*Eye controls:* There are a number of ways to make controls for actuating moving eyes. A couple of popular ways to do this will be presented.

The first one is a cross bar or 'teeter totter' style control. This is perhaps the simplest way to actuate the movement of the eyes. A cross bar is made out wood, plastic or brass stock (preferable to use a brass lever) that has a hole in the center and holes drilled in either end. The center hole is a clearance hole. A screw goes through the center hole, attaching it to the control stick (with a washer or two between the cross bar and the control stick), allowing the cross bar to rock back and forth like a 'teeter totter'. Looking at the illustra-

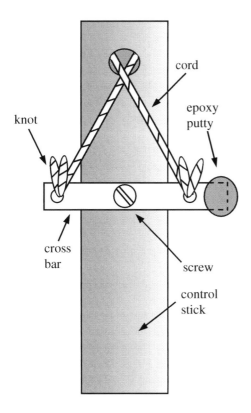

### Front View

*Cross bar* or *teeter totter* style eye control

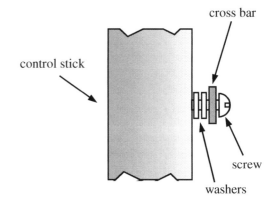

### Side View

Side view of *cross bar* style eye control

the head. The cords 'cross' each other inside the hole in the control stick.

The cords are run through screw eyes on either side of the eye mechanism and then in turn to a screw eye on the synchro bar. (See illustration below)

tion on this page, you can see that one end of the cross bar needs to be slightly longer than the other. This allows a place for the thumb to move the cross bar up and down. You could also add a little epoxy putty on the end where your thumb will be pushing on the cross bar for comfort. (See illustration this above. A right handed cross bar control is shown in this illustration)

File all of the edges of the brass cross bar smooth. Make sure there are no burs or sharp edges in the holes that the cords will connect to or the cords will get frayed and cut. The other ends of the cord go up through a hole in the control stick, through the neck, on up into

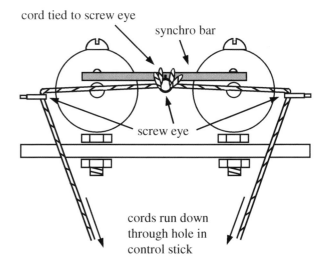

### Rear View

Cord connections inside head for *cross bar* control

By pushing the cross bar up and down on the control stick, the cords will be pulled back and forth through the screw eyes inside the head, which move the synchro bar back and forth, causing the eyes to move right and left. Simple, but effective.

fits the 1/8" brass rod) will fit into. (See illustrations this page). This can be done with a table saw or router table with a bit the right width. You will need to use a jig that will hold the control stick safely while making such a cut. *You don't want to injure yourself or lose a finger in the process!*

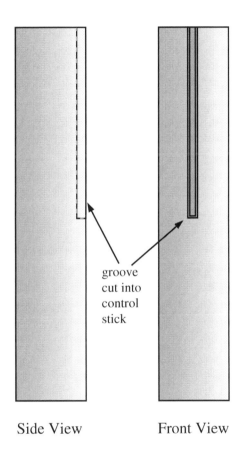

Side View          Front View

Cut a slot into the control stick for rod control

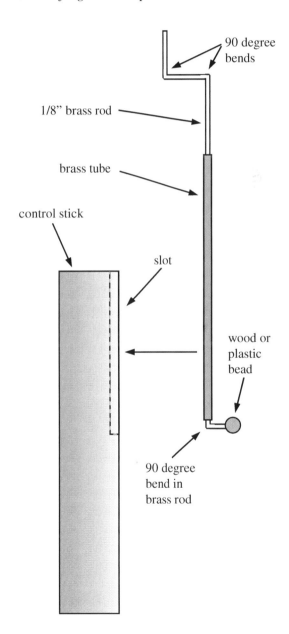

***Rod control eye mechanism:*** The other popular way of actuating the eye mechanism is with a ***rod control***. A rod goes up through the control stick and moves the eyes back and forth as needed. You need a 1/8" brass rod and a brass tube that fits over the brass rod for a rod style eye control.

The first thing to do is cut a groove in the control stick that the brass tube (the one that

Brass rod (with appropriate bends), in brass tube

Brass tube is glued into slot on control stick

Take the 1/8" brass rod and make a 90 degree bend in one end. Insert the other end of the brass rod into the brass tube. Two more 90 degree angle bends will also need to made at the other end of the brass rod as shown in the illustration, at right.

The 1/8" brass rod and tube assembly is bonded into the slot in the control stick. (See illustration previous page) This can be done with two-part epoxy (syringe type from hardware store) or with some epoxy putty. You can also use epoxy putty to cover over the brass tube to fill in the exposed gap from the slot. You can smooth the epoxy putty level with the outside surface of the control stick. This mostly a matter of cosmetics, so it is a matter of personal preference as to whether you do this or not. You must be careful not to get any epoxy putty on the 1/8" rod itself.

You will also need a slightly different set-up on the back of the eye mechanism to make the rod style eye control work. Bending some 1/16" brass rod in just the right fashion, can be the easiest way to go on this. (See illustration below and top right) The loop in the 1/16" brass rod makes a place for the 1/8"

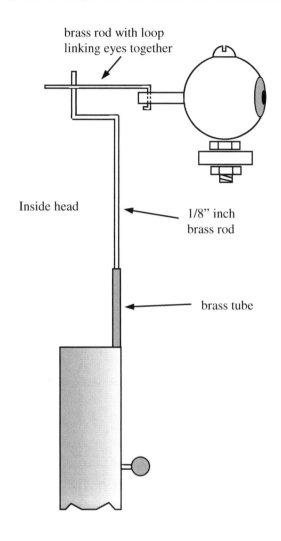

Side View

Rod control for moving eyes

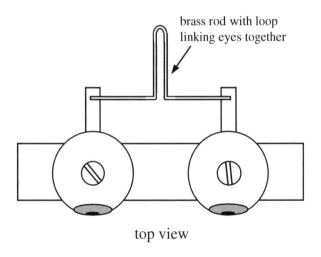

top view

Syncro rod with loop attached to eye posts

brass rod that comes up from the control stick to fit into.

If everything is lined up well and installed correctly, the rod style eye control is now ready to operate. By pushing the eye control on the control stick to the right, the eye turns to the right, and vice versa. You could also put the eye control on the back or side of the

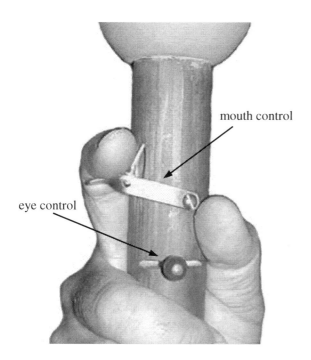

'Rod style' eye control (with mouth lever)

control stick if you wanted to. Placement of controls is a matter of preference, and also, what will work best with other controls on the control stick.

### Self-Centering Eyes

Many vents like to have the eye mechanism self-center when the eye control is not being used. Famous vent Paul Winchell, reportedly purposely chose not to have self-centering eyes so he would be forced to keep them moving (a steel pin or nail can be put near the eye controls so one knows when the eyes are centered). Again, it's really a matter of personal preference. There are many, many ways that self-centering eyes can be accomplished. A few different ways will be presented.

***Self-centering mechanism #1:*** This first one is very simple. It involves a single spring that returns the eyes to center. One end of the spring is attached to the synchro bar (or one

of the eye posts) and the other end can be attached to a screw eye or wire loop on the back of the head (trap-door). (See illustration below)

The tricky part of this arrangement is carefully attaching the spring to the trap-door just as you are closing the trap-door on the head. Another way of attaching the spring would be to make a small bracket that attached to the side of the head (on the inside) that was bent towards the back of the head (near where it would have been attached to the trap-door). That way you can open and close the head without worrying about the spring.

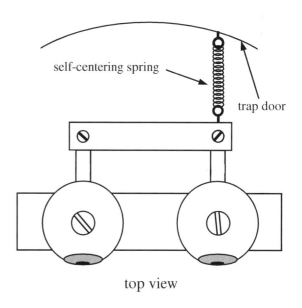

top view

Self-centering mechanism

***Self-centering mechanism #2:*** The second method involves using two springs in place of the eye posts. This is a very simple and effective self-centering mechanism.

To make this work, holes are drilled into the eyeballs so that the springs can be glued in place. Corresponding holes are drilled into a thicker, wood synchro bar, with the springs likewise glued into place. The way this works is that when the synchro bar is moved (right or left), the eyes will turn in synchronization and there will be some tension in both of the springs. The springs naturally want to go back to a straight position and thus self-center the eyes. Try it. You'll like it! (See illustration below)

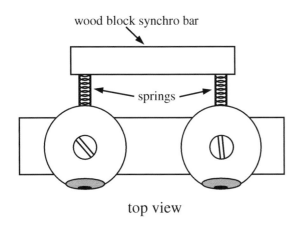

wood block synchro bar

springs

top view

Self-centering mechanism #2

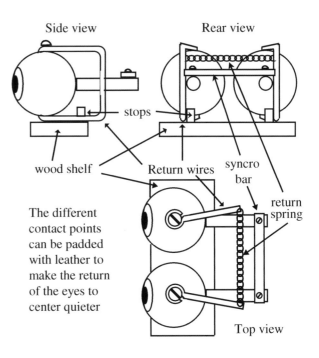

Side view          Rear view

stops

wood shelf     Return wires    syncro bar

return spring

The different contact points can be padded with leather to make the return of the eyes to center quieter

Top view

Self-centering mechanism #3

***Self-centering mechanism #3:*** The third method has return wires (made from bent brass rod or piano wire) that rotate on the same axis as the eyeballs. A central spring pulls the return wires towards each other and against the two stops attached to the eye shelf. (See illustration above right)

·  To understand how this mechanism works, imagine pulling the synchro bar to the left with your finger (the eyes will look to the right) or eye control (cord or rod style). As you do so the dowel in the back of the left eye will push the left return wire away from it's 'stop'. At the same time the right return wire is held in place by its ***stop*** and because it is not moving, tension is building up in the return spring. If you let go of the syncro bar the return spring will pull the left return wire back to its ***stop*** and the left eye dowel with it,

which brings the eyes back to center. The same basic thing happens if you move the eyes in the other direction. The hardest part of the whole setup is getting the ***stops*** in the right place and the right tension on the spring. Once it is set up you shouldn't have to fuss with it for quite awhile. (See illustration above)

### Raising Eyebrows

Raising eyebrows is a very popular animation and can simulate surprise or amazement. It is in some ways one of the easier mechanisms to install. As with so many of the animations, there are many ways this can be done. Two popular methods will be presented here.

The first step for either method is to drill some holes in the head, at the outside edge or corners of where the eyebrows would normally be painted on. These should be clearance holes so that a 3/32 or 1/8" brass rod

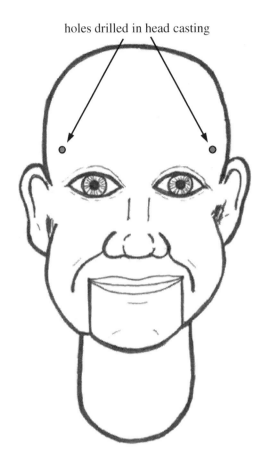

holes drilled in head casting

Drill holes for eyebrow brass rods

eyebrow. It is a compound angle. This takes a little fussing, but will eventually conform the way you want it. Repeat this step for the other eyebrow.

On the inside of the head slip a brass sleeve about 1" long over each of the brass rods. Slide them back towards the inside of the forehead temporarily. Now make another 'L' shaped bend in each eyebrow rod as shown in the illustrations. These will face each other when the eyebrows (outside the front of the forehead) are in the resting position (not raised). You will also need a loop at the end of each eyebrow rod for attaching the spring and cord. Spring tension needs to be just enough to easily pull the eyebrows back to their rest position after being raised.

(depending on what size you use) can pass through and rotate easily in the holes with little or no play. (See illustration above) The precise angle that you need to drill these holes at depends on which method you use. Read both methods through completely and study the accompanying illustrations to see what angle the holes need to be drilled at.

***Eyebrow method #1 (pulls up):*** Both methods use the same brass rod stock to actuate the eyebrows. A 3/32" rod is first bent into an 'L' shape. Set one of the rods into one of the holes that was drilled into the head (right or left) for the eyebrows. You will now see where the eyebrow rod needs to be bent to conform to the shape of the forehead of the head casting and a curve that looks like an

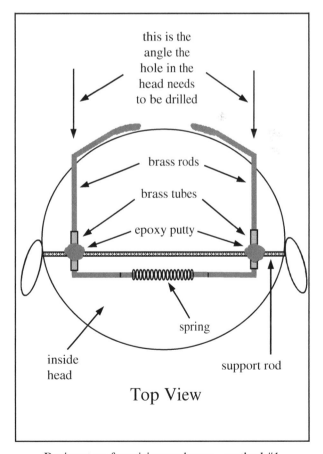

Basic set up for raising eyebrows - method #1

Note: pulleys and cords not shown in this drawing

The eyebrows will be actuated by means of cords. The cords run up over pulleys and down to control(s) on the control stick. With the basic setup, only one cord goes down to the control stick. (See illustrations previous page and below) You can use separate cords and controls if you want to be able to operate each eyebrow individually. It is probably more common, however, to have just the one control operating both eyebrows.

Some figure makers like to put brass tubes or sleeves in the holes on the head casting where the brass eyebrow rods go through. These can be reasonably short and are epox-

ied in place before inserting the eyebrow rods in place. This can make for a longer lasting mechanism.

***Eyebrow method #2 (pulls down):*** Method #2 is not a lot different than method #1. The biggest difference is that the 'L' shape on the eyebrow rods inside the head is bent in the other direction, i.e., facing outward instead of inward. Thus the pulling on these downward will cause the eyebrows to raise.

The other fundamental difference is that you will need two springs instead of one to pull the eyebrows back to the rest position. One additional bend at the end of the eyebrow rod will act as a stop. This will contact the support rod and stop the eyebrows in the rest position. Gluing a piece of leather to the

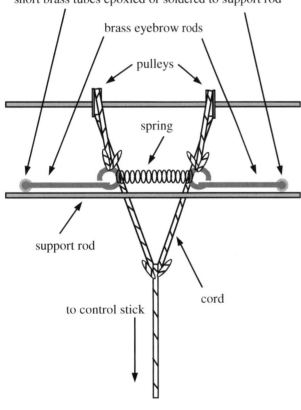

### Rear View

Rear view of setup for raising eyebrows - method #1

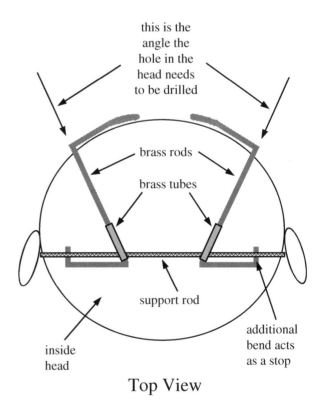

### Top View

Basic setup for raising eyebrows - method #2
Note: cords and springs not shown in this drawing

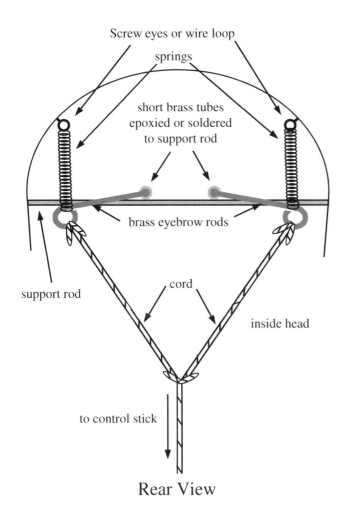

Screw eyes or wire loop

springs

short brass tubes
epoxied or soldered
to support rod

brass eyebrow rods

support rod

cord

inside head

to control stick

## Rear View

Rear view of setup for raising eyebrows - method #2

support rod where the eyebrow rod contacts it will help keep things quiet.

***Eyebrow coverings:*** The part of the eyebrow rod on the outside of the head can be covered with a number of things. One of the easier things to do is to cut some felt or fake fur (fabric or craft store item) to the right length and width and sew it into a tube. It is then glued onto the eyebrow rods. This looks pretty good and also makes a soft covering for the eyebrow rods making them less likely to scratch your paint job on the head later on. It would be best to wait to glue these in place until after you have painted the head.

Some figure makers like to use a hard material. You could form and shape some Magic Sculp over the eyebrow rods and let it set up. Make sure you leave enough clearance between the sculpted eyebrows and the forehead of the figure. You can later paint the Magic Sculp eyebrows whatever color you wish. (See Chapter Eight for painting info)

***Control(s) for raising eyebrows:*** Both methods #1 and #2 use a single cord going down to the head stick. You can hook up the cord to a simple lever the same as was done with the mouth control. Or you can get a little fancier and make a slot in the control stick with an appropriate lever as was shown for the mouth control on page 132. Another possible arrangement is shown on page 151.

It is also possible to modify this basic arrangement and have a cord and control that actuates each eyebrow mechanism separately. You would hook up a cord to the back of each eyebrow rod, and hook up a right and left lever on the control stick right next to each other. This is really a luxury and certainly not necessary for raising eyebrows.

### *Winkers*

There are two basic types of winkers that are installed in pro-style ventriloquist figures, to make the eyes wink or blink as needed. There are soft, doe skin winkers, and the other type is rigid shell winkers. Doe skin winkers have been covered in other figure making publications (the best being Joel Leder's figure making books). Rigid shell winkers have not been covered before in any previous figure making books that the author is aware of. Rigid shell winkers take a fair amount of precision or they simply will not work or work very poorly. There's a lot you can get away with on doe skin winkers because they are flexible. Not so with rigid shell winkers. An attempt will be made here to give the basics, as many have asked how they are done. As with so many things, however, experience is the best teacher. Take the basics that you learn here, and then experiment as much as you can until you find the best way that works for you.

First you need to make wire frames for the eye lids. Piano wire can work well for this. Try to get some that is at least 20 gauge wire (.045 dia.), which is pretty strong. With piano wire, the larger the number, the thicker the wire. Contact a local piano technician (who does re-stringing of pianos) and ask if you can have their bass string clippings from restringing. These usually get discarded anyway, so they will most likely be glad to get rid of them. If you can get these clippings you will get a range of gauges or diameters. These can be useful not only for winkers but other mechanics inside the head as well.

The piano wire needs to be formed and bent as shown in the illustration below left. The large curve (that conforms to the shape of the eyeball) is done first and is made by wrapping the wire around a pipe of the right diameter (usually smaller than the eyeball as the piano wire will spring back some). Then the bends on the ends of the piano wire are made. One end has a 90 degree bend. The other has two 90 degree bends and then a loop at the end of the wire. Use a combination of *Vise Grip*® pliers, round *needle nose* pliers and regular pliers to make these bends.

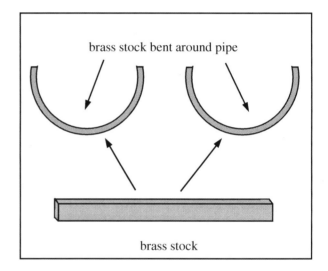

brass stock bent around pipe

brass stock

Flat brass stock formed for support frames

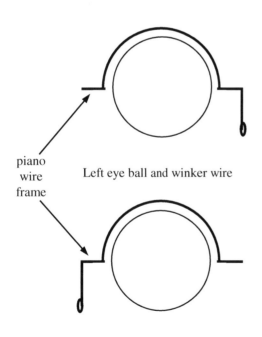

piano wire frame

Left eye ball and winker wire

Right eye ball and winker wire

Top View

Winker wire frames conform to shape of eyeball

After the wire frames for the winkers are made, you will also need to fabricate some support frames that the piano wire frames will be connected to. These can be made from flat brass stock and are similarly formed by bending around a piece of pipe the right size. (See illustration above) Before making the bends, drill a clearance hole in the center (same diameter as the screws that are used for eye pivots; see illustration next page). You can drill the clearance hole after making the bends, but it is usually easier to do so beforehand.

This arrangement for shell winkers can be set up onto an eye tray. This works best if a shallow groove is made in the eye tray where the support frames will go. The groove can be made on a router table or possibly a table saw. Do not hold the material for the eye tray with your hands when making this slot. Secure the eye tray to a larger piece of material (some plywood) or use two 'push sticks'. This can be very dangerous to cut without using the right precautions. (See illustration next page to see the slot on the eye tray)

The support frames are held in place on the eye tray by the same screws that hold the eyeballs in place. By using two nuts, you can lock the support frame securely while at the same time have the eyeballs rotate freely. Take one eyeball and one support frame and temporarily secure them to the eye tray. Drill pivot holes into the support frame, one on each side. The pivots holes need to be drilled at the exact center or midway point in relation to the eyeball. This is critical. The pivot hole must be 'dead on' center both up and down and from side to side. If this is not

done right, the shell winkers will not work correctly. This is *the* hardest part of the whole setup. Small corrections can be made later by bending the brass support frames, but it is better not to have to do that at all if you can help it.

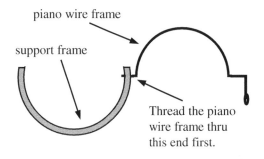

Attaching piano wire frame to support frame

After drilling the pivot holes for the one support frame, remove the eyeball and support frame and repeat the process for the other eyeball and support frame. After the other side is done, you can attach the piano wire frames to the support frames. You start by *threading* the short end of the piano wire frame through the 'outside' end of the support frame. (See illustration above) Do this very carefully so as to do as little damage as possible to the pivot holes in the brass support frames. After both piano wire frames are attached to the support frames, you can secure them as well as the eyeballs, to the eye tray with the screws and nuts as shown. (See illustration next page)

The next step is to attach the rigid shells to the piano wire frames. The rigid shells can be made of a number of materials. The most popular has been **brass** shells or **ping pong** ball shells. Ping pong balls can be purchased at a toy or sporting goods store.

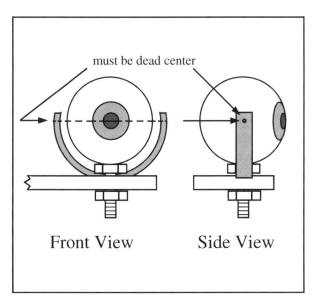

Pivot holes for winker pivots must be drilled dead center in relation to where the eyeball is.

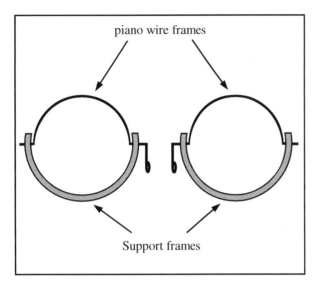

Support frames and wire frames for shell winkers

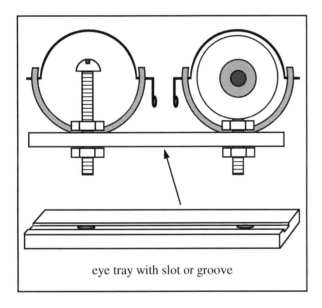

eye tray with slot or groove

Winker support frames attached to eye tray
Note: one eyeball not shown for clarity

Brass shells can be made with a jewelers *dapping* block, which is a metal block with many different sizes of half sphere shapes milled into it. An eyelid shape is cutout in brass and is then placed on the dapping block over the sphere of the right size. A corresponding round punch or die is used to ham- mer the brass into the dapping block which forms a half sphere shape.

Ping pong balls shells can work fine if the eyeballs you have made are the right size for them. You can also use the 'bubble stock' acetate sheet to make eyelids (available from A-R Products; see suppliers list). The famous McElroy figures used ping pong balls for eyelids and lasted for many years, so it can be a suitable choice for rigid shell winkers.

The rigid shells are then bonded to the piano wire frames. Brass shells can be sol- dered to the piano wire frames (some figure makers prefer brass rod in place of the piano wire). Ping pong ball shells are glued to the piano wire frames. With the acetate bubble stock shells, **Plastic Welder** (come in a syringe-type applicator like 5-minute epoxy) works well. *Use with adequate ventilation!* Mix in a little 'Cab-O-Sil (see Chapters Five and Six) to make the Plastic Welder into a paste. Ping pong ball shells can be bonded with two part epoxy (thickened with Cab-O- Sil), epoxy putty or possibly one of the craft glues. Always do a test to make sure the materials and adhesives you have selected will bond well.

When bonding or soldering the rigid shells to the piano wire frame, you need to suspend the shells up off of the eyeballs by 1/32 to 1/16 of an inch. One way is to set one or two thickness' of additional shell material tem- porarily under the shells you are bonding in place. The idea here, is that when all is said and done, the rigid shell winkers are 1/32" to 1/16" away from the eyeballs. The rigid shell eyelids need to be able to clear the eyeballs without any rubbing when the eyelids open and close.

The piano wire frames are attached near the rear of the winker shells. This keeps the the piano wire frames and glue (or solder)

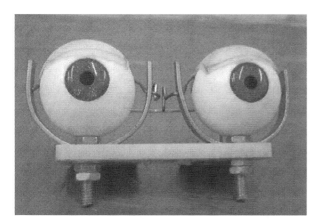

Rigid shells attached to piano wire frames

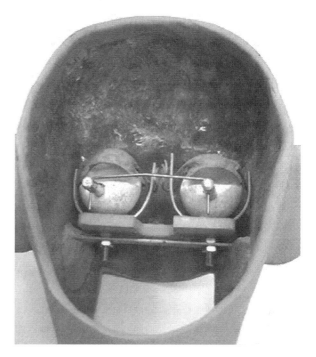

Eye tray and winker assembly inside head casting

Side view - rigid shells attached to piano wire frames
Rigid shells have been painted with primer in this photo

from hitting the eye sockets when everything is installed. (See photos above) You will probably have to sand or grind away a little of the top of the eye sockets on the head casting. You need enough clearance for the rigid shell winker to operate smoothly with no rubbing.

***Winker actuating mechanism:*** After the rigid shell winkers are installed and move freely around the eyeballs and eye sockets,

you need to make the actuating mechanism to open and close the eyelids. This can be done with a ***rocker*** or ***pulley*** setup. Either arrangement can work just fine. Rockers can be made from flat brass stock and pivot on a a pivot rod bonded in place above the eye and winker assembly. One end of the rocker is attached to a piano wire or cord linkage that pulls on the loop end of the piano wire winker frame. A return spring pulls the rigid shell winkers back open when released. The other end of the rocker has a cord attached that goes down to a lever on the control stick. (See illustration next page) Each individual winker has this setup and is controlled by pulling a single lever on the control stick. You can wink one eye by pulling on one lever, or close both at the same time by pulling on both at the same time.

The winker mechanism could also be done with a pulley system instead of a rocker set-up. The pulleys would go above the eye

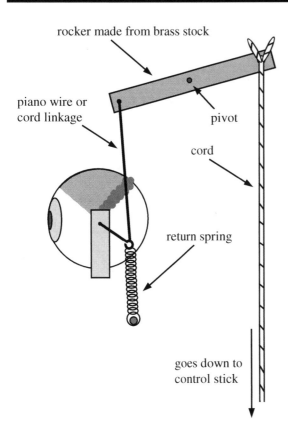

rocker made from brass stock

piano wire or cord linkage

pivot

cord

return spring

goes down to control stick

Winker actuating mechanism.

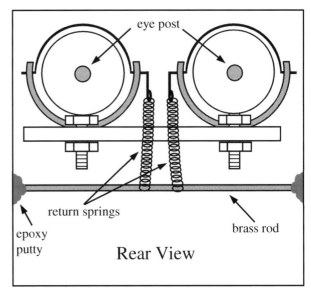

eye post

return springs

epoxy putty

brass rod

Rear View

Winker return springs attached to brass rod

and winker mechanism as was done with the rocker style setup. The pulleys are on a pivot rod that is bonded to the inside of the head casting with epoxy putty.

The levers for the winkers are done the same as the lever(s) for the raising eyebrows. A slot is made in the control stick. A slightly wider slot can be made so that the two levers have enough room to operate without problems. If you are installing winkers *and* raising eyebrows, you can make a larger slot yet in the control stick to accommodate all three levers. You can put some spacers between the levers so they will not be too close together or make individual slots for each lever in the control stick. (See illustration next page) There are literally hundreds of differ-

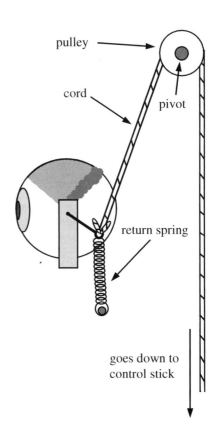

pulley

cord

pivot

return spring

goes down to control stick

Winker actuating mechanism - pulley style

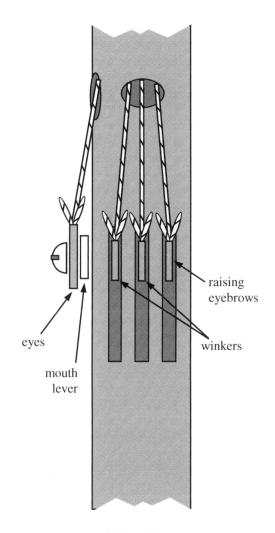

Side View

*One possible setup for levers on control stick*

mechanism is changing the design of the synchro bar that connects the eyes to move in unison. This basically involves setting up the synchro bar with a telescoping mechanism and a corresponding return spring. This is one of several ways to make the eyes cross.

A brass tube is glued into a small wood block, and a brass rod (that just fits into the brass tube) is glued into another small block. These small wood blocks are attached to the the eye posts with screws. The rod will telescope or slide back and forth inside the brass tube. The return spring on the bottom of the eye posts keeps the eyes in the normal synchronized position. (See illustration next page)

This set-up allows the eyes to go from side to side normally (in synchronization), until a

ent configurations for levers and controls on the control stick. Every figure maker has their preference.

### Novelty Animations

There are a number of animations that could be considered novelty animations. A *brief* overview of these will be considered next.

***Crossing eyes:*** This is a comedy effect that can be a lot of fun. The main part of this

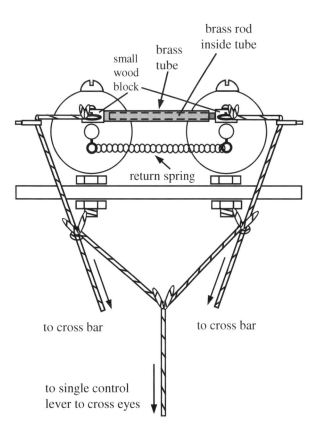

*One method of doing crossing eyes mechanism*

Crossing eyes can be fun!
Photo courtesy Rick Price

control. Crossing eyes can also be done with a rod style eye control with some slight modifications. The basic principle is the same.

***Flapping ears:*** Flapping or wiggling ears is another comedy effect that can be a lot of fun. When you pull on the control, both ears can flap forward, and then back when you release the control. If not overused, an audience will enjoy this special effect, mostly because it is totally unexpected.

The first step is to cast some separate ears. (See Chapters Four, Five and Six for information on mold making and casting) You can also cast just the ear portion of your head mold. Some small brass hinges are bonded to the ears. Then the hinges are in turn bonded to the side of the head in such a fashion that the ears bend or hinge forward towards the front of the face. (See illustration next page)

control lever is pulled for the eyes to cross. There are the two cords that would normally pull the eyes from side to side which are still controlled by the cross bar on the control stick (described earlier in this chapter). Attached to these two cords is another piece of cord that has some slack in it. Then, in turn, a single cord is attached to the middle of this cord and goes down to a singular control on the control stick. (See illustration previous page) Pulling on this single control causes both of the eye cords to pull equally and eventually overcome the tension of the return spring, allowing the eyes to cross. When you release the control lever, the return spring brings the eyes back to normal. After they have returned you can operate the eyes normally (from side to side) with the cross bar

Flapping ears can be fun too!
Photo courtesy Rick Price

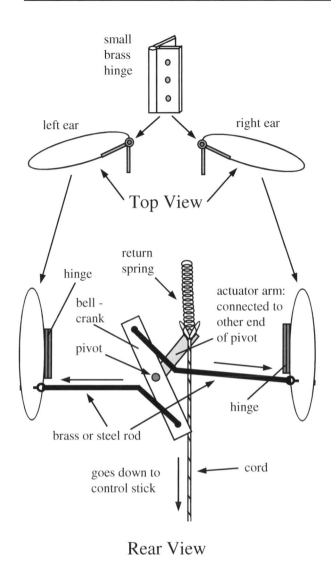

Top View

Rear View

One way to do flapping ears

The actuating mechanism is a little tricky but not too bad. (See illustration above) When the actuator arm is pulled downward by the cord, this causes the bell-crank (made from flat brass stock) to rotate. As this rotates, the brass or steel rods attached to the bell-crank assembly are pushed outward toward the ears. Because the ears are hinged, they will be pushed forward by this motion. A return spring pulls the bell-crank assem-

bly, and thus the ears, back to the normal position. A control lever could be put on the back of the control stick as this is not a feature that will be used as much as the mouth, eyes, eyebrows or winkers.

***Stick-out tongue:*** A tongue that sticks out of a figure's mouth will get a lot of attention and can be a humorous animation! Again, if not overused, this is a great effect and can be a tremendous amount of fun.

One basic set up for a ***stick-out tongue*** is shown in the illustration below. One of the more important things to keep in mind is that the tongue has to have a slight downward angle as it travels out of the mouth. The reason for this is that when the mouth is fully

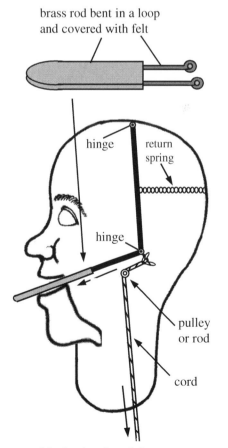

Mechanism for stick out tongue

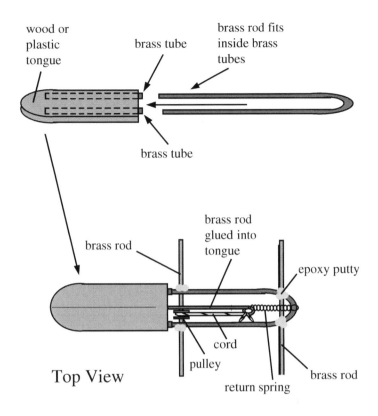

wood or plastic tongue

brass tube

brass rod fits inside brass tubes

brass tube

brass rod glued into tongue

brass rod

epoxy putty

cord

pulley

return spring

brass rod

**Top View**

Alternate method for stick out tongue

You can also set up the stick-out tongue mechanism so that it rides on a track instead of resting against the jaw piece as it is moving. This setup strongly resembles a trombone slide. This is a better arrangement if the tongue is not going to be made out of a soft material (it is also a more reliable mechanical arrangement), as the tongue will not rub against the jaw piece as it moves in and out of the head.

If the tongue were cast out of plastic or made of wood, you could bond a couple of brass tubes on the inside of the tongue that will act as tracks. Then you could use a corresponding brass rod bent in a *horseshoe* shape that fits inside the brass tubes. The tongue can then slide back and forth on the brass rod. (See illustration at left)

The brass rod (the one bent in the shape of a *horseshoe*), is bonded to

open, the inside area where the tongue and teeth are located will be at an angle. The *stick out tongue* of necessity has to follow this same angle.

For this first method, a tongue can be fashioned from some bent brass rod in the shape of a tongue, covered with some red felt (a local fabric store item). The mechanism hinges in two spots (see illustration previous page). When the cord is pulled downward, the mechanism that the tongue is attached to moves forward or towards the mouth opening, thus in turn causing the tongue to stick out of the mouth. The return spring retracts the mechanism and pulls the tongue back inside the head. With this method the tongue rests and slides on the jaw piece. Needless to say, you have to open the mouth before operating the stick-out tongue feature.

More fun! Sticking out tongue
Photo courtesy Rick Price

some larger gauge brass rods that are secured horizontally on the inside of the head. The horseshoe-shaped brass rod does not move. Only the tongue moves, sliding back and forth on the horseshoe-shaped brass rod. The actuating mechanism for a stick-out tongue with a track set up would work much the same as the first one with a cord and pulley set up. (See illustrations on pages 153 and 154 for details)

***Upper lip sneer:*** This effect causes the upper lip to move up slightly, exposing the upper teeth. This makes it look like the figure is sneering, smiling or combined with other effects (raising eyebrows or winkers) can emulate a few other emotions. The upper lip can be moved by itself or in combination with operating the lower jaw when performing, for different effects.

There are two basic things that have to go into place to make this mechanism: **1.)** Suspended upper teeth (the upper teeth do not move; only the upper lip moves with this animation). **2.)** A moving upper lip. The upper lip is much like the jaw piece in the way that it is hinged and moves in the head casting, except that is moves up instead of down.

The upper lip is a separate casting (just of the upper lip), and is essentially just a shell. You could make side pieces for the upper lip casting the same as was done for the lower jaw piece, however this is not necessary. The upper lip could possibly be cut from the head casting itself, or a separate casting of just the upper lip could be made from the head mold (as described earlier on page 124). Many of the same principles that apply to creating a lower jaw that fits and works well, apply to the upper lip casting. (See Appendix A)

Bonded to the upper lip shell are two brass rods that have the ends bent in a loop to act

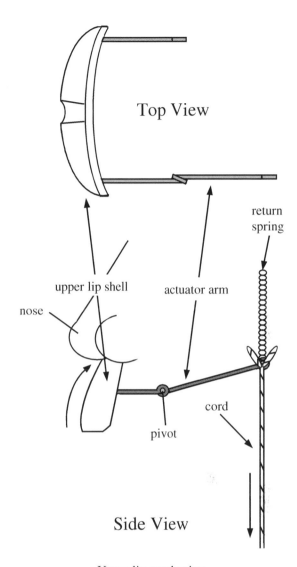

Upper lip mechanism

as pivots. One is made longer, extending towards the back of the head and becomes the actuator arm for the mechanism. (See illustration at right) To this is connected the cord and the return spring. Pulling downward on the cord causes the upper lip to move upwards and expose the upper teeth (which will be described shortly). The return spring pulls the upper lip back to the normal position, hiding the upper teeth once again.

When the upper lip goes up, it goes behind the nose and cheeks on the inside of the head

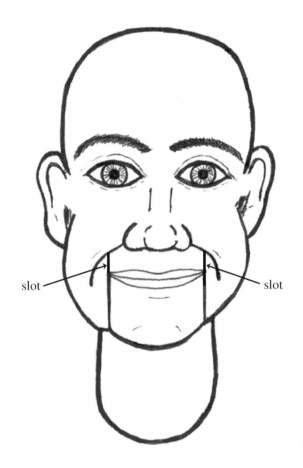

Upper lip has slots similar to lower jaw piece

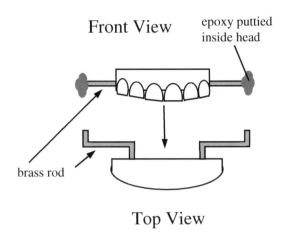

Upper teeth casting mounted to brass rods

casting. The sides of the upper lip ride in a slotted cutout, very much the same as the lower jaw does. It is very important the slots or cutout for the upper lip on the head casting be parallel and straight or else the upper lip will bind when it goes up and down. (See illustration above)

The upper teeth could be sculpted, a mold made and then cast in urethane plastic. Or they could be directly modeled out of Sculpey, Magic Sculp or other similar medium and later painted. The teeth are attached to brass rods that are bonded to the inside sides of the head, thus suspending the

teeth near the mouth opening. (See illustration above)

It is best if the upper lip mechanism is installed first. Then you can see clearly where the upper teeth need to be mounted inside the head. If you do this just right, you can arrange it so the moving upper lip brass rods will sit against the stationary brass rods (that hold the teeth in place) when in the rest position. You can glue some leather in place on the rods supporting the teeth to help make things quiet as the mechanism is being used.

### All-Direction Eyes

All-direction eyes is a novelty feature and is set up so that the eyes can not only move from side-to-side, but up and down or a combination of both. This is a fairly complex mechanism, which can be quite the challenge to install and have work correctly. There are a number of ways this could be done. Here is one possible way of setting up the mechanics for all-direction eyes:

The eyes are first of all set up to rotate on two different axis or pivots. One of the main

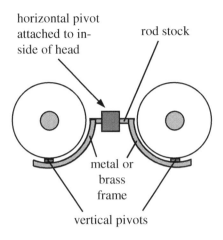

horizontal pivot attached to inside of head

rod stock

metal or brass frame

vertical pivots

## Rear View

Frame work and pivots for all direction eyes
Note: synchro linkage not shown for clarity

## Top View

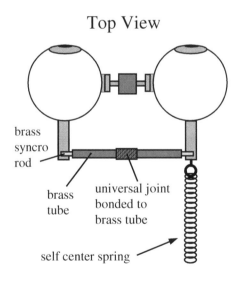

brass syncro rod

brass tube

universal joint bonded to brass tube

self center spring

Detail of synchro linkage and self-centering spring

parts of this mechanism is the framework that supports the eyes. Study the accompanying diagrams and illustrations carefully. This frame has a horizontal rod that rotates in a

horizontal pivot (which is bonded to the inside of the head near the bridge of the nose and essentially supports the entire **all-direction** eye mechanism), that allows the eye mechanism to go up and down. On the bottom of this framework, there are vertical pivots which allow the eyes to move from side-to-side. (See illustration at left) Needless to say the precision of these two axis (horizontal and vertical pivots) has to be flawless.

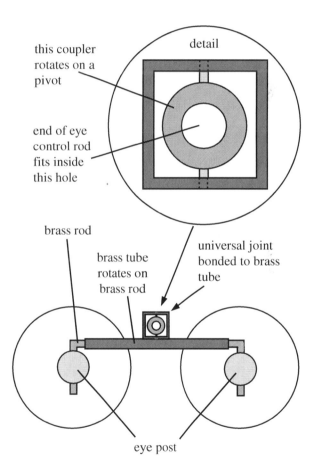

this coupler rotates on a pivot

detail

end of eye control rod fits inside this hole

brass rod

brass tube rotates on brass rod

universal joint bonded to brass tube

eye post

## Rear View

Detail of universal joint and related linkage
Note: other parts of mechanism not shown for clarity

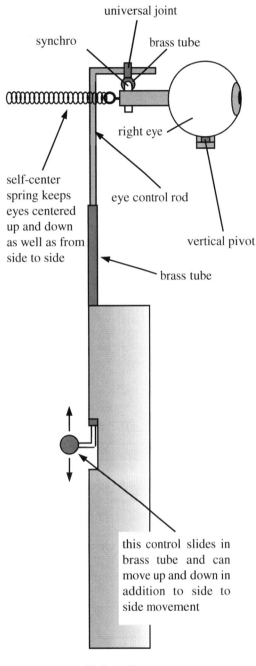

universal joint

synchro

brass tube

right eye

self-center spring keeps eyes centered up and down as well as from side to side

eye control rod

vertical pivot

brass tube

this control slides in brass tube and can move up and down in addition to side to side movement

## Side View

Complete all-direction eye control linkage

In order for all of this to work, a special setup needs to be fabricated so that the rod eye control can connect to this special eye mechanism. The goal here is to have it set up so that a single control on the control stick

can move the eyes in all directions. There are several ways that could be accomplished. Here's one possible way to do that:

The side to side movement is synchronized with a typical brass rod synchro bar. This brass rod synchro bar has a brass tube on it that is allowed to rotate freely. Attached to the brass tube is a special little *universal joint*. (See detail in illustration, previous page) This can be fabricated from larger brass rod and other brass stock.

The small brass bearing or coupler, pivots inside the universal joint frame. (See illustration previous page) With the combination of the brass tube and the universal joint, the end of the rod eye control can turn from side to side and go up and down as well, as the control on the control stick is operated. The self-center spring not only centers the eyes from side to side, but also from up and down motion too. The rod eye control rotates (side to side motion) in a brass tube mounted in the control stick (as is does for a simple moving eyes control described earlier in the chapter), but it also slides up and down inside the brass tube, to move the eyes up and down. A thorough study of the diagrams and illustrations will give you the basics on this some what complex mechanism.

### *Mechanics and Animations summary*

Installing the various mechanics and animations inside a head casting can be both very challenging and rewarding. Again, start out with the simpler mechanics and progress towards the more complicated mechanics as you gain more experience. You could add one additional animation to each head that you build possibly or try to improve on a previous animation that you have installed, that might not have worked quite as well as you hoped. Keep at it and you will succeed.

A book can only give you basic principles of how this all works. It is really only through much experimentation (trial and error) that you will get good at fabricating and installing the various mechanics and animations. Do not get discouraged if things do not turn out perfectly the first time you try your hand at different animations. This is actually a good thing. You will learn something from each new mechanism that you try. You will not only find out what doesn't work, but more importantly, what does! Most accomplished figure makers have worked at it for years and years, perfecting the way they make eyes move, or mouths move, or eyebrows raise, eyes blink, etc. So take your time. Don't rush your figure making projects. Strive always to do quality work. With some determination and a little practical experience, you can be very proud of the figures you have made!

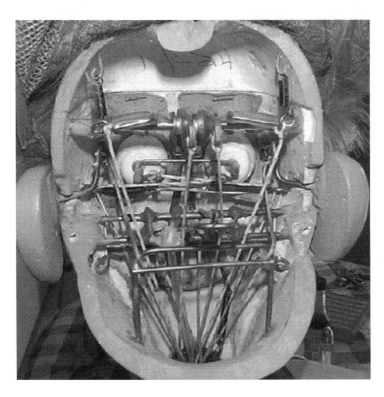

How many animations can fit in one head?
It depends on the skill of the figure maker.

Photos courtesy Rick Price

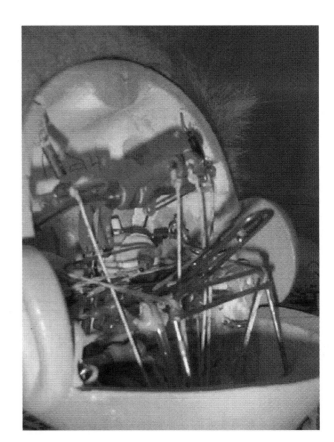

# CHAPTER EIGHT

# PAINTING & BODY CONSTRUCTION

Painting your figure can be one of the most important steps in the figure making process. Let's say your original model was sculpted very nicely with a lot of character. The mold you made of the model was excellent, and the casting of the pieces were flawless. But then the paint job was, well,..... not so good. A bad paint job can really detract from all of the other hard work that you did.so take your time and do a good job.

The first step is to wash the parts to be painted, to remove any remaining release agent left over from the casting process. This is very important for good paint adhesion. Add several drops of liquid dishwashing detergent to about four cups of warm water in a plastic pail or bowl. Swish it around to mix it with the water. Take a clean rag and immerse it in the solution and then wring the rag out well. Carefully wipe off all of the parts that are to be painted. Then take some clear clean water, without any detergent, and use another clean rag and wipe off the parts one more time. Let dry completely.

The paint job on a figure is only going to be as good as the final sanding that you do on the cast parts prior to doing any painting or sealing. A good paint job will not cover over a roughly sanded figure. Spend some time and examine each of the pieces that you are going to paint, and look for any imperfec-tions that need to be sanded or patched. You will need to patch any holes, voids or small air bubbles left over from the casting process. Spackle, wood dough, or Magic Sculp can be used, depending on what materials you made the castings from. It is best to use a patching compound that is about the same hardness as the casting. Otherwise, as you start to sand, one material will sand away quicker than the surrounding material or vice versa. This makes it extremely difficult to 'feather in' or blend your patching job. A quick test will tell you what you need to know in this regard.

It is a good idea to sand the entire part (head, hand or foot), to actually scuff or etch the entire surface that will be painted. A casting fresh out of a mold can be too smooth, which can cause problems with paint adhesion. Sanding (etching) is one of the most important steps in prepping a casting!

### *Primer Coat?*

A primer is only needed on certain types of casting materials, or with certain types of paint. For example, a fiberglass casting (head, hands or feet), made with polyester resin can have problems with acrylic paint sticking. A good primer can stick to the polyester resin fiberglass casting just fine, but acrylic paint will not stick well to many of the primers available. One way around this is to make up a hybrid mix of primer and acrylic paint. You can take some Acrylic Latex Primer, and mix it 50/50 with some acrylic paint. The Acrylic Latex Primer will stick to the polyester fiberglass casting, and because it has acrylic paint in it, your top coat of acrylic paint will bond to the primer.

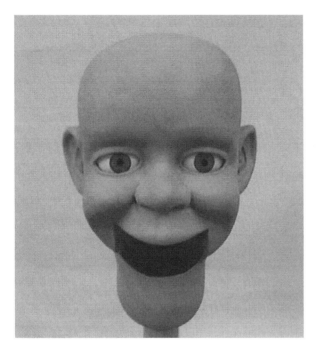

Cast head primed with a couple coats of gray primer
Note: mouth not yet installed in this particular figure

You should fully test the primer and paint that you intend to use, to verify that the primer bonds well to the casting and that the paint bonds well to the primer. Do a scatch test, first of the primer after it has dried for a few days, and then try to scratch the paint after it has dried for a few days on top of the primer. It should not scrape off easily. The bond gets a little more tenacious after a few weeks when they have cured even more yet. A urethane casting usually does not need a primer when using acrylic paints.

### Painting the parts

You may be under the impression that it is next to impossible to do a satisfactory paint-ing job on your figure by hand, without using a bunch of expensive spray-painting equipment. Spray-painting can work well, but the equipment is somewhat expensive and takes time to learn how to use and maintain properly. It may interest you to know that many of the top figure makers do not use any type of spray-painting equipment, and paint their figures strictly by hand, with a brush. It is not only possible to do a good paint job by hand, but it is probably a lot easier than you think.

Vent figures are typically painted with either acrylic or oil paints. Either type of paint can work well if done properly. Acrylics are much, much, easier to work with, are available at most any craft store, art store or super store like Wal-Mart, and cost much, much less than a good set of oil paints and related supplies. Oil paints can take a long time to dry, take much patience, and there will be a sizable learning curve to make them work for you.. Although acrylic paints are much easier to use, they can be deceptive as to when they are really dry. They can appear to be quite dry, but in reality they are still tacky under the surface and need to fully dry before sealing the paint or using the figure (lips sticking together when you open and close the mouth is one evidence that the paint has not fully dried).

***Acrylic Paints:*** Acrylic paints are available at most craft stores or art stores, etc., and come in bottles, tubes, and small jars. Any of these types can work well, and provide a good, durable paint job. Most stores that carry these have acrylic paints with a few pre-mixed fleshtones available. Although you could use these, you will usually find that the dried shade of flesh tone is not that great. So, the best thing is to mix your own flesh tones. Keep in mind that acrylic paints always seem to dry slightly darker than the shade they are when they are wet.

For mixing your own Caucasian skin tones, purchase some white, burnt sienna, bright red, and bright yellow. Start with a fair amount of white paint and start adding some burnt sienna until you start to get something that resembles a tan or beige color, getting close to a flesh color. Then add a very small amount of bright red to make it a little more pink. Finally add a very small amount of yellow to level out the pinkish tone and bring out a more true Caucasian flesh color. A good skin tone on a vent figure is usually darker than you think it should be.

For mixing other types of skin tones, you will mostly need to use some common sense. For African-American and other somewhat darker skin tones, you will need to add more brown paint to the mix. For Native-American skin tones, not as much brown would be added as for African-American skin tones, but you would add a little more red to the mixture. For Asian-American skin tones, adding a little more yellow to the Caucasian paint mix above, would be mostly all you needed to do.

Be sure to mix up more paint than you think you need. You will be painting the head, the hands and possibly a pair of feet. If you need some paint later for touch up you want to be sure you have the same shade, so mix plenty of flesh tone paint. Paint a little bit of this paint on a part of your figure that won't show and let it dry completely. Notice the difference in shade between the dry paint and the wet paint in the jar. Make sure this is acceptable to you. As with all other aspects of figure making, this mixing of flesh tones is learned by doing. Keep experimenting until you get the color you want.

You can apply a base coat of paint with a slightly dampened paint brush. A sponge can also work well. Many figure makers use a stippling technique and are purposely not trying to make a smooth paint finish, but rather slightly textured. This keeps the paint from looking too shiny when dry. If the paint is too smooth, it will shine too much under stage lighting or other such harsh lighting situations.

Stippling basically involves dabbing lightly with the end of the brush bristles as opposed to drawing the brush back and forth over the area to be painted. A light texturing will start to show up as you stipple with the brush. Again, you can do a textured or stippled effect with a small sponge or sponge brush (craft store item). Paint the entire head, hand or foot, one coat, using this technique and allow them to dry. With acrylics, it is really best to let the paint dry until the next day between coats. Doing three coats of paint is usually adequate for a durable paint job and good paint coverage. Be sure to wash your brushes out well with water after each coat of paint.

If the acrylic paint is too thick to work with, it can be thinned with an acrylic thinner or extender (available where you buy the acrylic paints). Because the paint is now 'wetter' so to speak, it will take a little longer for the paint to dry. This gives you more time to work with the paint. The bottles of acrylic extender are fairly inexpensive. Mixing with water is not recommended, as that can affect the quality of the paint and the bonding of the paint to the casting.

Look at any really nice figure, and you will notice some very subtle highlights on the forehead, nose, cheeks, ears, etc. This is some slight shading, usually a pinkish tone, that is applied and blended to these areas. Take a small amount of your mixed flesh tone that was used for your base coat and add a little bright red to it. Take a brush and dip it into this mixture and dab most of it onto a piece of scrap paper. Take the brush and dab or stipple the highlight color onto an area you want highlighted such as a cheek.

Start at the center of the highlight area and work outwards. The idea is to have darker amounts of this pinkish shade towards the center and then fade and blend into the flesh color surrounding the highlighted area. Another trick is that if you get too much highlight, you can come back later after the highlight paint dries, and then stipple and blend with your base flesh tone color. If worse comes to worse, you paint over the area with more flesh tone, completely covering it, and start over.

On the hands and feet, you have the option of having the whole piece the same flesh color, or adding a little dab of white to your flesh tone for highlighting the fingernails and toenails.

Allow the head to dry for a day before doing the final detail work. The details include the lips, teeth, tongue, eyebrows, and a little eyeliner to accentuate the eyes.

The eyeliner or outline of the eyes can be done with burnt sienna, burnt umber or a mixture of the two depending on how dark you want to go. You will need a small artist brush to do this. Takes a steady hand and a little patience. The eyebrows can also be painted with a similar shade, however, it tends to look better if they are closer to the color the hair is going to be. So use the wig you have selected (see Chapter Nine) for a reference to help you match the eyebrow color. The nostrils can be done with a little flesh tone with a slight amount of burnt umber, which makes it a little darker in color.

The lips, tongue, and inside of the mouth can all be painted the same basic color. A small amount of bright red is mixed with the flesh tone color to produce a shade suitable for these areas. The addition of small amounts of burnt sienna, bright yellow and possibly burnt umber can help level out the tone to a more pleasing shade that best emulates the lips, tongue or gum areas. The teeth can be a slight off-white color. Take some pure white paint and tone it down just slightly, with very, very small amounts of burnt umber and turners yellow. Remember, you are only trying to make it off-white, and not like tooth decay!

Detail work on eyebrows, eyeliner, lips and nostrils

As was mentioned, acrylic paints dry quickly to the touch, but take some time to be fully dry. If you are going to seal the paint job with a matte acrylic spray, you should wait 5-7 days before doing so to be on the safe side. If you seal it too soon the paint cannot fully dry. If using a sealer, apply 2 or 3 really thin coats. Some figure makers like to use a sealer, some do not. It is easier to touch up a paint job if it has not been sealed.

*Oil paints:* The techniques for using oil paints are not that much different than the acrylics. The mixing of the colors is basically the same. Oil paints are more chemically oriented than acrylics, so you have to add the right ingredients to get the oils to paint nicely and dry in a reasonable amount of time. Also, oil paints come in different grades as far as quality goes. Get the best quality oil paints you can afford.

Oil paints directly out of the tube will be too thick. You need to add paint thinner to thin them down. When starting off with the titanium white, mix in some paint thinner (odorless is nicest to work with) until the paint is the consistency of cream or a good quality house paint. Mix up enough white to paint all the parts of your figure several times.

Then mix up a base flesh tone, as was described in the acrylic paint section, by adding small amounts of burnt sienna until you start to get something that resembles a light tan or beige color, getting close to a flesh color. Then add a very small amount of cadmium red to make it a little more pink. Finally add a very small amount of naples yellow to level out the pinkish tone and bring out a more true flesh color. You may have to add more thinner after adding this additional paint.

A few drops of cobalt drier are also added to the mixture to hasten the drying process. Mix well. Follow all of the same basic steps that were outlined for working with acrylic paints, doing the base coats, highlighting and detail work. Let the paint dry after each step. You will need to wash your brushes out in paint thinner instead of water when you use oil paints.

Painting your figure is an exciting step in the figure making process. Your figure's per-sonality really starts to emerge as the paint brings out the features that you sculpted in the original model. In fact, you will see some personality come out in the painted figure that you did not see in the original sculpture or casting of the head. While you are waiting for the paint to dry, you can start working on a body for your figure.

### Body construction and assembly

If you have cast a body by one of the methods in Chapter Six, the first step would be to make any necessary cutouts in the body. The neck hole needs to be cut out of the top of the body for one. Also, a cutout needs to be made in the back if the body was not cast with an opening in it.

Before cutting out the neck hole, you first need to know how big a hole to make. To determine the exact diameter for the neck hole, cut a hole in some scrap wood and then sand the edges to take off any sharpness. Next, take the head and test the movement of the neck in the hole of the scrap wood. It should be readily apparent if you need to make this hole bigger or smaller. Experiment a little until you are satisfied that you have the correct hole size. (See illustration below)

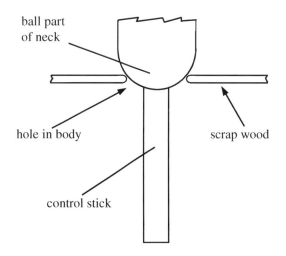

Neck hole, not too big, not too small....., just right!

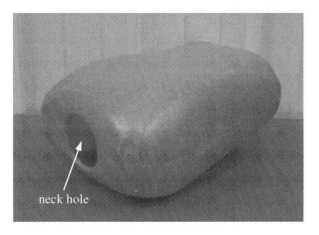

Hole cut out in fiberglass body for neck to fit into

perhaps, as you can always make it bigger later if necessary. If the opening in the back of the body is too small however, the control stick can collide with the remaining part of the back, limiting the full range of motion for the head. The idea is to have the hole in the back big enough so that no matter what angle you put the head, the control stick will not get hung up by the body. Drill a hole big enough for the saw blade and use a saber saw or small-bladed hand saw to make the cutout.

Mark where the hole is going to be on the cast body with a pencil or with a permanent marker. Drill a hole big enough for a small saw blade to fit into near the inside of the line you just drew. Use a hand-held saber saw or small-bladed hand saw and make the cutout. It is also possible to use a circle cutter or hole saw commonly available from the hardware stores or home building supply centers.

For the cutout on the back of a cast body, mark a line where you want the back opening to be. You might want to cut it a little smaller

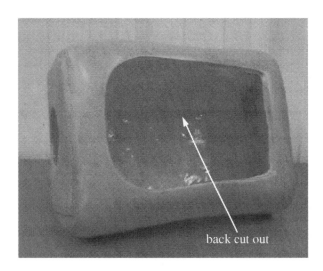

Cut out in back of fiberglass body casting

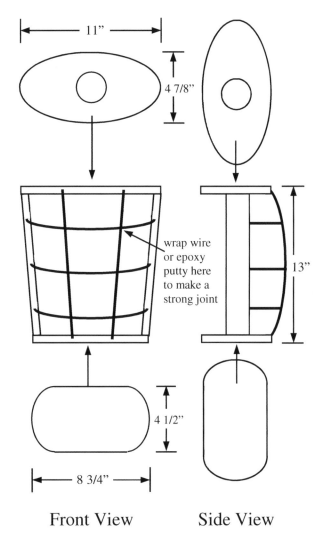

Front View          Side View

Body style 1

Wood framed body with wood sides and wire on front

Carefully sand any cutouts you made and the seams on the cast body. Some like to leave the bottom part of the body open when they make a cast body and then later attach a piece of wood to this area. It can make it easier to attach the cloth portion of the legs to the bottom of the body later (a simple staple gun can work just fine for this).

### Wood-Framed Bodies

If you have not made a cast body, a **wood-framed body** can be constructed without too much trouble. Many finely constructed figures are made with wood-framed bodies. It's simply a matter of personal preference. There are several different ways that a wood-framed body can be made. A few different ways will be described and you can choose a style that appeals to you.

One thing that many of the different wood framed bodies have in in common is a wood top piece and a wood bottom piece. Where they differ is in how the top and bottom pieces are connected and what's in between. Here are a few possibilities:

(1) The top and bottom pieces are connected with two wood side pieces (glued and screwed together) and then some wire (like coat hanger wire) is attached to the front for shape and support. Drill holes in the wood for the coat hanger wire to go into and epoxy into place. Where the wires cross in the middle, you can wrap a piece of smaller gauge wire or some epoxy putty to give the wire framework more support. (See illustration previous page)

(2) The top and bottom pieces are connected with two wood side pieces (same as the first body style) and then some wood ribs either cut straight or curved (for a more natural body contour) are attached to the front and sides for shape and support. (See illustration this page)

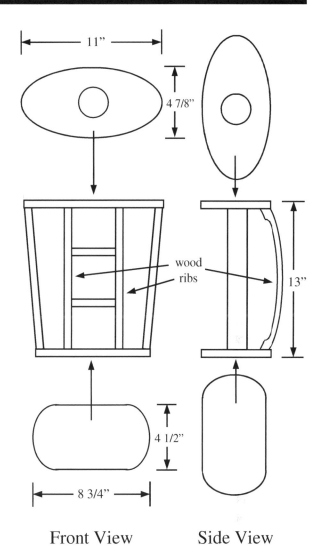

Front View          Side View

Body style 2
Body with wood ribs in front

(3) The top and bottom pieces are connected with 1/4" or 3/8" dowels. The dowels are space apart a few inches going around the front and sides. (See illustration next page)

(4) The top and bottom pieces are connected by a fiberglass or resin cast front and sides (all one piece). This is a cross between an all cast body and an all wood-framed body. The top and bottom pieces are wood and the front and sides are cast. The advantages are: a nicely sculpted contoured body, yet you can still put staples into the top and

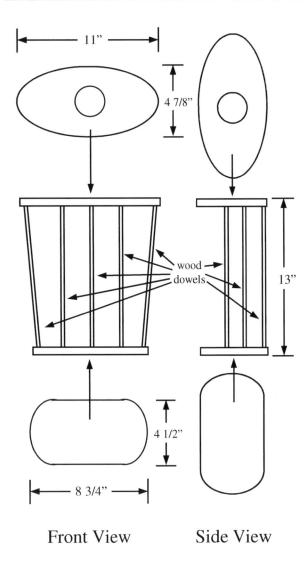

Front View          Side View

Body style 3
Body with wood dowels throughout

bottom pieces easily, for attaching arms and legs later.

The first step in all four of these examples would be to fabricate the wood top (shoulder plate) and bottom pieces. Purchase some clear 1" X 6" pine about 4' long (actual size is 3/4" X 5 1/2" by 4', the way lumber is measured). Trace the patterns provided (see end of this chapter) onto the wood. Cut one piece out for the bottom piece and two for the top piece. The second piece for the top or

shoulder plate can be done a few different ways to reduce weight. **1.)** Cut an oval out of the second piece so that it is open in the center and will effectively only be about a 1" strip. Glue to top shoulder piece with carpenters glue. **2.)** Cut out only partial pieces that go near the shoulders and glue to top shoulder piece with carpenters glue. Bevel and round the edges for this shoulder plate for a more natural look to the finished body. (See illustration next page for details)

Put the glued up top piece into a vice and shape the contour of the shoulders with a wood rasp, portable or table-mounted belt sander or other similar tools as needed. Cut a hole out in the top piece the right size for the neck (determine the size of hole the same way as described for the cast body). Sand off any sharp or rough edges on both the top and bottom pieces.

To make the body a little nicer, you can add a little padding as needed. A layer of cotton batting sandwiched between two layers of muslin fabric can be wrapped around the body. Fabric stores also carry a variety of pre-quilted or stuffed fabrics that will work. This padded fabric or material can be stapled and or glued in place on the body with a flexible type of craft glue made to use with fabrics.

*Neck hole lining:* Place the head on the body, and turn the control stick, moving the head from side to side (the ball part of the neck rides in the hole in the body). The neck against the body will have some friction and thus make some noise. There will always be some noise because of this, but it can be made a lot quieter.

Figure makers generally use some type of soft material to help quiet things down. Soft leather, felt, or fleece (a very soft fabric item), have all been used by various figure makers. Leather or chamois (automotive

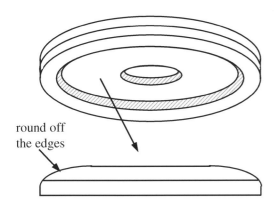

round off
the edges

Oval wood shape with center cut out
and glued to top shoulder plate allows
more room for rounding edges of top

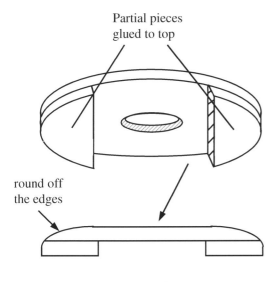

Partial pieces
glued to top

round off
the edges

## Front View

Top pieces or shoulder plate for wood frame body

cover the neck hole by about 1/2" to 3/4". Glue it in place on top of the body covering the neck hole. Try not to have any glue where the neck will contact the material (leather, felt or fleece), but rather, just outside of this region of the neck hole. If you use a glue that stays soft or rubbery (such as some of the craft glues or contact cement), that's not as critical.

After the glue has dried, you can cut a hole in the material (or just cut an 'X' through the middle) to allow the control stick to pass through easily. Some dust the area with a little talcum powder to cut down on friction. Depending on what material you use, you won't need anything. Do not use any oil or silicone spray as these will build up, collect dirt and make a greasy mess. Also, silicone tends to wander and will end up in places you don't want it. Silicone will cause 'fish eyes' if you try to refinish your figures paint job at some point and will give you a lot of grief.

***Cloth arms and legs:*** After the body is completed, you can make the cloth arms and legs that the hands or feet can be attached to. Buy a good quality muslin from a fabric store. Take a cloth tape measure and find out what the diameter of the wrist is on the hand casting. Take the measurement at the end of the casting where the cloth will be attached. Take this measurement and add one inch for seam allowance. This is how wide you need to cut the muslin cloth. Do the same for the feet (at the ankle opening) if you have cast some feet.

For the arms, the length for the muslin needs to be such that when all is said and done, the fingertips of the hands hang down to the seat of the body or just slightly past. It is suggested that for your first figure, cut the

store) can be purchased locally. Felt and fleece materials can be purchased at a local fabric store.

Cut out a circle (can also be square) of one of the above materials just large enough to

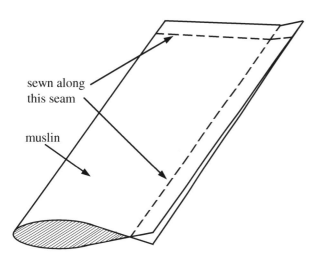

sewn along
this seam

muslin

Muslin fabric folded and sewn, one end left open
Cloth part of arms and legs are done the same

muslin longer than what is needed. You can cut some off, just before you attach the arms to the body. Some figure makers like arms that are longer than this and some like the arms about the same length as the body (as described above). Edgar Bergen's figures, Paul Winchell's figures, and other figures have short arms like this. It looks fine on a vent figure and is less obtrusive.

Fold the muslin material in half and sew along the top and the one side. Sew 1/2" in from the edge. This is called sewing with a half inch seam allowance. If you're not good at sewing, get a friend or relative to sew these for you. Leave the one end open. (See illustration above)

The same can be done for the legs. The muslin tubes need to be long enough so that the combined length of the cast foot and muslin is about 18" inches from the heel of the foot to the bottom of the body. This combined with body and head measurements should make a nice 40" figure. You can also make the top of the leg tubes bigger around than they are where they connect to the top of the foot casting.

Leave the muslin inside out (with the seams on the outside) for the next step. Take the open end of the sewn muslin arm (or leg) and place it over the wrist of the hand casting (or ankle of a foot casting). Keep sliding the fabric, bunching and gathering it as necessary until the top end (which is sewn closed) meets the open end of the wrist. Take a rubber band to hold the muslin firmly against the end of the wrist temporarily.

Wind some thread around the muslin and the wrist (specifically where the indentation or groove is). Put numerous windings of strong thread around the muslin, precisely where the indentation in the casting is. Take some craft glue or white glue and brush it onto the tightly wound thread. The glue and thread combined like this are very strong together (same principle as glass cloth and resin). Be careful not to use too much glue or it will soak through to the muslin and will show on the finished arm or leg when you turn the muslin back right-side-out. You mostly only need enough to keep the thread from unwinding. Let the glue dry completely before turning the muslin arm back right-side-out. This is the method the author first presented in his kit-building instructions back in 1994. This produces a very professional looking and durable attachment of the muslin to the cast hands or feet. (See illustrations and photos next page)

Repeat the above steps for the other hand casting, and/or foot castings if you have them. The beauty of the above method is that this also seals the opening of the hand or foot casting while at the same time securely attaching the muslin to the hand or foot castings. When you go to put the stuffing in the arms or legs, it won't go down into the hands or feet, taking up extra stuffing.

Groove in wrist

muslin tube bunched and gathered over end of hand

strong thread wrapped tightly around muslin where groove is and glue applied to thread

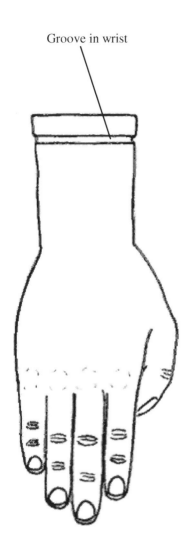
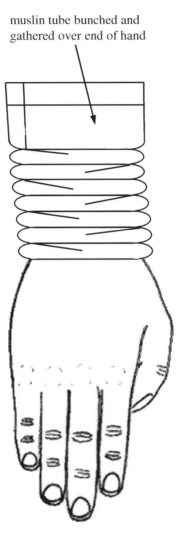
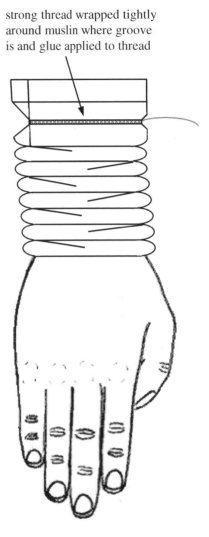

Cast hand with groove in wrist

Muslin tube set on end of hand

Thread wrapped around groove

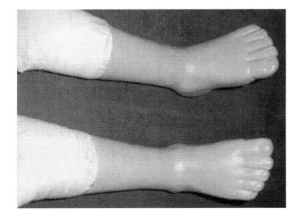

Muslin attached to feet castings

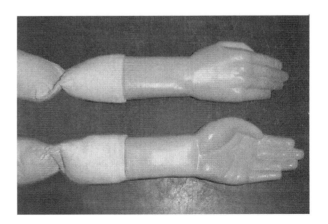

Muslin attached to hands and an elbow joint sewn

Purchase some toy/doll stuffing from the fabric or craft store to stuff the arms and legs with. Begin slowly to turn the muslin tubes right-side-out and start filling the arms and legs with as much stuffing as they will hold, ever so slightly over stuffing them. Keep in mind that the stuffing will tend to settle, so it's better to over stuff a little than to under-stuff. Some figure makers put in an elbow joint, some do not. Legs are generally much nicer if they have a knee joint.

If you are going to do an elbow or knee joint, they are basically done the same way. You stuff the muslin about halfway up the arm or leg and then sew across the muslin twice (two separate lines of sewing), one half inch apart. So the elbow or knee joint is effectively one half inch of muslin with no stuffing in it. See photo previous page. Then stuff the remainder of the muslin tube as necessary.

Finally, take the open end of the muslin (this is where having a little extra comes into play), and fold the end over one inch, and then fold again one half inch. This creates several thickness' of muslin which makes it nice for attaching the muslin to the shoulders or the legs to the bottom of the body. The folds in the muslin arms should be such that the hand will hang properly at the side of the body when attached. The folds for the legs should be such that the feet are pointing ever so slightly outwards, to have a natural appearance. Sew the folds together on the ends of each individual arm or leg so they will not come apart later.

To attach the arms or legs to a wood-framed body, a simple staple gun will suffice. Arms are stapled near the top outside edge of each shoulder. The legs are stapled close to

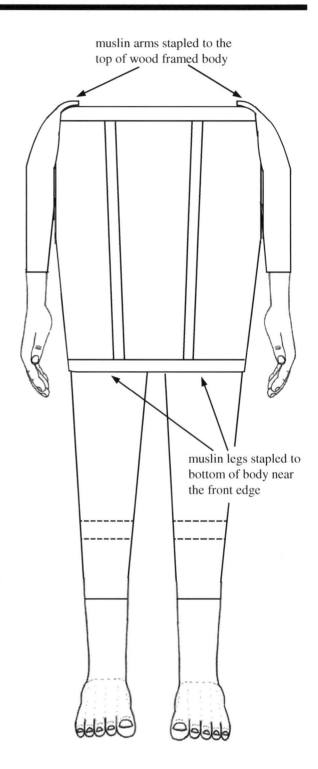

muslin arms stapled to the top of wood framed body

muslin legs stapled to bottom of body near the front edge

Arms and legs stapled to body
Screws or cord can be used on a cast body

the front of the bottom wood piece on the body.

Staples would not be a good idea on a cast body. Three to four small screws with matching nuts will work for attaching the arms or legs to a cast body. Three per arm and four per leg should be sufficient. Try to find a low profile pan head screw, size 6 or 8. These should be just long enough to go through the body with enough threads for the nuts to go on. Put the head of the screws on the outside. After attaching the arms and legs to the body with the screws, take a small amount of two-part epoxy putty (or Magic Sculp) and cover the end of the screws where the nuts are. This will protect your hands from any sharp edges on the screws when operating the figure.

You could also use some heavy cord in place of the screws. Some eyelets from a fabric store could also be set in the fold at the end of the arm or leg for extra strength where the holes in the muslin fabric will be.

If you did not make cast feet for your figure, you will need to make muslin legs that have the shape of a foot on the end. The length of the foot should be 5 1/2" to 5 3/4" from heel to toe. The length of the leg would still be about 18" from heel to the bottom of the body. (See illustration top right) Allow for a half inch seam allowance when making the pattern. Sew the muslin as was outlined for the arms and leg tubes. Turn the sewn muslin legs right-side-out, stuffing the feet and legs as you go. Attach to the body as outlined above.

### Painting and body construction summary

As with anything else, the more figures you make, paint and construct bodies for, the

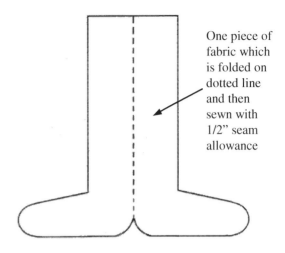

One piece of fabric which is folded on dotted line and then sewn with 1/2" seam allowance

Muslin legs with feet

better you will get at it. With each figure that you make, you will learn something from the process. You will see better and easier ways of doing things each time. It's an ongoing process that never really ends. Don't be afraid to try something new or a different way of doing the same thing. Shakespeare once said, "Our doubts are traitors, and make us lose the good we oft might win by fearing to attempt." Or in other words, sometimes we don't try new things because we're afraid of failing. The truth of the matter is, we will never know what great things we can do until we try. There are various inventors whose greatest achievements were labeled 'happy mistakes' or 'smart mistakes'. They weren't afraid to experiment and try new things. Walt Disney said that a lot of people were under the impression that he made few mistakes because of all his success. He indicated that the reality was that he made lots of mistakes. The only difference was that he kept at it, and kept at it, so that in the end he had plenty of successes to go along with the mistakes.

Now with your figure painted and the body constructed and assembled, your figure is really starting to look like more than just parts everywhere. You have come a long ways and should congratulate yourself! It is getting very close. Adding a wig, clothing, a few finishing touches and you will have a completed vent figure uniquely yours, with a personality that you created. What could be more exciting! Very soon, you will be able to show everyone the fascinating work of your hands. The final chapter concludes with the finishing touches that are needed to complete your figure.

After awhile your shop will be full of all kinds of parts, molds and figures in various stages of construction.

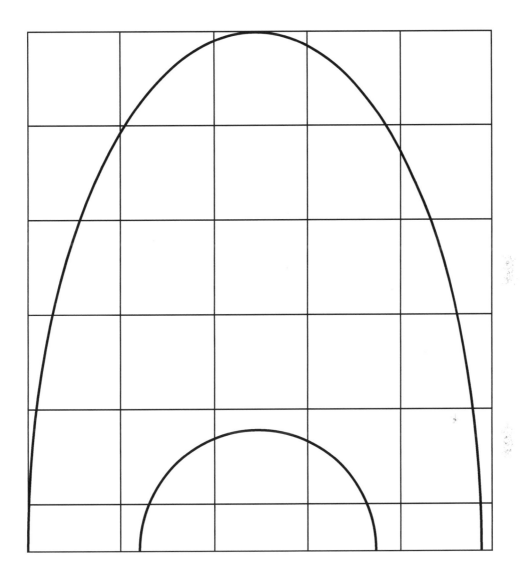

Half pattern for top of body. Make two photo copies of this,
scotch tape together and use for tracing outline onto wood.

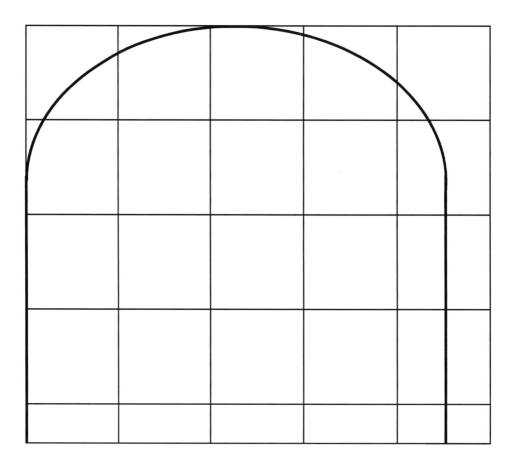

Half pattern for bottom of body. Make two photo copies of this, scotch tape together and use for tracing outline onto wood.

# CHAPTER NINE

# *FINISHING TOUCHES*

This is it! The last few steps to complete all your hard work. This chapter is kind of a catch-all for those little finishing touches that need to be done in completing your figure. Your figure may need a wig, a beard or mustache, fuzzy eyebrows (instead of painted ones), clothing, shoes, etc. Some of these items may seem somewhat trivial, but oftentimes, it is these little things that really bring out your figure's personality.

After your figure has some of the above finishing touches, he or she will need to be clothed. Is your figure going to be sporty, sophisticated, scruffy, a clothes hound, or??? They sometimes say that 'clothes make the man or the woman'. Likewise your figure's personality can be altered quite a bit just by the clothes you decide to put on them. So give this a fair amount of consideration when you begin looking for clothing items for your completed figure.

### *Hair for your figure*

Wigs come in all different sizes, styles, colors and quality. Needless to say, the better the quality of the wig, the better it will look and hold up over time. This is not to say you cannot find an inexpensive wig that will work just fine.

Some places to check for inexpensive wigs are local magic shops and novelty or costume shops. You have to inspect the wigs from these places to see if they will work or not. Typically these wigs are some of the cheapest available and sometimes the quality is just too poor to be used. These type of stores also usually carry fake mustaches, beards, eyelashes, etc. These can be glued onto your figure's face with super glue or contact cement as needed (use the glue or cement sparingly).

Other places you can sometimes find inexpensive wigs is at a *thrift store, flea markets, etc.* Some of these are top quality wigs that are still in very good condition. They typically only need to be washed to be usable again. Wash in warm or cool water (use mild shampoo or Woolite®). Don't use hot water as that does funny things to synthetic wigs.

Check with a beauty supply store or a beauticians school in your local area. They sometimes have a good source to get wigs at a reasonable price. Also, hair dressers, barbers and styling salons, can get wigs at discount prices. Finally, you can purchase a new wig from a store that specializes in the sale of wigs. Most larger cities have several good wig shops. You could also order a wig through mail order or on the Internet. Lacy Costume Wigs in New York has some wigs that are fairly inexpensive (see suppliers list at end of book) and are of reasonable quality. You don't need the 'best of the best' for a figure, but it needs to be good enough.

A petite or children's size wig (much harder to find and more expensive usually) is what you want if at all possible. This will be much closer to fitting your figure's head. Many wigs will be over size on your figure and will need to be adjusted or altered.

On some wigs there is a hook and elastic that you will see near the back label of the wig. The elastic can be pulled tighter and the hooks attach to the tape slots (a little hard to see, as it just looks like a piece of ribbon sewn along the edge of the wig skull cap) to hold it in place. Sometimes, adjusting this tighter helps quite a bit and might be all you need to do. Chances are, however, it will need some alteration of the skull cap before it fits half way decent. The skull cap is the woven part of the wig on the underneath side that the hair, synthetic or real, is attached to.

Figure makers generally fit a wig in one of two ways: **1.)** Fold and gather small portions of the skull cap, and sew together. **2.)** Cut small portions of the skull cap away to make the wig smaller. This takes greater care as sometimes when you make cuts in the skull cap, it can start to fall apart in places. So sometimes it is a combination of the two methods that is needed to fit a wig properly.

***Wig fitting method 1:*** The front of the wig you generally want to leave alone and not alter. Place the wig on the figure's head and see just how much too big the skull cap is going over the ears. Start by gathering some of the skull cap in the middle of the wig. Hold the wig inside out and take a 1/2" or 3/4" pinch at the middle of the wig cap so the fold is running from front to back. This fold or gather should be anywhere from 2-4" long. Take some needle and thread and sew the fold in such a way that it will not come undone. It's kind of like creating a fold in a

curtain or drapery. The difference is you are sewing this fold together so it will stay put. After the fold or gather has been sewn, you can also fold it to one side or the other and sew it in this position inside the wig skull cap. This will help it to lie flat inside the wig.

Keep taking sections in on the skull cap (making folds and pulling them together with needle and thread) until the wig fits as well as it can. This makes it possible for a larger wig to fit a smaller head. This is how it is done in the wig shops. The nice thing about this method is that if you make a mistake, you can remove the thread and try again, redoing the fold.

***Wig fitting method 2:*** This method basically involves cutting the skull cap to make it smaller, thus making the wig smaller. With this method it is best to glue or velcro (see 'Using velcro to attach the wig', next page) the front and middle part of the wig in place first before you actually start cutting. After those parts are secured, check the fit of the skull cap near where the sideburns would normally be and over the ears. Cut away small portions of the skull cap as needed until it fits nicely around these areas.

Keep working towards the back of the head and finally near the back of the neck cutting and trimming the skull cap as you go. Even on a female vent figure, the wig will look best if the skull cap fits around the ears nicely. With this method you will probably want to glue or attach velcro as you do each section so things are held in place, making for a more accurate fitting of the wig. The disadvantage to this method is that it's possible to cut too much away. So take your time and cut away only small amounts. You can always cut more off, but you can't put more back on!

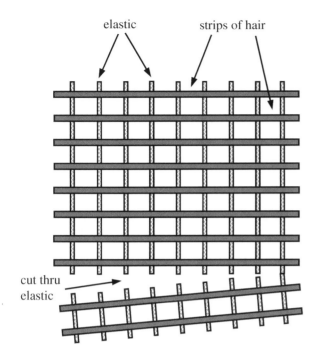

elastic      strips of hair

cut thru elastic

Cutting thru elastic parts of skull cap to trim wig

Also, take note of how the wig skull cap is constructed. They are done different ways. Many have the strips of hair connected by elastic. If you cut through the strips of hair, the wig is more likely to fall apart somewhat as you trim it. It is better to cut through the elastic strips. (See illustration above) You also have to be careful not to cut the hair of parts of the wig that will be remaining as you are trimming this way. Take your time and be sure of exactly what is getting cut as you go.

***Using velcro to attach the wig:*** Using velcro to attach a wig to a figure's head makes it easy to take the wig on and off again when needed. Squares or patches of velcro are attached to the head and wig in a few key places to secure it in place on the head.

Purchase some one inch wide ***velcro*** strips (it comes as a pair of strips, one that is a ***hook*** piece and the other is a ***loop*** piece)

from your local fabric store. Take some of the velcro strip, with the hook and loop pieces pressed together, and cut a piece 1" to 1 1/2" long. Now you have one hook piece and one loop piece the same length. The hook piece is hard, the loop piece is somewhat soft. The hook piece will be glued to the head and the corresponding loop piece gets sewn to the wig.

Determine where the center front part of the wig will sit on the head and make a small pencil mark there. Make another mark 1/4" back from that on the head. This is where the leading edge of the velcro ***hook*** piece will be glued. Temporarily set the hook piece of velcro near this second mark and trace the outline of the velcro with a pencil. This area needs to be roughened with medium to coarse sandpaper. Now take the hook piece (the hard piece) and glue it to this area with a very thin layer of 2 part epoxy (syringe type from the hardware store) or super glue gel. Put the matching soft piece of velcro aside temporarily.

Velcro will also need to be put in a few other places as well. Some good places to put them are: just above the back of the neck, on the crown of the head, above the ears near the sideburn areas and one on each side just behind the ears. Cut as many sets (hook and loop) of velcro pieces (1 to 1 1/2" long) as are needed. Glue the hook pieces (the hard piece) with epoxy or super glue gel to the areas just described. (See illustration next page for details) Let the glue set thoroughly.

After attaching all of the ***hook*** pieces to the head you will need to attach the corresponding ***loop*** pieces of velcro to the inside of the wig. Put the wig back onto the head and take note of where the ***hook*** velcro pieces (already attached to the head) line up

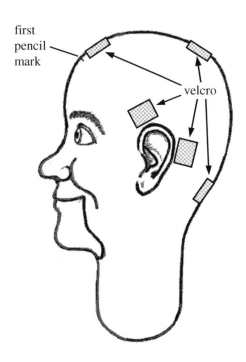

first
pencil
mark

velcro

Velcro 'hook' pieces glued to head casting

with the skull cap. This is where you need to sew the corresponding loop pieces of velcro to the skull cap of the wig. Take some needle and thread and sew the loop pieces to the skull cap as needed. If you are not comfortable doing this, get a friend or relative who is good at sewing to do it for you.

The sets of velcro should hold the wig in place quite well. You can add additional pieces of velcro in strategic places if needed. The beauty of attaching the wig this way is that it is easy to take on and off for cleaning or styling as well as gaining access to the trap door for adjustments or repairs. ***Note:*** You should use care when pulling the wig off of the head, grasping the loop pieces and pulling on them as opposed to pulling directly on the wig. The woven part of the skull cap can be somewhat delicate on some wigs.

***Wig styling and cutting:*** Unless you are experienced at cutting hair, it would be best

to take your figure (with the wig attached) to a barber or hair salon to get it cut and styled. This is also a great way to get some good publicity if you are a performing vent. Call the local newspaper and let them know about the event (check with the hair stylist first to make sure they are comfortable with that arrangement). Also, make sure you take it to someone you trust who will do a good job cutting and styling the wig. If it gets cut too short, it will not grow out again! A good wig shop in the larger cities can also cut and style your figure's wig.

If you do end up cutting the wig yourself, use a good pair of thinning shears for the majority of the cutting and styling. This will make it easier to blend the cut. There are also some good books and videos available at many public libraries, that can help you learn some basic hair cutting techniques. Just like so many things, it is mostly a matter of learning the principles and then practicing.

It is not recommended to use hair spray on synthetic wigs. Brush it gently with a nice hair brush and then use clean hands to gently lay down whatever stray hairs are out of place. Some of the stray hairs will just have to be cut. As the figure is used for performing, you will occasionally need to brush out the hair again and trim the stray hairs if needed.

It is best if you do not leave your figure sitting out, as dust will collect on the wig and make it necessary to wash it. Noted figure maker, Rick Price, uses a special fabric bonnet that goes over the figure's head and ties in the back. The figures are stored in a suitcase or trunk with the bonnet in place. When you remove the figure from the case and remove the bonnet, the wig should be in pretty good shape.

*A side note on wigs:* If you want a figure with shorter hair, it is not necessarily imperative that you purchase a short hair wig. Some of the long hair wigs do not cost any more than a short hair wig. These sometimes have a nice, small, skull cap as well. In any case, don't pass by a wig with long hair until you've had a good look at it first. Since you have to trim, cut and style a wig anyway, it really doesn't matter how long the hair on the wig is to start with.

### *Dressing your figure*

One main thing to remember when clothing your completed figure is that you need to cover the places where the muslin arms and legs meet the hands and feet, as well as the ball and socket neck joint of the body. Long sleeves and pant legs take care of the arms and legs. Turtle neck sweaters/shirts or dress and casual shirts that have nice collars work well to hide the ball and socket neck joint. When you buy dress shirts or casual shirts, they usually have a cardboard or plastic insert underneath the collar to help them hold their shape. You can leave these in place so the collar will continue to stay in place and look nice while the figure is manipulated.

Other than that, you can really dress your figure any way you want. Of course, the best thing would be to dress your figure according to the character you have sculpted and created. An older man or older lady figure would certainly dress differently than a little boy or girl figure. A country rube would dress differently than a sophisticated gent, and so on. Do some 'people watching' at a shopping mall sometime to get some clothing ideas. You never know what kind of characters you will see at the mall! You are bound to get some good ideas this way.

Some perfectly good clothing can be found at various thrift stores. Check out the various local swap meets, flea markets and rummage sales. Again, there are oftentimes some nice items that you can get at a low price. Also look for close-outs and sales at local clothing and discount stores. Try to anticipate when the stores will be closing out certain items that you would like to have. Winter clothes at the end of the season just before spring and summer clothes near the end of summer just before the fall, etc.

It is best if you can try the clothing on your figure first before purchasing. The clothing sizes for your figure could be anywhere from size 4 to size 6 in children's size clothing depending on what size you made your figure. Also, the cut of the clothing and sizes can vary slightly from manufacturer to manufacturer. Don't take the tags off of purchased clothing until you have had a chance to try the clothes on the figure. Or.........the best way would be to take the figure with you to the store to try the clothing on for good general fit, and.....to get some real attention. You never know. It might help you get a booking for your next performance!

The pants that you choose might possibly be too snug in the waist, but that's okay because you will probably be cutting a short slit in the back of the pants to accommodate control stick movement anyway (described shortly). The length of the pants may need to be shortened, either by rolling up the cuff or cutting the pant legs shorter and hemming them (bribe a friend or relative who does sewing if you are not skilled at doing this). The same can be done if the sleeves on a jacket are too long. Usually, shirt sleeves will bunch up nicely especially on knit or certain stretch fabrics. Also, the ends of long shirt sleeves usually are elastic in nature or have buttons on the sleeves. This helps to keep the sleeves from coming past the wrists of the hands on your figure. In some cases, you will still have to alter the sleeve lengths on some clothing items.

***Shirt or Jacket Slit:*** For the jacket and/or shirt you will also need to cut an appropriate vertical slit down the middle for your hand to go through to operate the figure. Place the shirt or jacket on the body and note where the top of the hole in the back of the body is and where the bottom of the control stick is. What you want is about a 6 to 8 inch vertical slit centered in this area, in the back of the jacket or shirt. Some will want a larger slit, some may want to try to get away with a smaller slit. It's up to you. The idea is to have the slit big enough to get your hand in and out easily, as well as having enough room for movement of the head stick in all positions.

*If you want to do a professional job on the slit, here are a couple of suggestions:* To keep the slit from splitting or ripping further, do a ***bar tack*** (a 3/8" to 1/2" long stitch made several times in the same place with a sewing machine) at the top and bottom of the slit. (See illustration at right) To keep the edges of the slit from unraveling, use a sewing machine to do an overcast stitch or wide zig-zag stitch. It's a little tricky sewing these stitches on the edge of the cut fabric this way, but can be well worth the effort. Again, find

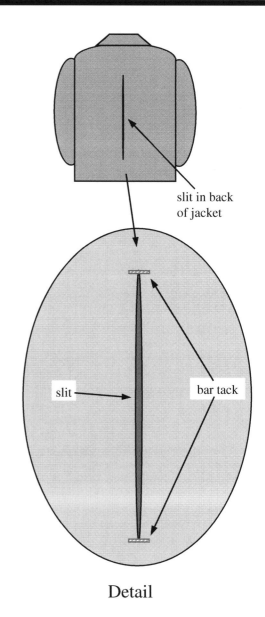

slit in back of jacket

slit

bar tack

Detail

Detail of 'bar tack' at ends of slit in a figure's jacket

a friend or relative who does sewing if you are not skilled at doing this. You might be able to find someone to do this inexpensively by a student or instructor at a college class on sewing or tailoring.

***Fitting the pants:*** The pants on most vent figures are cut in the back to allow for full movement of the control stick. Make a cut a few inches down the back of the pants at the waist band. Sew a *bar tack* (the same as you did for the slit in the shirt or jacket) at the end of the slit to keep it from getting bigger. Put the pants on the body and fold the flaps that this slit creates to the inside of the opening in the back of the body. Staple these flaps in place to the inside of the body with a staple gun. Velcro could also be used if you wanted to have the pants be easily removable.

If you want your figure to wear a belt, it will be necessary to cut the belt. Cut out a section near the opening in the back. Staple the ends to the inside of the body where the pants are already stapled in place. The belt will still function as normal at the front of the pants, and can be buckled and unbuckled.

If it is a cast resin or fiberglass body, it would be easiest to use velcro to hold the pants in place. This would be done in a similar fashion as was described for attaching the wig. Glue some hook pieces (the hard pieces) with epoxy or super glue gel to the inside of the body (use some coarse sandpaper and roughen the areas first to help it adhere properly). Sew the corresponding loop pieces to the flaps on the back of the pants. The flaps are then pushed firmly in place where the velcro has been attached. (See *'Using velcro to attach the wig'* section on page 179. Also see photo below)

***Socks and shoes:*** Of course if you have a 'country rube' type figure, they do not necessarily need to wear socks or shoes, and can just go barefoot. Besides, it would be nice to show off those nicely cast feet if you made some! (See photo next page)

Again, a local thrift store can be an excellent place to find used clothing items in good condition, including shoes. In fact, if they have a little bit of wear, so much the better. They will look more natural that way. Generally speaking, shoes that are slightly larger in size will look better on a vent figure. If they are too small they will look odd. Purchase ordinary socks at a discount store. Check the feel of the material that the socks are made of. Some materials are somewhat slippery in nature which will make it harder for the shoes to stay on. It would probably be best to get some 100% cotton socks if you can.

As was mentioned earlier in this publication, many parts of the body on a vent figure are proportioned differently than that of a human. Look at a picture or movie clip of Charlie McCarthy, for example. You will notice his feet are short in comparison with what a real boy's feet would be. But he is a good looking figure and it works. The feet of your figure have probably been made shorter than a real foot would be (from heel to toe), so they might be of necessity a little on the wide side in comparison with their length. When you are shoe shopping for your figure, you might need to look for shoes that are slightly wider than normal.

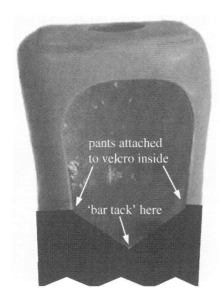

pants attached to velcro inside

'bar tack' here

Attaching pants to a cast body

Finished figure showing off his bare feet

In general, cast feet will hold shoes better (they actually stay on the feet!) than stuffed muslin feet will. If the stuffed feet on the figure have a continuing problem with this, you could put some velcro on the heel of the muslin feet (**loop** pieces sewn in place) and the heels inside the shoes (**hook** pieces glued in place). See *'Using velcro to attach the wig'* section starting on page 179.

The shoes do not have to be of really good quality, since your figure will probably do very little walking around! They just have to look nice. For some real fun, you could take the feet into the shoe store before you attach them to the figure's body (if you made molded feet). Of course, then you might have some explaining to do!!! It will definitely make for an interesting conversation.

### Closing thoughts

Well, if you have come this far and have done all of the steps to complete a pro style vent figure, you should take a bow. It is quite the accomplishment! There's is nothing like the feeling of owning and operating a figure that you built yourself. You will have a great sense of pride that is hard to describe.

Figure making is a strange, wonderful and intriguing art form all at the same time. You end up going through many different creative processes in the adventure of trying to create a pro style vent figure. Some are painful, some are immensely satisfying. If this is your first figure that you have made, I can probably guarantee it won't be your last. Even if you found part of the building process to be frustrating at times, you will usually find yourself drawn to come back and build another figure. Most who get bitten by the figure making bug never recover. It's hard to explain, but it has happened to many people who were perfectly normal prior to their being bit by the bug!

As you have seen throughout the pages of this book, there are many different materials and techniques available for this interesting craft. The goal has been to give you, the reader, a working knowledge of a variety of materials and techniques to help you get started in this fascinating art form. As has been stated before, the rules in figure making are, there are no rules! Keep experimenting. Find what works best for you.

Talk to other figure makers as you can. Be willing to share what you have learned with others. Accept the fact that there will be some mistakes along the way. Refuse to get discouraged! Your next attempt with a certain process or technique is bound to be better. No book can replace practice and experience in figure making. It does take time. Don't expect to learn it all overnight. But most of all............, enjoy the journey. The journey of learning and perfecting your craft at what ever level you strive to be at.

I know that if you are patient and persevere you are sure to have success with your figure making projects. I would sure like to hear about it! Please send a birth announcement, photos and any details you wish to relate of how you built your figure.

If you want to see the latest exciting things the author is up to, please stop by and visit his *Web Site* at:

www.puppetsandprops.com

I would like to wish you the best of success with all your figure making adventures, and I sincerely hope this book has helped you along the way.

Happy figure making,

Michael Brose

**Write to me at....**

**Puppets and Props**
P.O. Box 250
Pomerene, AZ 85627

"Good night, Winch."                    "Good night, Jerry."

# Appendix A
## Fitting the mouth

Fitting of the mouth or jaw piece is really one of the most important areas of figure making. The mouth being the most used part of the figure, and smooth operation being so critical for performance, you need to take a fair amount of time to make sure it is done correctly. The aspect of parallel lines for the mouth opening in the head and jaw piece was covered in Chapter Seven. This is very important and if you haven't already done so, you should read the information about this starting on page 123, before proceeding.

There is also the aspect of aesthetics, which is very important. A well fit and well designed mouth or jaw piece can really make the difference on how attractive or homely you finished figure is. Some older figures (and some barely a few days old) have some really poor fitting work done on the mouth. This all quite preventable with a little care. The two main aspects in relation to aesthetics are: **1.)** The very bottom of the jaw piece under the chin, right next to the neck. This can leave a huge gap when the mouth opens if not done correctly **2.)** The arc or curved areas on the side of the jaw piece, and the corresponding areas surrounding the jaw on the head casting. This area usually looks fine when the mouth is closed, but can look a little strange or have unsightly gaps when the mouth opens, if improperly designed. Take the extra time to do a good job!

To start, the first problem, (gap under the chin on the bottom of the jaw piece) is probably the easier of the two to correct. You can sometimes also use this method to fix such a problem with an existing figure. To do this, the jaw needs to already be installed in the

head on an axle, rotating freely. Add some patching compound such as wood dough, Bondo (auto body repair material) or Magic Sculp to the area shown in the illustration. The material that you use depends on what the jaw is cast out of. Magic Sculp is a hard material and does not sand as easily as some other materials. Try to use a compound that is about the same relative hardness as the jaw piece is. This will make it easier to sand and blend the edges.

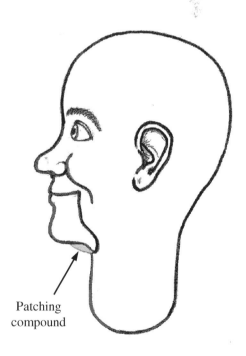

Fixing gap under chin with patching compound

Swing the mouth open and closed as you add the patching compound. What you want is for the compound to almost contact the bottom of the mouth opening in the head, as the jaw opens and closes. It takes a little fussing to get it just right, but when you do, there will be hardly any gap between the jaw and mouth opening in the head casting. If done correctly, you should see the same amount of gap when the mouth is open as when it is fully closed. This same amount of gap should be present throughout the entire travel of the mouth opening and closing.

The other way to do this is to put on slightly more patching compound than is needed, or in other words, slightly *overfill* the area to be patched. This should be done with the mouth fully closed. Then, as you carefully push the mouth or jaw piece open, the excess will be scraped off (by passing through the bottom of the mouth opening in the head), precisely where it needs to be removed. When the material has set up, you can sand the area you patched. Going this way will make for a very nice, thin gap throughout the travel of the mouth. You may have to do some minor 'fill in' patching and sand again, but overall not too much additional work.

The second item on the list is the arcs on the sides of the jaw. The best way to do this is when you make the clay model of the head. There are two ways to do this. **1.)** Take a previously made mouth or jaw piece from one of the figures you have made that works really well, and set it in the clay. **2.)** Make a mockup or model that indicates where the arcs need to be.

The ***first way*** of establishing the arcs is easiest if you use a modified jaw. Here's what you do. First, make a casting of this existing jaw (the one that works really well) in a material that is easily carved, like wax or plaster (see Chapters Two, Four, Five and Six). You can then make a generic model that will fit quite a number of vent figure heads that you might make. The front of the lips

can be carved away as well as a good portion of the chin area. Only carve away enough to give you room to sculpt the new look you want for the next head you are going to sculpt. Don't carve away the arc areas on the sides of the jaw or the well fit bottom area of the jaw (that was described earlier). All you really need from this modified jaw is the sides (where the arcs are) and bottom area near the neck (described above).

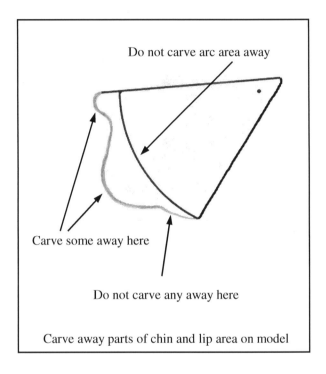

Do not carve arc area away

Carve some away here

Do not carve any away here

Carve away parts of chin and lip area on model

This generic jaw can be used for many different heads that you sculpt. Simply place it in the clay model of the head (make sure it is perpendicular to the face and head stick). Sculpt the rest of the face and sculpt the features of the jaw such as the lips and chin. Do not alter the bottom area near the neck (see illustrations previous page and this page) or the arc areas on the sides. The clay that you sculpt on the head around the jaw should conform to the arcs already present in the generic jaw piece.

The sides and bottom of the jaw piece are essentially a template to follow. To finish the process, take a sculpting tool and make vertical lines where the arcs are, and a line where the very bottom of the jaw is. In other words, you are making a thin visible outline in the clay (right next to the jaw model) that clearly shows where the jaw is. This outline will be visible in the mold and later on the castings of the head. Then it will be real easy to know where to make your cuts in the head casting later on.

After you make a mold and have removed it from the head sculpture, you can carefully remove the modified jaw from the clay head. If all is in tact, you can make a mold (see Chapters Four and Five) from this jaw which now has the bottom lip and chin sculpted in clay. When the mold is complete, you can cast a jaw that will precisely fit the castings of the new head (after the mouth area has been cut out, of course). The arcs should line up nicely and there should be very little gap near the bottom part of the jaw piece when opening and closing. There will only be minor fitting or refining if any, when installing the cast jaw piece in the head. (See Chapter Seven).

The **second way** to establish the arcs is to make a mockup of what you need. How? First draw two lines at right angles and an arc on a piece of paper. Use a compass (from local office supply outlet) to draw the arc. (See illustration above right) You can make the arc with a radius of 1 1/4" from the center of the right angle. This is just a place to start from. You can certainly use a dimension that you come up with on your own. The corner or center of the right angle is where the pivot will end up being.

Then draw two extra lines next to the first two lines. These should be about 3/16" away

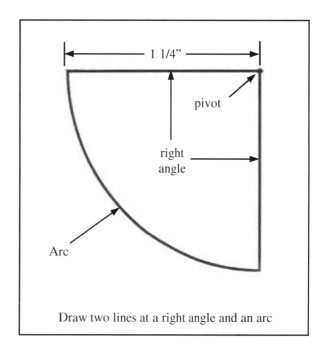

Draw two lines at a right angle and an arc

from the first two lines that were drawn. (See illustration below) If you want, you can erase the first two lines, as they are no longer needed. Do not erase the pivot area or the arc.

Use the drawing that you made as a pattern. Trace the pattern over two pieces of

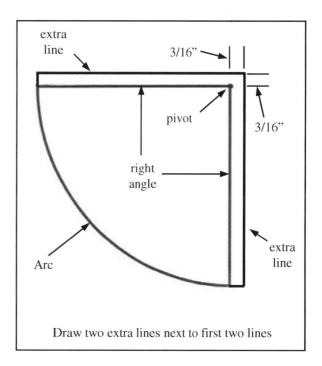

Draw two extra lines next to first two lines

Plexiglass® or thin plywood. Carefully cut out the pieces following the outline of the pattern. Sand the edges only enough to take off any undue roughness. Be careful not to change the shape of the 'arc' area in particular. These two cut out pieces (Plexiglass or plywood) should be the same size with matching arcs and matching right angles. Make sure the pivot is clearly marked with a permanent marker.

Next take a block of wood and glue it between the two cut pattern pieces. (See illustration below) Use a square and a flat work surface to make sure that the pieces are glued on squarely in all directions. An alternate method would be to use three dowels instead of the wood block. These could even protrude out the side of the cut pieces and

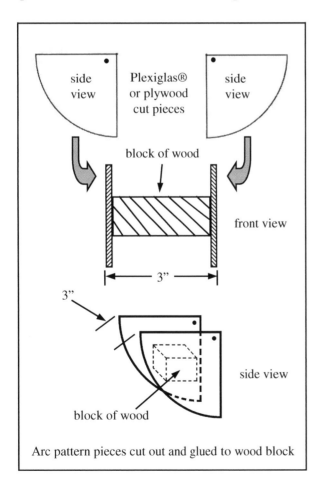

Arc pattern pieces cut out and glued to wood block

trimmed later. The important thing, whether using the wood block or dowels, is that the two cut pieces (Plexiglass or plywood) be the same distance away from each other, no matter where it is measured. In other words, getting everything square and true is the key to all of this working properly.

This *arc* model that you have made can be set in a clay model of a head you are sculpting. This little device will establish where the arcs on the sides of the mouth should be, the corners of the mouth and the approximate placement of the bottom of the jaw opening in the head.

As was done with the existing jaw 'that worked well' (described earlier) and was used for establishing where the arcs will go, make lines in the clay indicating the outline of the jaw. Take a sculpting tool and make vertical lines where the arcs are, and a line where the very bottom of the jaw is. In other words, you are making a visible outline in the clay that clearly shows where the jaw is. The line on the bottom of the jaw can have some curve to it for aesthetics. Likewise the corners of the mouth near the bottom of the jaw can be rounded as well. These outlines will be visible in the mold and later on the castings of the head. Then it will be easy to know where to make your cuts in the head casting.

After a mold has been made of the head, you can remove the arc model from the clay. You can now use this arc model to help make a jaw model. First, use the head mold to cast the front part of the jaw (See Chapter Seven, pages 123 & 124). This should be cast pretty thin. Glue it onto the front of the arc model. Glue in a top piece and sculpt teeth and tongue as described in Chapter Seven. Install an axle in this model (where the pivot points are marked) and temporarily glue the jaw in place in the matching head casting (which you have made a cutout in the mouth area). Use the method described earlier using patching compound (clay could be used) to fill in the area under the chin near the very bottom of the jaw piece.

Carefully remove the jaw from the head casting. Make a mold of this perfected jaw piece which now has the correct arcs and correct shape for the bottom of the jaw. Now when you make more castings of the head and jaw you should have a jaw or mouth piece that fits pretty nicely in the head. When it is installed and you open and close the mouth, the arcs on the side will match well with the arcs on the head casting. Also, the bottom of the jaw should have just the right amount of gap throughout its travel when the mouth opens and closes. Making a precision mouth can be a lot of work, but well worth the extra effort involved.

"N - E - S - T - L - E - S...,  Nestles makes the very best...,.  Cho - colate!"

# *Appendix B*
## *Vacuum Chambers*

You can often find a good used vacuum pump that will work just fine. It is very important to find one that pulls 29 In. Hg (inches of mercury). Do a thorough search through your local yellow pages (or go to the public library where they have all kinds of yellow pages), and try surplus outlets, scientific equipment, etc. You can also do an interenet search to see what companies handle vacuum pumps and which ones carry used units. You can get *new* vacuum pumps from Graingers (suppliers list), probably around $300-$400.

Obtain a heavy walled cooking pot as you might find in a restaurant (this will be the chamber). A scrap piece of 10" to 12" diameter PVC pipe from a construction site also works well (but this would require making a sealed bottom piece). PVC pipe walls should 3/4" to 1" thick for safety. The top can be made out of clear Plexiglas® or Lexan®. This material for the top should also be 3/4" to 1" thick for safety reasons. You will need a release valve, a vacuum gauge (if the vacuum pump doesn't already have one), hoses and fittings for making connections.

Drill two holes in the Plexiglas®. One will be for the release valve, the other for a connector fitting that connects a hose from the Plexiglas to the vacuum pump. This is wher the air will be drawn out of the chamber. You could make the connections (release valve and intake connection to the pump) on the side of the vacuum chamber if it is made from PVC, as it can be drilled fairly easily. Trying to drill holes in a heavy walled cooking pot is another matter entirely. In any case, all such connections (whether on the Plexi-

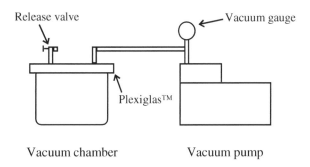

Vacuum chamber and pump- Basic components

glas® top or the side of the PVC chamber), should be sealed with silicone caulking or other suitable sealant to prevent any air leaks. If you have such air (actually vacuum) leaks, you will not be able to pull 29 In. Hg., and get a good vacuum.

It will be necessary to make a gasket that fits between the rim of the pot (or PVC pipe) and the Plexiglas® lid. This could be cast out of silicone, urethane rubber or even silicone sealant. The important thing is that you get a good seal when the vacuum pump is used to pull a vacuum on the vacuum chamber. Sometimes just a heavy layer of Vaseline will seal it adequately.

If you use a vacuum chamber to pull the air out of the silicone it will be necessary for the mixing cup to be 2 to 3 times larger than the volume of silicone you will be mixing. After mixing the silicone put the container in the vacuum chamber. Put the lid on and turn on the pump. Watch the gauge and see that it pulls to 28-29 In.Hg. If not, check for leaks in the chamber, hose or connectors. If everything is okay, after a few minutes the material will start to rise and then fall down again.

Keep watching and wait until the bubbles and mass of material rise to their highest point, after which the mass will collapse and fall back down to the original level in the mixing container. After it collapses that way, let the pump run anywhere from 30 seconds to about 2 minutes. Open the release valve and turn off the pump. Pull off the lid when the air pressure has equalized. The silicone is now ready to be poured.

You will notice that even after the material has risen, collapsed and continued under vacuum for a few minutes, you will still see bubbles popping in the silicone. At this point, what you are seeing is not air, but rather a 'boiling' of the material. Not a serious thing, but if you let it keep going that way, you are merely boiling off chemicals in the silicone resin (which are needed) and are no longer removing any air. It looks like air, but the scientists who research this sort of thing say it is not. ALL materials will **boil** so to speak, under perfect vacuum. So don't be fooled by this peculiar phenomenom.

For the scientifically curious, here's a few more facts related to vacuum science: To clarify the measuring of vacuum, in the U.S. it is "inches of mercury" written as In. Hg. The standard is, atmospheric pressure is 0, and a perfect vacuum is 29.92126 In. Hg. Using the metric system, '760 mm Hg absolute' represents atmospheric pressure, and '0 mm Hg absolute' represents perfect vacuum. A micron equals .001 mm Hg. A really good vacuum pump is rated in microns. But don't necessarily let that influence your decision making when you are looking to buy one. The needs for pulling air out of silicone aren't as critical as some other, more sophisticated applications. The most important thing is that it will pull 29 In. Hg.

As has been mentioned, you can use silicone without a vacuum pump. A low viscosity silicone (a thin consistency silicone) will let the air bubbles rise to the top and most of the time will produce a satisfactory mold. Using a vacuum pump, however, will undoubtedly ensure the best results.

# Suppliers List

In *section one* of this suppliers list, the products are listed first, in alphabetical order. Under each product heading in section one, (e.g. **Latex Rubber)**, you will find the *name* of the suppliers who carry that product. You can then go to *section two* where you will find the address, phone numbers, e-mail addresses and web sites (if available), for that particular supplier.

## Section One - Products & Suppliers

### Aqua Resin
- The Compleat Sculptor, Inc.

### Burlap
- Burman Industries, Inc.
- The Compleat Sculptor, Inc.

### Cab-O-Sil
- A-R Products, Inc.
- Continental Clay Company
- Burman Industries, Inc.
- Polytek Development Corporation

### Carving Wax
- Dick Blick Art Materials
- Silpak, Inc.

### Epoxy Resin
- The Compleat Sculptor, Inc.
- FIBRE GLAST Development Corp.
- Polytek Development Corporation
- Silpak, Inc

### Ease Release 2300 (and other release agents)
- A-R Products, Inc.
- BJB Enterprises
- Burman Industries, Inc.
- The Compleat Sculptor, Inc.
- Polytek Development Corporation
- Smooth-On, Inc.

### Extend-It
- A-R Products, Inc.
- Smooth-On, Inc.

### Eyes
- G. Schoepfer Inc.
- Van Dykes

### Fiberglassing materials
- The Compleat Sculptor, Inc.
- FIBRE GLAST Development Corp.

### Hemp (casting fiber)
- Burman Industries, Inc.
- The Compleat Sculptor, Inc.

### Jiffy Mixers
- FIBRE GLAST Development Corp.
- Silpak, Inc.
- Burman Industries, Inc.

### Klean Klay
- Burman Industries, Inc.
- The Compleat Sculptor, Inc.
- Art Chemical Products, Inc.

### Latex rubber
- A-R Products, Inc.
- Douglas and Sturgess, Inc.

## Light Cast
- Russ Simpson Company

## Magic Sculp
- Magic Sculp
- The Compleat Sculptor, Inc.

## Mold Key Knife
- The Compleat Sculptor, Inc.

## Neoprene (liquid)
- Chicago Latex

## No.1 Pottery Plaster
- See 'Plaster' heading below.

## Plaster (Plaster, Hydrocal, Hydrostone, etc.)
- Burman Industries, Inc.
- The Compleat Sculptor, Inc.
- United States Gypsum Company

## Plaster Bandages
- Burman Industries, Inc.
- The Compleat Sculptor, Inc.
- Silpak, Inc.

## Release Agents
- BJB Enterprises
- Burman Industries, Inc.
- The Compleat Sculptor, Inc.
- Polytek Development Corporation
- Smooth-On, Inc.

## Scales
- The Compleat Sculptor, Inc.
- Continental Clay Company
- Burman Industries, Inc.

## Sculpting tools
- Burman Industries, Inc.
- Continental Clay Company

- Dick Blick Art Materials

## Silicone Rubber (RTV)
- Alumilite Corporation
- BJB Enterprises
- Burman Industries, Inc.
- Polytek Development Corporation
- Silpak, Inc.
- Smooth-On, Inc.

## Urethane foam (rigid)
- BJB Enterprises
- Burman Industries, Inc.
- Polytek Development Corporation
- Smooth-On, Inc.
- Silpak, Inc.

## Urethane paste
- Polytek Development Corporation
- Smooth-On, Inc.
- A-R Products

## Urethane plastic
- Alumilite Corporation
- BJB Enterprises
- Burman Industries, Inc.
- Polytek Development Corporation
- Russ Simpson Company
- Smooth-On, Inc.

## Urethane rubber
- BJB Enterprises
- Burman Industries, Inc.
- Polytek Development Corporation
- Smooth-On, Inc.

## Vacuum pumps
- Alumilite Corporation
- Graingers

## Wigs
Lacy Costume Wigs

# Section Two - Suppliers contact info

**Alumilite Corporation**
315 East North Street
Kalamazoo, MI 49007
e-mail: world@alumilite.com
http://alumilite.com

Mold release, latex gloves, dry resin fillers, urethane resin, roto casting machines, Dow Corning silicone RTV, super casting kit, vacuum pumps and vacuum chambers.

**A-R Products, Inc.**
11807-7/8 Slauson Ave.
Santa Fe Springs, CA 90670
(562) 907-7707  Fax (562) 907-7708

They carry the # 74 Latex and 'bubble stock'. In addition to these items, they carry several other latexes, Extend-It, Plasti-Paste and other Smooth-On products, silicone RTV, urethane rubber, urethane plastic resins, several mold releases, clay, wide variety of mold making and casting materials.

**Art Chemical Products, Inc.**
P.O. Box 678 1019 Salamonie Ave.
Huntington, IN 46750
219-356-2328  Fax 219-356-2328
e-mail: info@kleanklay.com
http://www.kleanklay.com/

Featuring Klean Klay, a sulfur-free clay in different hardnesses and a variety of colors.

**Burman Industries, Inc.**
14141 Covello Street, Suite 10-C
Van Nuys, CA 91405
(818) 782-9833  Fax (818) 782-2863
http://www.burmanfoam.com/

Burlap, hemp (casting fiber), silicone RTV, urethane rubber, urethane plastic resins, mold releases, clay, and a wide variety of mold making and casting materials. Will sell smaller quantities on most items than you can get from most suppliers.

**Chicago Latex Products**
**345 E. Terra Cotta**
**P.O. Box 395**
**Crystal Lake, IL 60039**
**815-459-9680**
e-mail: spartan@mc.net
http://user.mc.net/~spartan/cl.htm

Liquid neoprene and some other latex casting and molding materials.

**The Compleat Sculptor, Inc.**
90 Vandam Street
New York, New York 10013
(212) 243-6074  Fax (212) 243-6374
http://www.sculpt.com

Mold key knife, armature wire, calipers, dry pigments, water base clay, Chavant Clay,

Klean Klay, Sculpey, Super Sculpey, plaster, silicone rubber, urethane plastic, sculpting tools, wide selection of release agents, a wide variety of mold making and casting supplies. books, videos.

## Continental Clay Company
1101 Stinson Boulevard N. E.
Minneapolis, MN 55413
1(800) 432-CLAY
email: continentalclay@uswest.net
http://www.continentalclay.com

Klean Klay, sculpting tools, Cab-O-Sil, Plaster bandages.

## Dick Blick Art Materials
P.O. Box 1267
Galesburg, IL 61402-1267
(800) 933-2542  Fax (800) 621-8293
http://www.dickblick.com

Balsa Foam®, carving wax, plaster bandages, silicone rubber, urethane plastic, and many more useful tools and supplies.

## Douglas and Sturgess, Inc.
730 Bryant St.
San Francisco, CA  94107
(415)-421-4456 Fax (415) 896-6379
e mail: Sturgess@ix.netcom.com
http://www.artstuf.com/

They carry a similar line to A-R Products, plus many other items of interest.

## FIBRE GLAST Development Corp.
1944 Neva Drive,
Dayton, OH 45414
http://www.fiberglast.com/

A very complete line of fiberglassing materials and related supplies. A very good selection of fiberglass cloth, mat, epoxy and polyester resins, release agents, instructional videos and books.

## G. Schoepfer Inc.
460 Cook Hill Road
Cheshire, CT 06410
(203) 250-7794  Fax (203) 250-6939

Glass and plastic eyes. Some nice eyes but a bit pricey!

## Graingers Industrial Supply
Most big cities have a Graingers location nearby. Check their web site for a local address near you.

http://www.grainger.com/Grainger/homepage.jsp

Vacuum pumps, and all sorts of industrial tools and supplies.

## Lacy Costume Wigs
505 8th Ave NY, NY 10018
1-(800) 562-9911 Fax (212) 695-3860

Wigs suitable for vent figures at reasonable prices. Call for a catalog.

**Magic Sculp**
2639 Voleyn Street
Carmichael, CA 95608
http://www.magicsculp.com

Magic Sculp in various size packages.

**Polytek Development Corporation**
55 Hilton Street
Easton, PA 18042
(610) 559-8620  Fax (610) 559-8626
e mail: sales@polytek.com
http://www.polytek.com

Polygel plastic-75 (mother mold material and possible head casting material). Platsil 71-20 silicone RTV. Also carries a full line of mold making and casting materials as well as their catalog which is also a small mold making manual.

**Russ Simpson Company**
21906 Schoenherr Road
Warren, MI 48089
(313) 771-2768

'Light cast' urethane.

**Silicones, Inc.**
P.O. Box 363
211 Woodbine Street
High Point, NC 27260
(336) 886-5018 Fax (336) 886-7122
http://www.silicones-inc.com

GI-1000 and other great silicone rubber RTV materials. Call for a local distributor.

**Silpak, Inc.**
P.O. Box 2830
169 Alantic Street
Pomona, CA 91768
(909) 595-6191 Fax (909) 598-2446
(Silpak cont'd)

http://www.silpak.com

Carving wax, plaster bandages, urethane plastic & foam, silicone & urethane rubber, epoxy, release agents, etc.

**Small Parts, Inc.**
P.O. Box 4650
(13980 NW 58th Court)
Miami Lakes, FL 33014-0650
1(800) 220-4242
www.smallparts.com

They carry brass rod, tube and flat stock as well as many small tools, parts and accessories.

**Smooth-On**
2000 St. John Street
Easton, PA 18042
(800) 762-0744  (610) 252-5800
Fax (610) 252-6200
http://www.smooth-on.com

Silicone and urethane RTV rubber, numerous urethane resins, rigid urethane foam, Plasti-Paste (for making mother molds), mold releases, fillers, a very good mold making and casting instruction booklet (only $3.00 and jam packed with info!)

**United States Gypsum Company**
125 South Franklin Street
Chicago, IL 60606-4678
1(800) 487-4431  (312) 606-5380
e-mail:  industrialgypsum@usg.com
http://www.usg.com

Call for nearest supplier of plaster, hydrostone, hydrocal, etc.

**Van Dyke's**
P.O. Box 278
39771 S.D. Hwy. 34
Woonsocket, SD 57385
(605) 796-4425  1(800) 843-3320

Glass and plastic eyes, mold making compounds, Cab-O-Sil, 2-part epoxy modeling
compounds, felt and leather.

## *E-mail lists for Vents and Figure Makers*

WORLDVENTS:  http://groups.yahoo.com/group/WORLDVENTS/

Figure Making list:  http://groups.yahoo.com/group/ventfigures/

## *Useful Figure Making URL's and Vent related Web sites*

**Vent Haven:**  http://www.venthaven.com/

**Puppetry Home Page:**  http://www.sagecraft.com/puppetry/index.html

**International Ventriloquist's Association**:  http://www.inquista.com/

**Gary Koepke's Figure Making Resources:**  http://bellsouthpwp.net/g/k/gkoepke/fig.htm

**Figure Making Info:**  http://www.puppetsandprops.com/FigMakInfo.html

Manufactured by Amazon.ca
Bolton, ON

21511655R00111